The Last Best West

An Exploration of Myth, Identity, and Quality of Life in Western Canada

The Last Best West

An Exploration of Myth, Identity, and Quality of Life in Western Canada

Edited by Anne Gagnon, W.F. Garrett-Petts,
James Hoffman, Henry Hubert, Terry Kading,
Kelly-Anne Maddox and Ginny Ratsoy

New Star Books /// Vancouver /// 2009
and

Textual Studies in Canada

Thompson Rivers University

New Star Books Ltd.
107 3477 Commercial Street
Vancouver, BC
V5N 4E8
Canada

1574 Gulf Rd., #1517
Point Roberts, WA 98281
USA

info@NewStarBooks.com
www.NewStarBooks.com

Published in collaboration with Textual Studies in Canada, Thompson Rivers University. 900 McGill Rd., Kamloops, BC, V2C 5N3

Publication of this work is made possible by grants from the Social Sciences and Humanities Research Council of Canada.

Designed by Dennis Keusch
Printed and bound by Imprimerie Gauvin, Gatineau, QC.
This book is printed on 100% post-consumer recycled paper.

Library and Archives Canada Cataloguing in Publication

The Last Best West : An Exploration of Myth, Identity and Quality of Life in Western Canada / edited by Anne Gagnon ... [et al.].

Co-publ. with: Textual Studies in Canada, Thompson Rivers University
Includes bibliographical references.
ISBN 978-1-55420-044-3

1. Canada, Western–Civilization–21st century.
2. Canada, Western–Intellectual life–21st century.
I. Gagnon, Anne C., 1951-

FC3219.L38 2009   306'.09712090511   C2009-901302-9

Contents

Acknowledgments

This book came together with the support and enthusiasm of many. Since this book flows out of the Last Best West Conference organized in September 2007 by the Centre for the Study of Canada at Thompson Rivers University, our thanks begins there, noting especially the work of Director Anne Gagnon, and members Ginny Ratsoy, Kelly-Anne Maddox, Terry Kading and Martin Whittles, as well as supportive work by Jim Hoffman and Brigitta O'Regan, among many others. We also acknowledge our contributors, first to the conference, and subsequently for their professionalism and for graciously meeting our deadlines. We also thank our anonymous referees for their helpful, constructive reviews. Special thanks go to our colleagues Henry Hubert, for his expert copy-editing, and Dennis Keusch for layout and design. We are also indebted to Rolf Maurer at New Star Books for his support; to Thompson Rivers University's Community-University Research Alliance (CURA), The Mapping Quality of Life and the Culture of Small Cities research group and its Director, Will Garrett-Petts; and to the Social Science and Humanities Research Council of Canada for an Aid to Conference grant that helped fund both the conference and this book.

The editors have made every effort to obtain copyright permission for photos and images; if any errors or omissions have occurred, we will correct them in any future reprinting of this volume.

Terry Kading

Introduction

I s the "West" in Canada just a geographical point of reference and set of topographical images (from the wide open prairies to the Rocky Mountains), or does the term convey something even more dissimilar from central or eastern Canada; or have nationalistic and/or globalizing forces had a leveling and homogenizing effect, rendering us in the West "just like the rest"? The idea for first a conference and then this edited collection arose out of a shared sentiment that there was still something quintessentially "Western Canadian" that distinguished and separated living in this region from all other Canadian regions. What this distinctiveness would be defined as, and comprised of, we left as open as possible in soliciting the participation of numerous disciplines and approaches to the question of "the West" and being a "Westerner."

The conference, entitled *Still the 'Last Best West' or Just Like the Rest: Interrogating Western Canadian Identities* (held September 13-16, 2007 at Thompson Rivers University, Kamloops, B.C.), dealt with a variety of political, social, cultural, literary and artistic issues, with session themes as varied as "paradigms of the West," "de-constructing Western identities," "selling the West," "questions of identity in Alberta," "First Nations and colonizers," "narratives of the West," "imagining Alberta culture," "education in the West," "voices muted and exalting," "Western portraits of immigrants, migrants and settlers," "Western literature and politics," "visual representations," "post-peasant sensibilities from the Canadian prairies," "creating Canada," to "political discourses." In collaboration with the Community-University Research Alliance (CURA) Mapping Quality of Life and the Culture of Small Cities research group, based out of Thompson Rivers University, and with a focus drawing largely on Western Canadian small city experiences, our conference was supported by presentations on "mapping culture and social change," "space and performance," "second life and online community building," "museums, galleries and quality of life," and a keynote address on "Arts and Quality of Life in Five Western Canadian Communities." Supplemented by art exhibitions (including a student roundtable on the creation of an art exhibition), a readers' theatre (comprised of student participants), webcasts of roundtable discussions, and local tours of a long-established working ranch and a First Nation's museum and heritage park, the conference became a revelatory confrontation with the depth and diversity, both intellectual and visual, of all things "Western." With examinations of the past to the present, expressed in a myriad of forms, the conference revealed for interrogation the novel experiences and creations that have forged the concept of the "Last Best West."

This collection is comprised of a sampling of the diverse presentations from our conference. The subtitle, "An Exploration of Myth, Identity, and Quality of Life in Western Canada," expresses our recognition of the limits of our enterprise to date. For instance, where Alberta and British Columbia figure prominently in the collection (as they did in the conference), Saskatchewan, Manitoba, the Yukon, and the Northwest Territories are only peripherally represented, and remain to be more fully integrated into the several understandings of the West elaborated in this collection. Further, while we share a sense of a unique experience to being in the West within a larger Canadian context, the extent to which there are qualitative differences arising out of the particular geography, patterns of immigration, contact with First Nations peoples, and provincial and urban dynamics in direct contrast with "the rest" remain to be substantiated. Our work, then, lays out the variety of approaches and unique research initiatives, with a novel focus on small urban centres, rural education, regional representations and identities, theatre, literature and film, visual representations, and quality of life issues, allowing for multiple lines of inquiry and discussion involving other provincial and regional experiences. The term "exploration" captures the initial, original and tentative character of the works we have brought together, establishing the bases for further research, deeper comparisons, more debate, and ultimately revision from both within Western Canada and from without.

This work is divided into three parts, each addressing distinct themes concerning our understanding of "the West." Part One, which we have entitled "Talking West," examines the topics of regional ideologies, theorizing the West and linguistic constructions in our ongoing efforts to understand and adapt to living in this region. Rachel Nash's "Are the Rocky Mountains Conservative?: Towards a Theory of the How 'the West' Functions in Canadian Discourse" examines the contemporary Canadian discourse where the term "the West"—as well as iconic Western Canadian images such as the Rocky

Mountains—have become associated with Conservative politics. Nash analyzes and critiques this prominent discourse with reference to several other semantic understandings of the West that ultimately challenge the Conservative conception and reveal the broader complexity of the West. Tanis MacDonald's "Gateway Politics: West meets west in Kristjana Gunnars' *Zero Hour*" offers a distinct interpretation of Gunnars' work. Gunnar subverts elegiac convention to challenge traditional notions of "reading the west" in Canadian literature, and positions the fecund Pacific forest as the landscape of death and disaster, offering the semi-arid prairie city as a site of consolation and eventual renewal. MacDonald's article, on the other hand, considers Gunnars' use of the city of Winnipeg's tourist slogan "Gateway to the West" to connote a gateway to aesthetic practice and practical mourning. Yaying Zhang's "What is the Chinese-Canadian Accent?: Ideologies of Language and the Construction of Immigrant Identities" uses the bilingual experiences of Chinese immigrants in a medium-sized city in Western Canada as sources of evidence for understanding the dialogical process of ethnic identity construction in Canada's smaller communities. Where many studies have examined immigrant experiences in metropolitan cities in Canada, few have focused on immigrants in smaller communities and how their cultural positioning and identity construction intersect with their appropriation and negotiation of bilingual practices. Within this novel focus Zhang also examines how immigrants' linguistic practices, or rather, perceptions of their linguistic practices, create cultural proximities or distances in the nation and raise questions of who belongs in multicultural Canada. Taken together, "Talking West" provides new insights into political, literary and immigrant representations of life in the West.

Part II, entitled "Peopling West," concerns issues of identity and culture in the West. Kimberly Mair's "Subjects of Consumption and the 'Alberta Advantage'—Representations of Wiebo Ludwig in the Theatre and the Media, 1997-2005" examines media representations of Wiebo Ludwig in the context of the image of Alberta as a rogue and grassroots Western Canadian province to the extent that this image abates dissent that is internal to the province. Mair argues that the ongoing process of normalization of institutional power relations in Alberta under Klein's Progressive Conservative government was maintained despite the destabilizing potential of media coverage of Ludwig's struggle with the corporate energy sector. For Mair the active participation of Ludwig himself in the construction of self and other representation through these same narrative practices played a role in keeping controversy over oil and gas industry activities in public discourse, which contributed to an eventual convergence and identification with debates over Canada's ratification of the Kyoto Accord on Climate Change, opposition to new well development proposals, and conflicts between the oil and beef industries in Alberta. Gloria Filax's "Unruly Alberta: Queering the 'Last Best West'" expands on this conflict over the Alberta identity by examining popular notions of identity in that province and how these are altered by sexuality and gender. Filax observes that Albertans are often portrayed as an alienated bunch of rednecks, entrepreneurial and self-reliant, and Alberta is often referred to as oil rich "Saudi-Alberta" and "natural" Alberta, where the cowboy is often mobilized as a symbol of Alberta-ness that gestures to a common past. Filax argues that much of the idealism associated with these images has been achieved through exclusions, and she highlights modern challenges to cultural norms of sexual and gender appropriateness such as k. d. lang and the drag-king group, "Alberta Beef."

Pamela Cairns' "Teaching Adventures in Seymour Arm: A Case Study of Rural Education" develops a greater understanding about the nature of rural teaching by comprehensively examining the schooling experience in Seymour Arm, British Columbia. Where rural schooling has not been adequately documented in our history books and the nature of isolated rural schooling is changing with increased access to technology and a population that continues to become more urban in nature, Cairns emphasizes rural education as a valuable area of inquiry as a part of both our educational and our social histories and utilizes interviews and other primary sources to explore the history of the community and the nature of teachers' experiences in the Seymour Arm schools. A unique addition to the area of culture and identity is our inclusion of the transcript from a keynote panel discussion from our conference, entitled a "Roundtable on Defining Quality of Life and Cultural Indicators for Small Cities." This roundtable reports on and discusses recent research on "quality of life" and cultural indicators specific to smaller communities, emphasizing how indicators sensitive to municipal scale are not only crucial measures of each community's cultural health, but when developed and implemented in consultation with key stakeholders become vehicles for social cohesion and change. Our transcript includes a post-roundtable analysis and critique by Mark Seasons (University of Waterloo) on the issues raised in the discussion. The intent of this roundtable and critique is to initiate a national dialogue, helping both to refine existing quality of life reporting systems and advance the relevance of cultural indicators for smaller cities locally, nationally, and internationally. "Peopling West," then, offers unique lines of inquiry and theoretical constructs that may be critically adapted to research in other provinces and regions on provincial identities, identity formation and cultural indicators.

Part III, "Picturing West," is comprised of investigations and critical commentary of artistic representations of the West through photography, theatre, and film. Kalli Paakspuu's "Photojournal Rhetorics of the West" examines how in Canada the transformative value of a photograph was quickly recognized for nation building, but the early photograph tended to reproduce the contradictory relations between industry, settlers, and Indigenous communities as a particular future was envisioned and contested. Canadian Harry Pollard photographed Blackfoot and Blood peoples with a photojournalistic aesthetic that became a site of meaningful encounter resulting in a photography that decentred dominant European discourses. Paakspuu argues that Harry Pollard's dual "citizenship," as member of the professional photographic fraternity of Alberta and as honorary chief of the Blackfoot, enabled him to mediate two separate referential worlds. Paakspuu focuses on Pollard's photography and a new definition of the West through a photojournalism where a visual narrative style subverts the binary opposition between an "us" and "them"–between Europeans and Indigenous Peoples. Ginny Ratsoy's "Re-viewing the West: A Study of Newspaper Critics' Perceptions of Historical Drama in a Western Canadian Small City" examines something rarely studied in scholarly work on Canadian theatre: newspaper reviews. With an eye to local newspaper reviewers' perceptions of the use of historical material for dramatic purposes, Ratsoy analyzes their responses over two decades to a series of plays produced in Kamloops, plays in which the small city and/or its citizens figure prominently. Ratsoy finds a congruence between academic and journalistic criticism in which both revel in perceptions of difference and construct home-grown drama as creatively reflecting historically distinctive, even eccentric, notions of the West.

James Hoffman's "Community Engagement and Professional Theatre in the Small City in British Columbia" challenges the notion that professional theatre companies in small cities would seem at first glance to be well positioned to engage the life of their communities, and questions how deeply they can actually become involved with the very real issues and directions of their own small cities. Hoffman's article looks at the genre of professional theatre as it has developed in Canada and as it functions in Kamloops, Prince George, and Nanaimo,

5

and the degree to which its formation somewhat limits community engagement, and he asks for a rethinking of that genre. His article finishes by examining several examples of professional theatre companies radically committed to community, ones that might serve as a model for a truly community-engaged professional theatre in a small city. Mervyn Nicholson's "Babes in the Woods: Exotic Americans in British Columbia Films" examines British Columbia's mythic reputation symbolized by freedom, natural beauty, and natural bounty, and how this mythic conception rejects the aggressive, conformist, and restrictive lifestyle of the East and of the United States. Nicholson analyzes two major Canadian films that deal with this pastoral myth of British Columbia, where both feature Americans escaping from the United States: Philip Borsos' *The Grey Fox* (1982) and Sandy Wilson's *My American Cousin* (1985). Nicholson argues that while very different, these two films share many features; in particular, both of them present and then deconstruct the British Columbia pastoral myth. But in an ironic and interesting twist, they both reconstruct it, so that British Columbia does indeed in the end emerge as a place of refuge and genuine innocence. Whether through a focus on the role of theatre, film and photography in Western communities, or a questioning of that role, the articles of "Picturing West" provide compelling (re)examinations of places, practices and works on or of the West.

The varied works within this collection cumulatively offer a unique panoramic understanding of Western themes. It is our hope that the eclecticism in subject matter, theory and approaches serves to enrich our understanding and appreciation of what "the West" has been and continues to be, the "Last Best West." More importantly, we hope this collection stimulates further critical inspection of various Western representations, provincial identities and creative practices that have gone unexamined in terms of their formation and significance in our towns, cities, and provinces/territories.

Part I   Talking West

Rachel Nash

Are the Rocky Mountains Conservative? Towards a Theory of How the West Functions in Canadian Discourse

As is so often the case, it was a crisis of sorts that brought the everyday under scrutiny. This crisis took place between my morning newspaper and me on January 23, 2006. On that day, the front cover of the *Globe and Mail* was almost completely taken up by an article entitled "The West Comes In," featuring a large, imposing photo of the snowy peaks of the Rocky Mountains. The piece predicted, correctly, that the Conservative party would win the imminent federal election (see Figure 1 below). Something bothered me very much about this, and not just typical small "l" liberal disgruntlement, displeasure at the coming conservativism to which I had already resigned myself. Rather, my quarrel was with the representation of the content. It had to do with the unproblematic equation of those mountains and the West with conservativism, a powerful and ubiquitous formula in contemporary Canadian discourse, but one that denied much of my own lived experience.

For the purposes of this article, let's think about discourse as the "characteristic ways of speaking, writing, and interpreting text in relation to recurrent social activities" (Stillar 12). Canadian discourse, then, has a recurring role for the West–exemplified in the *Globe and Mail* article cited above–that is consequential, I argue, even when it generally functions below the threshold of consciousness (perhaps, indeed, especially when it acts below the threshold of consciousness). Everyday representational habits may lull our critical capacities, as we rush on to other projects and the business of our lives. However, Stillar argues for the significance of everyday texts:

> No matter how mundane we may take these types of text to be, they all (a) exhibit complexity in terms of the linguistic resources we draw upon to make and understand them, (b) perform critical rhetorical functions for the

participants involved, and (c) powerfully summon and
propagate the social orders in which we live. (1)

It is function "c" in Stillar's list with which this article is most concerned. How do texts of Westerness, including images, stabilize our
social order, and to what end? Given attention, these *Westernisms* in
Canadian discourse have the capacity to tell us much about the nature of the Canadian West itself: how we have constructed it in our
collective imagination, how we have negotiated with both what we
have found here and made here, and how we have disputed each
other's interpretations. In that sense, this article, indeed this book,
must also be considered as yet another entry in our continuous mean-
ing-making, an ongoing conversation about the West. And, of course,
the fruit of our understanding does not terminate at the Manitoba/
Ontario border: in understanding more about any region of a nation,
we understand more about the complexities of the nation itself.

Let me briefly contextualize myself: I identify as a Westerner. I was
born in New Westminster, B.C. in the same hospital as my father. My
mother was born in Vancouver. My prairie-born grandfather climbed
the North Shore mountains as a labourer in the '40s and '50s, putting in the Vancouver waterworks, and encountering trees so big he
still talks about them. Family stories report that my Francophone
great-grandmother paddled her canoe to work, teaching school in St.
Boniface. My Icelandic immigrant great-grandparents stared at the
Saskatchewan sky and tried to figure out how to farm. As a child, my
paternal grandmother, poverty-stricken on the great plains, crossed
the 49th parallel again and again. These true but romantic references
reveal, I hope, not merely the factual basis for my identification as a
multi-generational Westerner, but also the breadth of my attachments
and my affection for them. Certainly, I'm not from any other place.

Given my strong sense of regional affiliation, this *Globe and Mail*
front page triggered in me not only a deep sense of misrecognition,
but, paradoxically, also an almost comical wave of textbook Western
alienation ("How dare they assume the West is alienated and conservative. Eastern bastards!")[1]. I recollected Stephen Harper's Etobicoke
roots, sharing the observation with anyone within earshot. A *West*,
one possible version of the West, was recognized on that front page,
but it wasn't my West, one which accurately reflects my history, communities, and life. It's someone else's idea of the West. This article is
both a rebuttal and an attempt to understand why this version of the
West has been so persuasive; it analyzes the catalyzing *Globe and Mail*

Fig. 1. *Globe and Mail* photo representing "The West"

front page and another Western text, exploring the language used to signify the "West," related Canadian Western icons, such as those Rocky Mountains, and how they function in Canadian discourse.[2]

In coming to terms with how the West means in Canada, I identify three dominant cultural metanarratives that play into the current signification of the West in Canadian political discourse. In order to organize the ideas that cluster together, I've given each metanarrative a provisional title: 1. the Wild West; 2. the North West; and 3. the Global West. In the following sections, I elaborate on each of these sets of cultural resources and how they interact with each other to form much of our current ideology of the West, before concluding with an examination of a current expression of Westerness in action.

The Wild West

Others working on questions of the meaning of the Canadian West in the public imagination have pointed out that our West has much in common with the familiar metanarrative of the American "wild" West, arising from our shared roots: a joined geography that was inhabited by aboriginal peoples neither American nor Canadian and that was exploited and settled by similar peoples during roughly the same period. And, indeed, ample evidence confirms that the familiar myth of the American West is, to some degree, continental, popularized and elaborated through Hollywood movies and dime novels, with an emphasis on masculine adventure and hardy independence. American Western icons such as the cowboy, the Conestoga wagon, the saloon, and the lumber jack all have comfortable homes on this side of the border as well, woven throughout our home-grown cultural products.

Brian W. Dippie refers to such icons as "trans-border," and his examination of Western-themed visual art leads him to state "when it came to Western myth, the distinction to be drawn was not between life north and south of the Forty-ninth Parallel, but between East and West" (522). Dippie concludes, "When it comes to the visual imagery of the American and Canadian Wests, it can be said, emphatically: one West, one myth" (530). However, others examining the relationship of myths across the North American frontier detect a similar but more nuanced interplay. In "'A Northern Vision': Frontiers and the West in the Canadian and American Imagination," William H. Katerberg draws on popular literature to support his thesis that there has been an easy transmission of Western myths across the Canadian-American border, an exchange that has gone both ways. Katerberg offers an example of this phenomenon in the form of Ronald Regan—the quintessential cowboy (i.e., "Western") president—and his love of the poetry of Canadian Robert Service. Through a close reading of Service's popular poem "The Shooting of Dan McGrew," Katerberg demonstrates the extent to which Service's work conforms to the genre of the Western, a connection which exemplifies the influence of Western myth on both Canadian and American frontiers (544-5).

And, while it might be possible to dismiss Service's poetry and cowboy art as mere nostalgic artefacts, a recent publication from award-winning author Sharon Butala shows how aspects of the continental Western myth continue to inform our understanding of the Canadian West. Through a mixture of personal observation, history, and current events, in *Lilac Moon: Dreaming of the Real West* (2005), Saskatchewan's Butala re-visits the meaning of Canada West, particularly the prairie provinces. While *Lilac Moon*'s touted focus is the Canadian West, throughout Butala spends much of her narrative energies on pan-North American Wild West topics in the abstract—alienation, toughness, and the landscape; and in the particular—rodeos, guns, and bison, albeit all within a Canadian context. In her epilogue, she comments,

> I think that for thousands of Western Canadians the
> *dream of the West* is not about oil or farming or even cattle,
> or block after block of houses that would be palaces in
> most of the world, but instead, to settle finally into a *real*
> *life* that is part of this unique North American world, the
> one that was here before the first European set foot on it.
> (220, italics in the original)

Noting the North American nature of her setting in this excerpt, Butala reminds us here and elsewhere of another key feature of Western discourse shared by the American and Canadian Wests: the intensifier "real," which frequently prefaces "West." Infrequently do we hear of the "real east," or "real Ontario," for example, while the "real West" is a relatively common pairing. This hackneyed doublet offers a promise of authenticity, a notion that the West is somehow more real than other jurisdictions. The position suggested by the use of a term such as "the real West," however casual, corresponds to the idea of wildness itself present in the moniker "wild West." The term "wild" provides not just a description of the storied unregulated norms of behaviour on the American frontier, but also of the shared geography of the North American West itself: a landscape many still imagine as purer, less interfered with by humanity, retaining qualities of a pre-contact idyll such as described by Butala above, where she subsumes the idea of Canada within North America. Thus the term "real," when used in the context of the "West," allows us to observe a shared set of values that deeply inform our understanding and use of the West in current Canadian discourse, and that link us in a fraught but inevitable relationship to our continental sister, the USA.

The North West
However, the Canadian West is not the American West, as Katerberg and Butala would be quick to agree. The most obvious way in which the Canadian West has been inflected differently from the American West is through the strong−shall we say magnetic− influence of another direction, and another rich semiotic field, the Canadian North. The North figures dominantly in pan-Canadian imaginary: in both cultural imagination and geographic fact, the North is, quite literally, the shared ground for Canadians; it is our unique common denominator. The North is frequently represented as mythic, silent and spiritual. Even more so than the West, the North acts as a site of purity in an increasingly contaminated world and, I would argue, the evocative spectre of drowning polar bears (an indisputable

sign of damage) speaks not so much to the ruination of the North as to the loss of global innocence.

In *Canada and the Idea of the North*, Sherrill Grace provides a reading of a popular culture text that draws heavily on the Northern mythos, encapsulating much of this set of cultural resources in action. A quick review of Grace's interpretation here provides a rough overview of how the North signifies in Canadian discourse. Perhaps not surprisingly to those who have monitored Canadian pop culture in the last fifteen years or so, Grace's text is a beer ad (see Figure 2). The Molson Dry ad she analyzes involves two separate images: the top picture is of three Inukshuks – those standing human-like forms made of rock, closely identified with the North; the bottom visual portrays a very refreshing looking Molson Dry label. The text reads: "When you have a chance to stand for something, don't sit down. Character wins." Grace contextualizes and parses the ad as follows:

> Molson Canada, which sponsored the August 1995 rock
> concert in Inuvik, advertised Molson Dry by evoking
> a sense of shared nordicity through the symbols of the
> Inukshuk and the Molson label. This image appeared as
> a full-page colour advertisement in newspapers and on
> television during the summer of 1995 and represented
> a clever appeal to national identity and patriotic spirit
> through the semiotics of cold, purity and pride. (72)

This ad demonstrates many of the qualities we associate with the North in general (strength, coldness, purity, spirituality, mystery), while also evoking putative Canadian qualities with which (potential) patriots/beer drinkers are invited to identify. This text suggests that we are a "stand up" nation (like the Inukshuks, which seem to *stand on guard*, echoing our anthem), a country of good fellow peacemakers who show up the world's bullies: references to this are made visually in the row of soldier-like inukshuks and in the verbal text. The close association of Canadian identity and nordicity exemplified in this masterful text, into which the beer brand insinuates itself, is no one-off, but rather reinforces the existing and powerful connection between Canadian identity and the North.

How then does the West fit into this set piece of "Canada = North"? Regardless of geographic accuracy (after all, because of Alaska, the Canadian Eastern Arctic is actually larger than the Canadian Western Arctic), North and West are often semiotic bedmates in Canadian discourse, sharing similar patterns of signification. Con-

WHEN YOU HAVE

A CHANCE TO STAND FOR SOMETHING

DON'T SIT DOWN

CHARACTER WINS

Fig. 2. Molson Dry beer ad.

sider, for example, the snowy peaks of the Rockies meant to symbol-
ize Westerness featured on the front page of the *Globe and Mail*. In my
estimation, they look cold, desolate, and pure enough to function as
signs of either North or West. And this overlap is critical, as the North
and West increasingly map onto each other in Canada, creating the
NorthWest. Even though her focus is the North, Grace herself recognizes this trend. Using the work of contemporary Canadian writers as
her evidence, she claims that "North has moved ever more West and

North" (43). Katerberg echoes her stance: "In the culture of Canadian nationhood...the West is 'NorthWest,' West of the Old World and North of the US" (553). This important function of the North in Canada is a gift of distinction conferred upon the West, rendering it different from the American wild West, a difference cherished by many Canadians.

The Global West

In speaking to a friend and colleague from China, I was able to understand further the workings of the term "the West" in Canadian political discourse. What Katerberg and Grace's arguments do not address is the resonance of the term "the West" in what I will call "global discourse."

Global discourse, in the way I mean it, is the language of free trade agreements and international protocols, where economic and political power seem to be synonymous. It is a discourse through which, for example, international students are recruited and deals of all kinds are made, a way of talking and thinking about the world through the lens of the marketplace.

In order to try to verify my experiential sense of this discourse, I turned to the Collins Cobuild corpus, known also as the Bank of English. The Bank of English is a database of modern English in use, consisting of instances of over 200 million words from contemporary British, Canadian, Australian and American sources such as television, radio, newspaper, ephemera, and transcribed speech. From this corpus, the online corpus concordance/collocation sampler (consisting of a mere 56 million words) allows Internet users to find the 100 words which most frequently collocate or keep company with a given word, in the way that "bee" and "honey" tend to be found together. If we take out words to do with climate change, a search of the word "global" reveals one other significant group of collocates belonging to the register of business: "economy, market, system, fund" and "management."[3] This is the global discourse described here, one in which West acquires a whole new set of meanings, not divorced from what the "Canadian West" means.

And what particular meanings does the West have in this posited global discourse? I would suggest, rather bluntly: democracy, power, capital. In a have-not world, the haves are largely Westerners. Canada, of course, is a Western nation. While internationalists have long argued that North/South is a better index of have/have not, in real geographical terms, the East/West axis is, in fact, the direction that matters, rhetorically speaking. For example, often when we speak of "the West," this powerful abstraction includes nations such as Japan, because of their high level of prosperity and modernization, regardless of actual location on the map. And these commercial, pecuniary associations with the direction "West" may be ancient, as Grace reminds us in an earlier essay "Comparing Mythologies: Ideas of the West and North": the Western myth, she posits, has European origins in Columbus and the push for a passage to the Orient (248-9), which was, of course, an imperial and financial endeavour. In any case, "meaning" is not necessarily a logical issue; rather Bakhtinian resonances adhere to a term, and when we use the term "West" these "global" meanings are always unavoidably contained within it, even when we use it within a more localized Canadian context.

The Working West

So, let me now return to my initial beef: the use of "West" as a shorthand in Canadian political discourse to represent just a single version of Western Canada. As consumers of mainstream Canadian culture, we are all familiar with the association of the West with the Conservative party and, before that, and more powerfully, the Reform and Alliance parties. In any given national context, a regional tag would seem to be a disadvantage, an indication that the party's interests are limited and lack national scope. However, Katerberg notes the complexity inherent in cultural myth and the ways in which myth may exceed the localized or provincial context: "cultural myths can promote both national and regional, or 'limited' identities, and have continental and international resonances" (553-4). This quality of cultural myth is apparent in, for example, the bottles of maple syrup for sale at the Vancouver airport. Thousands of kilometres away from any actual sugar bush, the syrup has become a pan-Canadian sign (a little trinket of a myth of Canada that include voyageurs, Huron villages and sugar shacks) while still also representing specific regions of Eastern and "Central" Canada. Katerberg points out the relative and fluid nature of identities: "Distinctions between national, regional, and international identities break down on closer inspection, as all identities are 'limited'" (554). In the context of this discussion, Katerberg's assertion implies that, in some ways, all Canadians are Westerners; we all live in the greater West.

And this is how the term "the West" (and its attendant visual and verbal signification) functions in Canadian discourse: it is both a regional and a national identity – the Conservative party may be somewhat "Western Canadian," but it is also "Western and Canadian." This largely unspoken formulation is, like many successful rhetorical devices, both devastatingly simple and rather complex. It works, I hypothesize, to the advantage of the Conservative party to retain a Western tinge, a colouration, because the clusters of meanings associated with the word resonate positively with Canadian values (that is, our self-perception) and, more particularly, these values harmonize very well with the Conservative party's particular values.

To boil it down, the term "the West" carries with it a cast of meanings, many of them positive. The "wild West" suggests independence, adventurousness, and tenacity, along with a wash of dusty romanticism, and it reminds us of our kinship to the USA. This wild West is modified by ideas of the Canadian North, which influence what Daniel Francis calls "the mild West," adding other connotations, while also distinguishing it from the American West and mysticism, purity and mystery. Finally, in the field of global discourse, West connotes democracy, power, and wealth. If the Conservative party represents "Western" values within Canada, I understand how this combination is politically effective and appealing, even to those not from the regional West: many Canadians would (and clearly do) embrace a vision of Canada as a "Western" state by any measure, as a tough, independent, pure, prosperous, and powerful nation.

The Best Place on Earth?

Rather than ending here with a political analysis, I would like now to expand this reading of the West by demonstrating the scope of these ideas and how they may work in other less overtly political contexts. The actual text which caught my attention for further analysis is more mundane, and more highly regionalized than the *Globe and Mail* front page. I refer to a new variety of British Columbia licence plates called the "Winter Games Plates" (see Figure 3). The current standard issue plates—the ones you'll find on my car—feature the waving BC flag and the slogan "Beautiful British Columbia." For a slight annual fee, a kind of voluntary taxation, the new official Olympic and Paralympic Winter Games plates are available to all comers. Money from the extra cost helps to fund the upcoming 2010 winter Olympics in Vancouver-Whistler. The offer has been popular: even in my hometown of Kamloops, a remove from the Winter Games epicentre, local parking lots reveal many vehicles sporting the attractive new plates.

Let's consider the design of these license plates: in the background we have the iconic, almost *de rigeur* mountainscape. According to the plates' corporate authors, the Insurance Corporation of British Columbia (ICBC), this is no generic line of mountains. Rather,

Figure 3. B.C. Winter Games License Plate

> The mountain scene on the 2010 Winter Games plate
> is that of Garibaldi Park, located 13 km North of
> Squamish, 97 km North of Vancouver along Hwy 99 on
> the road to Whistler. The chosen plate design captures
> the spirit of the 2010 Winter Games while showcasing
> one of the most scenic and breathtaking areas between
> Vancouver and Whistler. The image was also used in the
> Vancouver 2010 Olympic and Paralympic Bid proposal.
> (ICBC website)

While a determined or interested person can find this information
on the ICBC website, or perhaps even recognize this particular vista,
the specific identity of this range is really beside the point. In practice,
the majority of people who encounter this image will simply equate
the mountainscape with Westerness, especially with BC, exactly like
the Rockies function on the front page of the *Globe and Mail*, perpetu-
ating this one-dimensional perspective on the West.

But what I'm even more interested in is the province's new official
slogan featured on the plates. All winter games plates read "The Best
Place on Earth," an expression also used over the last few years in a
domestic tourism campaign in which we British Columbians tell ourselves how great we are. However, the use of this "BC brand" on the
voluntary plates, and our willingness to fork out extra for these plates,
seems to me to be of a different order than its use in official government discourse. Through putting the plates, and thus the slogan, on
our private vehicles, ordinary people are quite literally buying into
this message. The public's willingness to endorse this motto means

that this is not merely a self-promotion ploy dreamed up in Victoria, but rather that this way of thinking about ourselves resonates with a good part of the population. Such self-aggrandizement is not necessarily new to the region: Laurie Ricou comments on this in a prescient passage from his book *The Arbutus/Madrone Files*, in which he reads a variety of Pacific NorthWest texts, including salmon, the Peace Arch, and various literary works. In this book Ricou notes that "tropes of excess … are themselves a staple of the NorthWest" (13). To make his point he quotes an earlier BC slogan – remember this one? – "Super, Natural," which, by today's standards, seems almost modest. In keeping with this pattern, the current tourism catchphrase of the Yukon, that supreme site of NorthWesterness, is "larger than life."

In the slogan "the best place on earth," the semiotics of the term the West – as I've been discussing in this paper so far – play out again, utilizing the three discourses in the construction of the Canadian West. First, the stereotypical characteristics of the "wild West" are realized through the sheer bravado expressed in this motto: the aggressive assertion "the best place on earth" demands a certain ruggedness from its interlocutor, a lack of fear about judgement and, on a provincial scale, almost pathological narcissism. This isn't a slogan concerned about offending the rest of the (lesser) world.

Second, the semiotics of the NorthWest are present in this motto in the idea of the West as the last stretch of uncontaminated, pure and wild land, a motif reinforced visually through the snowy, unpeopled mountains. The NorthWest at play here is not only a West modified by the North, as discussed earlier, but also a North modified by the West, rendering North as something more workable, domestic and familiar than the danger and malevolence often associated with the North proper. Margaret Atwood draws our attention to the dark side of the North through a series of lectures entitled *Strange Things*, where she cites the bloodthirsty Wendigo and our collective fascination with the doomed Franklin expedition – to name but a few of many cultural moments – as evidence of the creepiness Canadians have also come to relate to the North, but, I argue, not with the NorthWest we are dealing with here. Rather, through the lens of Westerness the nordicity underpinning this motto is unproblematic in its appeal, without the potential of danger usually suggested by the North proper. It is a place with which we, fairly unambiguously, are called to identify.

Third, the influence of global discourse appears in several ways. The prepositional phrase "on earth" situates the province on the global stage. Likewise, the rampant self-promotion and boosterism exemplified in this slogan clearly reflect global ad culture and the international marketplace: after all, the plate is for the Olympics, a "global" event, if ever there was one. The mountain image, as well, consists not just of mountains *per se*, but rather of "peaks"—a series of individual pinnacles—and, indeed, the language of individual achievement and competitive advantage borrows seamlessly and frequently from the alpinist. Further, the slogan "the best place on earth" echoes the title of the conference at which this paper was first presented, taken from an earlier exercise in promoting the West: "the last best West." Despite the positive tone of both slogans, they seem to emerge from a similar kind of anxiety, a fear of running out of the planet's resources and possibility: the fear, in short, of running out of West.

Finally, a note about the official 2010 Olympic emblem, a multi-coloured graphic interpretation of the Inukshuk, which appears right in the very centre of the Winter Games plates. Another whole paper could be devoted to this topic; however, let us very briefly review how the Inukshuk, called Ilanaaq by the Olympic organizing committee, exemplifies this argument about the sources of Westerness. The lone vigilant figure, meant to represent a guide, harkens to the hardy individualism of the wild West. The North is clearly present as this Northern regional image becomes a symbol of the West (thus further muddying North/West distinctions). Finally, global discourse is the whole *raison d'être* of the image, as Ilanaaq represents the West, lifting its crayola-coloured arms in a gesture of greeting from Canada to the global community.

Whither West?

In conclusion, I would like to point out the patterns explored in this chapter are surely the reason these slogans find such potent currency: they are not random. Rather, in order to be effective the people who put together and approved "the best place on earth" as BC's slogan were drawing upon pre-existing metanarratives. This slogan emerges from a similar cultural matrix as that from which the term "the West," and its various discursive adjuncts (both verbal and visual) accrue their meaning. For example, in a plain-spoken, folksy turn, Manitoba licence plates read "Friendly Manitoba." I doubt that we will see "Friendly BC" as a slogan in Canada's westernmost province, although it might be a nice goal. This difference in provincial attitude emerges from two different complex cultural histories of self-representation, both embedded within the West. But I would also point out that we Westerners are agents to some degree, not just stuck in a loop of re-representing, going back to the same semiotic well repeatedly; neither are we stuck in resentment or dis-ease, becoming upset at headlines. Instead, each time we select from certain semiotic resources, we re-inscribe and re-make that (non-identical) meaning, and here we have our opportunity. And so, the inflection of absolute superlative, "the best," says a lot not only about who we have been as a province, our "roots" as it were, but also about who we are now: in other words, what version of these stories or metanarratives gets told reflects quite sharply upon us.

My final exhortation takes its inspiration from Ricou. In *The Arbutus/Madrone Files* he writes, "definitions of the Pacific NorthWest region vary, shrinking and expanding as source and context alter. This book folds together many of these shifting, overlapping and disappearing maps" (5). I would expand that impulse to include all the West. What we need is not the stabilization of a brand or a regional stereotype offer, but rather flexibility and slipperiness as we continually negotiate the West. What are we doing here? In relationship to whom? We need to ask: what voices and range of experience are left out with every representational anecdote? What about the many recent immigrants to the West, both domestic and international? How does the West resonate for them? Or does it? Who, indeed, is left out of every shot of a remote mountainscape? And how might we re-envision our own space more inclusively and complexly without falling into easy clichés?

Notes

1. One of this article's reviewers observed that the Calgary and Edmonton papers are more likely to promote, on a regular basis, a simplistic, one-dimensional and conservative (dare we say Alberta-centric?) rendering of the West than the *Globe and Mail*. While not a regular reader of these papers, I am hardly surprised, and note how Western alienation actually supports a particular kind of West.

2. In his work *This is My Country, What's Yours?* Noah Richler folds the West, including Western alienation itself, into Greater Canada by proposing that Western alienation, ironically, is just a strong version of a larger pattern of Canadian myths of disappointment, of always being let down by a central power, suspicion and distrust (282).

3. The top 20 substantive words from the "global" collocate list, in order of frequency, are the following: warming, change, climate, scale, economy, market, system, fund, management, village, model, threat, temperatures, temperature, trade, ocean, markets, average, models, and business.

Works Cited

Atwood, Margaret. *Strange Things.* Oxford: Clarendon P, 1995.

Butala, Sharon. *Lilac Moon: Dreaming of the Real West.* Toronto: HarperCollins, 2005.

"Collins Cobuild Concordance and Collocations Sampler." *Collins Home Page.* HarperCollins. 14 June 2008. <http://www.collins. co.uk/corpus/CorpusSearch.aspx>

Dippie, Brian W. "One West, One Myth: Transborder Continuity in Western Art." *American Review of Canadian Studies* 33 (Winter 2003): 509-41.

Francis, Daniel. *National Dreams: Myth, Memory, and Canadian History.* Vancouver: Arsenal Pulp Press, 1997.

"2010 Winter Games Licence Plates." *Insurance Corporation of British Columbia.* 2008. Insurance Corporation of British Columbia. 14 June 2008. <http://www.icbc.com/registration/reg_spec_lic_ plates_opp.asp>

Katerberg, William. "'A Northern Vision': Frontiers and the West in the Canadian and American Imagination." *American Review of Canadian Studies* 33 (Winter 2003): 543-563.

Grace, Sherrill. *Canada and the Idea of the North.* Montreal: McGill-Queen's UP, 2001.

__. "Comparing Mythologies: Ideas of the West and North." *The Borderlands Anthology.* Ed. Robert Lecker. Toronto: ECW P, 1991. 243-262.

Richler, Noah. *This is My Country, What's Yours? A Literary Atlas of Canada.* Toronto: McClelland & Stewart, 2006.

Ricou, Laurie. *The Arbutus/Madrone Files: Reading the Pacific NorthWest.* Edmonton: NeWest, 2002.

Stillar, Glenn. *Analyzing Everyday Texts: Discourse, Rhetoric and Social Perspectives.* Thousand Oaks, CA: SAGE, 1998.

Tanis MacDonald

Gateway Politics: West Meets West in Kristjana Gunnars' *Zero Hour*

To write you this I have come to the Gateway to the West. Not because the West is intriguing. But because it is there: open, dry, with
little culture and much politics. And beyond the West there is the
ocean. The jungle. The rains. A place to long for. To think towards.

Kristjana Gunnars, *Zero Hour* (1991)

Go west, young man, and grow up with the country.

John Soule, editorial, *Terre Haute Express* (1851)

Part I: Thinking West

West as opportunity, west as philosophical destination:
the two quotations above suggest a dichotomy about
ideas of the west as the great good place in North
America and, more significantly, about the state of
mind that accompanies the decision to travel west–into the sunset,
towards the edge of the continent, and perhaps beyond everyday
experience. "Heading west" in order to seek a new beginning–be
that fresh start nationally inflected as John Soule asserts or spiritually
aligned as Kristjana Gunnars implies–suggests an engagement with
geography, including but not limited to the physical act of traversing
space: the choice to leave the centre for the margins. As a Canadian
literary trope, "going west" has often been proposed as an ontological
position as well as a geographical direction. Both Soule and Gunnars
gesture to this moment before "heading west" as a moment of preparation: the ontology of the west demands that the traveler becomes
something other than the usual self. To stand at the "Gateway to the
West" and to prepare to enter the new frontier is to re-think the nature of being, selfhood, and change. John Soule's famous 1851 advice
exhorting expansion into the western territories as an American op-

portunity for both adventure and financial gain[1] seems worlds away from Kristjana Gunnars' allusive and genre-challenging *Zero Hour*. Yet Soule's position as editor of the *Terre Haute Express* in the mid-nineteenth century indicates that he too was acquainted with a "gateway" view, and spoke from a place that was "open, dry, with little culture and much politics." Beyond geography, the western edge of the continent is an effulgent symbol of freedom in both the American and Canadian imagination, and Soule's masculinist advice can be read alongside Gunnar's philosophical peregrinations as historically and geographically situated notions of paradise.

The literary tendency to imagine the west as both prosaically "there" *and* mythically "beyond" is neither frivolous nor contradictory, but, rather, a philosophical position that informs the Canadian metanarrative, as Robert Kroetsch suggests, as paradoxically "disunified" and defined by resistance to unity. Where Soule's gateway points to opportunity for "growth" as social maturity and financial gain, in keeping with the American Dream, Gunnars' gateway is closer to the Kroetschian periphery, in which "doubt about our ability to know invades the narrative" (Kroetsch 23). In so much of Canadian literature, Paradise West is "a place to long for," but not necessarily a place at which one may arrive. Certainly decades of prairie literature affirm that Paradise cannot be found by rushing towards it, as Margaret Laurence's heroines – Stacey in *The Fire-dwellers*, and Hagar in *The Stone Angel* – discover upon arriving in Vancouver after years of prairie life: the West Coast is not so much Paradise found as it is Paradise deferred.[2] Furthermore, Gunnars makes it clear that arriving is never just a matter of buying a plane ticket or driving over the mountains. The problem with the west as Paradise is that it must be "thought towards," and in *Zero Hour* Gunnars offers an unrepentant philosophy of desire that is all too aware of the effort that thinking takes.

In *Zero Hour* Gunnars juxtaposes the stark prairie with the paradisal coast that lies beyond it, in a postmodern text that reaches beyond the nation-building ideals of "growing up with the country" to contemplate growing beyond the demands of culture. Offering fragments of life writing, philosophy, literary theory, and a particular reading of the geography of the Canadian West, Gunnars arranges these shards in a shatter pattern by exploring the traditional elegiac mode through a very contemporary obsession with nuclear annihilation. Although the book's publication in 1991 technically disqualifies it from being part of Jon Paul Fiorentino's definition of 21st-century "post-prairie poetics," Gunnars' intense exploration of the ways in which "the anxiety of geography … reshapes the context" of place declares *Zero Hour*'s position in post-prairie modality (Fiorentino 9).

Part narrative, part poem, part elegy, part philosophical treatise, *Zero Hour* is the first-person account of a woman's attempt to establish a satisfying mourning ritual in the aftermath of her father's death. The text engages with elegiac conventions of pastoral consolation even as it casts a doubtful eye on the Christian consolation on which such conventions lean. Gunnars' metaphor for the moment of her father's death is a nuclear explosion, the "zero hour" of her title, and the mourner must travel through the emotional equivalent of a nuclear winter. The narrator—who is explicitly identified in the text as a literary version of the author herself—describes an imaginative longing for that which lies "beyond the West" as a spiritual desire interlaced with a philosophical premise to move beyond her mourning self. But it is in Gunnars' inquiry into these types of vital elegiac paradoxes that *Zero Hour* finds purchase as a text that rewrites the west as it rewrites mourning. The geographical west is only coincidentally located near to the consolatory West, beyond which lies Paradise. The impulse towards Paradise is far more significant than movement towards it: longing trumps doing, and *Zero Hour* proposes a west in which the impossibility of consolation is yoked to a mappable certitude. In true postmodern fashion, the Gateway defines the West by refusing to define it. Were the protagonist of Gunnars' *Zero Hour* to actually "go west, young woman" in order to keep the country (and all its messy postmodern disunity) at her back, her arrival would undo the premise of the Paradise that lies "beyond the West"; i.e., beyond the space that mourning occupies.

The Gateway to the West as a philosophical space of preparation is wryly dismissed in Gunnars' initial description, but we cannot ignore that this dismissal echoes Northrop Frye's "where is here?" even as it reiterates Sir Edmund Hillary's existential claim about climbing Mount Everest: "Because it was there." This claim is made doubly ironic by Gunnars with the lugubrious implication that life in a Gateway city is a barely surmountable obstacle. Add to this a hint of Gertrude Stein's statement about her brief return to her hometown of Oakland, California in *Everybody's Autobiography*: "There's no *there* there." All things considered, this West may not be "intriguing," but it is most definitely "there." But, to return another version of Frye's question, where in this text is "there?" Even a postmodern prose-poem cannot entirely sidestep one of the most contentious points in working towards a thesis of the west in Canada: where does the west begin? At the ocean, interior, mountains, foothills, prairie? And whose west is it? The west "settled" by pioneers from Europe, or the west of the Indigenous peoples? Here Gunnars conflates notions of the west as stark prairie and lush coast as death and regeneration, and reconfigures what she calls "the disappointment, the heartbreak of the west" ("Was the West Ever One?" 119) into a post-prairie diasporic elegy. In *Zero Hour*, the end of a life is conflated with the end of consciousness, the western edge of a continental land mass, and the end of meaning.

Part II: The Poetics of Zero

Writing beyond expectations and the limits of genre is a career-long project for Gunnars. In an essay titled "On Writing Short Books" in her 2004 collection *Stranger at the Door*, Gunnars considers the popular expectation that novels must be lengthy tomes, and argues instead for the appeal of the "brief, intensely written, poetic narrative," citing Elizabeth Smart's *By Grand Central Station I Sat Down and Wept* as the ultimate Canadian example (*Stranger* 86). Referring to another "short book," Albert Camus' *The Outsider*, Gunnars observes that such books are often deeply allusive and "intergeneric," and furthermore, that the "brevity of narration is in itself a philosophical position" (86-87). Include Gunnars' contentions that such a short book "tends towards the fragmented, the poetic and the theoretical" and demands "to be lived with rather than simply read and put aside for the next one" (86), and it becomes clear that *Zero Hour*, though she does not name her own text in the essay, represents Gunnars' "short book": a brief, intense and highly allusive narrative. *Zero Hour*'s use of fragmentation – the shatter pattern, in keeping with Gunnars' explosion imagery – corresponds to Robert Kroetsch's idea that the postmodern novel treats the ongoing present as "the debris of something else" and any form of immediate experience as a digression from the "real" narrative of the past (*Stranger* 84). For Gunnars, this kind of book resists being "consumed" in the way that more realist novels are consumed: "Given that we cannot know the whole story, it would be absurd to try to master the narrative in all its parts and provide closure as well" (*Stranger* 85-86). Practicing this liminal "short book" form that negotiates the space between a novella and a long poem, Gunnars uses the metaphor of the father's death as a bomb to convey the "sense of living on the margin of 'big' history" (84): in this case, the "big history" of institutionalized and governmental violence that forms the subtext of *Zero Hour*.

The resistance to closure is important to reading *Zero Hour* as a contemporary elegy that considers the personal affect of mourning alongside the political implications of historical violence. Such explorations are not unknown in Canadian elegiac work, with Dennis Lee's *Civil Elegies* and Fred Wah's *Waiting for Saskatchewan* as two examples of long poetic sequences that fold the mourner's grief into troubled revelations of governmental policies of racism and war. However, the resistance to closure, and perhaps to consolation itself, is also a vital component of what Gunnars calls her own "poetry of belligerence" in her essay "Avoidance and Confrontation: Excerpts from Notes on a Longpoem Poetics," published in *Trace: Prairie Writers on Writing* in 1986. Asserting that writers of her generation inherited "the post-war language of crisis that comes with the nuclear age" (183), Gunnars describes her struggle to write two kinds of psychological and linguistic estrangement: "the 'permanent' alienation" of modernism "where things pass, imperceptibly or not, and there is a continual state of Stevesian 'flux' to contend with in existence" and a post-Hiroshima "social alienation" from "the company of the living" (180). Written with the fragmentation and the intergeneric allusiveness of the "short book," *Zero Hour* presents social and geographical alienation through two central metaphors: grief as the emotional equivalent of nuclear winter, and the West as a Paradise that lies beyond consolation.

The major literary allusion in *Zero Hour*, to the extent that Gunnars even glosses it in the book's title, is to French philosopher and semiotician Roland Barthes' idea of "degree zero writing" from his 1953 text *Writing Degree Zero*. Barthes debates the possibilities for language use that extend beyond stale reference, possibilities that he claims are realized only in the dictionary or in poetry, where the written word may be "reduced to a sort of zero degree, pregnant with all past and future specifications" and therefore "contains simultaneously all the acceptations from which a relational discourse might have required it to choose" (Barthes 48). Picking up on Barthes' idea of an "encyclopaedic" function of a word, Gunnars modifies Barthes' "degree zero writing" and declares that *Zero Hour* will be her attempt at "ground zero writing…writing in which the author does not know what to do" because the "writing is enacted exactly where the bomb fell" (*Zero* 10). Though the term "ground zero" was coined in the early days of the atomic age, Gunnars' use of the term to explore the literary practice of mourning predates the more recently popularized use of "Ground Zero" to indicate the remnants of World Trade Center towers in New York City. *Zero Hour*, written in 1991, was published ten years before the implications of locating "ground zero" as a site of mourning and regeneration was made culturally explicit to the reading population of North America. The metaphor is fundamental to Gunnars' notion of entering a space with the intention of establishing a mourning practice. Gunnars' "ground zero" functions as a symbol of physical annihilation and of spiritual emptiness, as well as a statement of poetics:

> If the mind were a nuclear reactor with a built-in safety
> shutdown mechanism, I could say my mind shuts down
> when thoughts of my father's decline and fall occur. All
> the meters instantly go down. All the arrows suddenly
> point to zero....You are left with a story that is not a
> story. A novel that is not a novel, a poem no longer a
> poem. (*Zero* 29)

Gunnars' concern with nuclear escalation have been a prominent feature in several of her texts. In "Avoidance and Confrontation" she vows to "write poetry that will help rechannel the ingredients of the Nuclear Age" (182), and nuclear disarmament acts as a major plot device in her 1989 novel *The Prowler*, and as a prominent thematic concern of her 1985 volume of poetry *The Night Workers of Ragnarök*. Given Gunnars' politics, the cameo appearance in *Zero Hour* of American physicist Richard Feynman as her father's dissertation supervisor at the California Institute of Technology is both highly appropriate and deeply ironic. Feynman worked on the Manhattan Project when he was a young and gifted scientist, and his image as a father figure to the narrator's father is an excellent example of Barthes' degree zero writing as writing that is "pregnant with possibility." If the portrayal of the narrator's brilliant geologist father is given over to elegiac encomium, then Feynman's historical legacy in the atomic age suggests a blip in this paternal praise.[3] Considering nuclear disaster as her most developed metaphor for violence, both historical and personal, the Icelandic-born Gunnars notes that "global nuclear escalation" is "an obsession in Scandinavia," but she is surprised to find the issue "woefully absent from Canadian letters":

> There has been talk of making the Nordic countries a
> nuclear-free zone, and discussion is constantly taking
> place on issues of world peace. I could not help noticing
> the insidiousness of the situation where a nation [Iceland] without armed forces, dedicated to peace, nonetheless cannot escape the effects of nuclear escalation. (*Night
> Workers* 4)

So Gunnars' proposal to "think towards" a Paradise West is as global as it is local, and as political as it is personal. Far from an instructional narrative of how to get to Paradise, Gunnars offers a contemplation of what it is to live at the "ground zero" of affect, writing grief as an emotional annihilation equivalent to a nuclear disaster: "when a world disappears, it takes away with it everything you are up to that moment. Your past is erased within a few minutes and you no longer recognize it as your own. Suddenly you stand up and find you have to start over. There is no you" (11). Declaring that she wants to write a book that demonstrates "loss without commentary" (25), the narrator offers a text that "steps outside of time" to get to the "zero" of grief (17). In *Zero Hour*, even the west coast–known as "the best place on earth" according to recent television commercials–becomes vulnerable to denatured science and to human frailty. Gunnars offers an anti-pastoral symbology that threatens Paradise West, emphasizing nuclear disaster as perverted entropy, and suggesting fruitfully that her spirituality does align on some points with geography. In their shared vulnerability to despairing annihilation, West does meet west.

Part III: Gateway and Ground: The Politics of Mourning

Gunnars' "Gateway to the West," and not coincidentally the gateway to her state of mourning, is the city of Winnipeg. As Deborah Keahey notes in *Making it Home: Place in Canadian Prairie Literature*, Winnipeg acts as a "transformative site" in *Zero Hour*, as the narrator "makes home" out of the strangeness of the city (48). The gateway function of Winnipeg, the fact that the city represents both west and not-west, emptied of "culture" yet filled with "politics," housing a speaker who is physically present but absented by her grief, makes the city not only a transformative site, but also a philosophical trope: a gateway beyond the limitations of the self. Like a pushpin in the map of mourning, Winnipeg as Gateway to the West marks the west as an elegiac space of annihilation and regeneration, particularly as Gateway's history of "much politics" forces the narrator to read a culture of profound mourning that lurks beneath her view of "little culture." In Winnipeg you are here, and only from here may you go west, young woman.

But before she can access this gateway, Gunnars' configuration of "the West" in her mourning narrative begins as a declaration of intention and location of place that confounds the tradition of pastoral consolation. The death of the narrator's father takes place in the lush of the Willamette Valley in Oregon. Geographically, botanically, climate-wise, our narrator is already immersed in the paradisal pastoral beauty of the west coast. But much depends upon how we view the west in this spiritual geography. The prairie and the coastal rainforest occupy positions on a map of mourning—points on a compass that we can read as Purgatorio and Paradiso, as though Gunnars is refashioning Dante's *Commedia*. Midway through her life's journey, she finds herself, not lost in " a dark wood of error" as Dante was, but, rather, in the stark landscape of grief. Moving east in order to think towards and eventually "beyond the West" is perhaps illogical, but *Zero Hour* configures the West as a spiritual destination, and the necessities of the mourning journey cannot be subject only to the force of logic. Spiritually and philosophically, this mourner's journey begins with the search for a space that reflects and even affirms her annihilated world. The Canadian prairies offer her a geographic demonstration of the paradoxical elegiac mode: space that appears empty but is historically and psychologically full, and is evocative of a profound absence that bespeaks a presence. Much of *Zero Hour* is occupied with aligning the ethos of the prairies with the narrator's mythology of mourning. While the narrator's geographical route is circuitous, her emotional route follows the fractured logic of mourning. Grief is pure affect, but mourning is a process that demands ritual, and literary mourning requires a mythic symbol; for the narrator of *Zero Hour*, finding the Gateway to the other world is first an idea, then a ritual, and then finally a geographic space.

Winnipeg was dubbed the "gateway to the west" during the 19th century, as Ontario politicians advocated for Western expansion. In the United States, the nickname was applied to both Fargo, North Dakota, and to St. Louis, Missouri, for similar reasons. The slogan is still used occasionally about Winnipeg, though the city's official slogan has become the non-historical, non-situated, giddily assertive "Winnipeg: One Great City!" This new slogan, blandly but vigorously proclaiming "greatness" without historical or cultural context, was hilariously parodied by visual and performance artists Shawna Dempsey and Lori Millan as "One Gay City!" in an inspired bit of lesbian culture-jamming in the late 1990s. Dempsey and Millan proved, among other things, that civic slogans are not mere cultural space-filler; that historical context, recent or ancient, matters when a community declares itself either Gateway or "great."[4]

Consequently, in *Zero Hour*, when the narrator holes up in the echoing empty rooms of an old mansion, adjacent to but safe from the floods and plagues of mosquitoes of Biblical proportions for which Winnipeg is infamous, her choice of mourning space is neither unmarked nor empty. The city insinuates its history upon the text, and disturbs the narrator's personal mourning with an overriding political urgency. Far from indulging in stereotypical regionalism that designates Ontario and British Columbia as great, wealthy, fruit-bearing green provinces separated by two thousand miles of dust and farms called the Canadian prairie, Gunnars' protagonist notes the unexpected greenness of the city, the gardens and lawns: beauty notable even in, or especially in, this purgatorial space. But Gunnars also notes that Winnipeg remains a "city of warehouses" (19), as it has been for more than a century: a storage and distribution centre for agricultural products of the prairies and for manufactured products from Eastern Canada. The idea that emotion may be stored and distributed at a later date has a great deal to do with rituals of mourning, and could suggest that Gunnars' empty mansion is another kind of "warehouse."

The mansion as metaphor becomes even more poignant and historically compromised as the narrator notes that the house was "built and owned by one of the owners of a warehouse during the heyday of the Exchange District" (20). The location of that mansion within the Gateway city says something about the guiding persona of Winnipeg in this text. Despite the fact that she feels as though her own past has been wiped away by the enormity of her loss, the narrator finds that her search for a space that is unmarked by grief is impossible. She comes to understand that she cannot find a personal space for mourning without unearthing a politicized space of mourning. Such politicized space fans out from her personal space in historical waves, including her neighbourhood, the city, the surrounding prairies, the west that leads to the West: all spaces haunted by the subtext of history. The beautiful tree-lined neighbourhood in which the mansion is situated, described by Gunnars as "an old estate located in a park of such mansions, secluded by three enormous gates through which you pass" (20), is immediately recognizable to current or former Winnipeggers as Armstrong's Point, on which the first mansion was built in 1845, and now more colloquially known as "the Gates." This Gateway to the West has its internal gates, and not everyone is welcome everywhere in this west. The original function of the metal gates was to lock out the undesirable working class that populated boom-town Winnipeg in the 19th century, when the city limits began to creep towards the exclusive homes of Armstrong's Point. Since the 1950s, the Gates have shared an east-west boundary with one of the most poverty-stricken areas of Winnipeg. The elaborate gates still stand at the borders of the neighbourhood, but they are no longer locked, not because the spirit of solidarity has seized the residents of Armstrong's Point, but because the gates were ineffective in keeping the privileged space separate, and residents have found that active police surveillance does what the psychological barrier of stone gates can no longer accomplish.

In *Zero Hour*, the empty mansion in which the narrator lives not only carries a legacy as ironic nostalgia for the city's commoditized "glory days" of the 1890s-1920s, but its riverside location in Armstrong's Point also suggests that the mansion sits on land that was much in demand by Métis and poor Scottish farmers from the 1840s to the 1860s, a site of contention in the Red River Rebellion of 1869-70. In the Manitoba Act of 1870, these peoples were issued "Manitoba Script" from the Federal Government, entitling the bearers to good farming lots lining the Red and Assiniboine Rivers. Such claims were never honoured, as the Manitoba Métis Federation reminded the Manitoba government in April 2006, when the Federation insisted that the province make good on its 135-year debt of river-lot land. Located on the banks of the Assiniboine River, Armstrong's Point would come under the terms of those land claims, as would various communities in and surrounding Winnipeg. In the present day, the gateposts of Armstrong's Point indicate a socio-economic, class-based, and racial border between the residents of the rooming houses on one side of the street (many of them of Aboriginal and Métis backgrounds) and the mostly white residents of the graciously aging mansions on the other. In the metaphor of the empty mansion, Gunnars' personal mourning practice runs up against historical echoes of mourned space that has already been stolen and recommodified.[5]

Gunnars inscribes the Aboriginal subtext of *Zero Hour* through the narrator's two encounters with the Cree community. The narrator, invited to watch the dance of mourning performed by a Cree woman whose father has died, admires the Indigenous culture's acceptance of and ritual to acknowledge "loss without commentary." While she knows she can neither appropriate nor imitate the dance, she remembers and records it as evidence of mourning that does not "launder emotions" (17); the Cree woman's mourning dance lives in the narrator's memory as the example she admires, but cannot follow. Later in the text, the narrator walks behind three Cree residents from the neighbourhood abutting the Gates and observes a teenage boy in the group beat a butterfly to death with his t-shirt. This is Winnipeg as Gateway: to an annihilated cultural past, to losses both personal and political, to pastoral consolation abutted onto the violence of poverty. The narrator realizes that the annihilation that she fears has already happened to Indigenous populations in Canada, in which thousands of people have been institutionally and governmentally estranged from their families and their cultures, in which communities were usurped by despair, and about which collective mourning has not yet finished.

Part III: Heartbreak of the West

It is possible to read the end of *Zero Hour* as quite conventional in terms of the elegiac consolation that it proposes. Completing the text as her ritual of mourning, Gunnars' narrator prepares to leave the mansion with the advent of fall; like Milton's swain in *Lycidas*, she will move on to "freshe fields and pastures new." However, as with many elegiac texts, *Zero Hour* debates the latitudes and paradoxes of consolation, and the narrator cherishes this definition sent in a friend's letter: "the only consolation I give you is that you will never get over it" (92). If the loss is world-destroying, as Gunnars maintains throughout *Zero Hour*, to what fresh fields can the mourner realistically move? For the final unmaking of this world, Gunnars turns to Norse mythology for an alternate view of Paradise. Valhalla, the warrior's heaven, is understood to be merely a way station for warriors (albeit a very pleasant one) until the true paradise, Gimli, emerges after the climatic battle of Ragnarök. Gimli is also the name of a town on Lake Winnipeg, just north of the city, and the largest settlement of Icelandic peoples outside of Iceland. The narrator attends a cultural festival there, presided over by the Viking statue that welcomes visitors to the town, and by the not-dissimilar physical person of Icelandic-Canadian scholar and poet David Arnason.[6] In *Zero Hour*, Arnason presides over Gimli like Odin after Ragnarök, reminding the crowd that it "must protect its own culture" (93). This is a different version of Paradise West, and the narrator 's image of "many hundred pairs of hands...clapping madly against the sun-laden blue sky" (93) seems to be the embodiment of heavenly approval, a surprise after the mournful tone of much of *Zero Hour*. It seems as though Ragnarök is over; we are in Gimli now.

But just as the repopulation of the west by immigrants from Scandinavia and all parts of Europe — those settler-invader populations — displaced but could not replace the Aboriginal peoples who originally hunted and lived on that land, so the making of the migrant's world, with its injunction to "protect its own culture," cannot quite dispel the politicized mourning to which the narrator has been awakened. In *The Prowler*, Gunnars calls Icelanders "white Inuits," people who are both foreign to and native of Scandinavia. While readers should take seriously Len Findlay's warning that many literary strategies to "self-Indigenize" in Canadian literature are doomed to merely "reinscribe diffusionist colonialism" (Findlay 372), we should take equally seriously Gunnars' discussion of the parallels between the Indigenous peoples who were removed from tribal hunting grounds on the prairies and the destitute Europeans who "were lured by false advertising" to farm and populate the Canadian West. These Europeans (including those "white Inuit" Icelanders) were so thoroughly "conquered by the West" that Gunnars finds that "the disappointment, the heartbreak of the West is still in the air" ("Was the West" 117-118). This similarity between those First Nations and immigrant populations who were "conquered" in different contexts by the project of Western settlement suffuses *Zero Hour* with profound historical grief. Gunnars' protagonist knows it is her task to show "solidarity with the grieving" (25) she has found at the Gateway, and demonstrate respect to the mourning that remains unconsoled, and largely unacknowledged, when her ritual has been completed. She remains in spiritual debt to the example of the Cree woman dancing her grief for her father: the gift of observing "loss without commentary." The death of the narrator's father has reminded her that *there is no zero on the clock. To get to zero, you have to step outside time*" (122; Gunnars' emphasis). The conflation of time and place, being at ground zero at zero hour, suggests that a history of annihilation, like a history of mourning, is always current and never fully consoled; it is never subject to commentary, but always in need of commemoration.

It is towards such needful commemoration that the final pages of *Zero Hour* builds, for, on the level of story, the ending of the text is more indicative of Gunnars' "combining of harmony and disjuncture" ("Avoidance " 182) than a completion of a narrative. Deborah Keahey suggests that the ending of *Zero Hour* is "massively confusing" with the sudden introduction of the narrator's son and his violin in a space of deep loneliness, as the beauty of the son's music suggests a final symbol of homemaking in a site that the protagonist is leaving (Keahey 49). Appearing to offer familial consolation and a generational resolution of mourning, the narrator's son, the boy "in whom all [her] father's hopes are bound" (127) enters his mother's mansion apartment just as he appears earlier in the text at his grandfather's bedside to offer the gift of his youth and resiliency in the face of despair (110-111). When the boy plays his violin for his grandfather, he plays European music and American jazz, and the music is clearly a gift for the narrator's dying father, who listens "raptly" (111). However, the key to reading the boy's appearance at the end of *Zero Hour* is also the key to reading the west (as prairie) as that space which both defines and refuses the West (as coastal paradise). When the boy appears again at the end of the text, the music seems to be a gift, but it actually functions to repay the narrator's debt to the Cree woman who showed her the dance of "loss without commentary."

In her reading of *Zero Hour*, Keahey discusses "Winnipeg's inscription as an empty present in which to recollect the past" (49), which is accurate as a description of personal mourning, but reading Winnipeg as both west and "Gateway" in Gunnars' narrative disunites even the conventional mourning narrative, and suggests that one grief can recognize another grief more readily than people recognize their own histories. Clearly, the Gateway is too bartered and betrayed a site to operate as a "place to think towards…to long for," but in the end Paradise is indeed postponed for the harmony and disjuncture of west meeting West in this poetry of belligerence. The story of the return gift begins with the narrator looking out of the windows of her now-empty mansion, seated at an angle so she can "see out of the Gate and into the streets closer to downtown" and note that "at five in the morning the streets of the Gates in Winnipeg are like a picture someone painted without people" (125-126). This "picture" refers to the "unpeopling" of early Canada as reflected in landscape paintings of the 18th and 19th century that "paint over" the Aboriginal presence. Thomas King parodies this artistic trope in his 1999 novel *Truth and Bright Water*, in which his "famous Native artist" Monroe Swimmer works as a museum restorer, ironically restoring not the paintings themselves, but rather restoring images of Aboriginal people who have been "painted out" of colonial Canadian landscapes, literally and figuratively.[7] Gunnars' evocation of the de-Indigenized landscape that is re-Indigenized, first by people "stumbling" and being helped by others into the various houses, and then by the figure of the narrator's son, is a reimagined acknowledgement of presence, again offered without commentary, like the mourning dance: at once unified by a past filled with grief and disunified by an uncertain present. Even the boy's offering of music is Aboriginalized. The violin is, after all, an instrument adopted by displaced Métis peoples in Manitoba and Saskatchewan, and when the boy himself appears, wearing a "Peruvian hat" (127), he appears from the other side of the Gates, walking through the current Aboriginalized space, moving through the gated boundaries into that space of mourning for the west, that politicized, stolen, and commodified space, and offering in the music an art that describes loss without commentary, a parallel to the Cree woman's dance. Paradise is postponed again as the text ends without movement to the West. Arrested in the Gateway position, "where" meets "there" in this place of "much politics"; at the Gateway, postcolonial Canadian west meets the spiritual West, and the heartbreak of this history cannot and does not step outside of time.

Notes

1. Soule's utterance is often attributed to Horace Greeley, founder and editor of the *New York Tribune,* who made it famous in his 1865 editorial. Debate rages on as to the original authorship, and I will not solve it here. However, for my purposes, the differences between Greeley's East-Coast position and Soule's more liminal "Gateway" position are significant, for the injunction to "go west" means something when uttered from the centre of the continent that it does not when uttered from the Eastern searboard.

2. Laurence is by no means the only Canadian writer to construct the west coast as an ambiguous paradise. Historical novels by Daphne Marlatt (*Ana Historic*) and Sky Lee (*Disappearing Moon Café*) suggest that the iconoclastic "freedom" of the West Coast was not available to female or Chinese immigrants to the coast in the late 19th century. Dorothy Livesay's 1944 long poem about Vancouver's industrial boom, "West Coast," notes that workers were "swept from farm and mine/drawn to the hungry suction of the sea." Malcolm Lowry's posthumously published *October Ferry to Gabriola* paints a picture of a west coast island retreat that is heavenly in its solitude, and hellish for the same reasons.

3. Given Gunnar's anti-nuclear politics, Feynman's inclusion in this text is startling, even more so as he is mentioned only in his capacity as the father's dissertation supervisor, and not as a pioneer of the atomic bomb. Oddly, but perhaps by design, his name is misspelled in the text, appearing on page 83 of *Zero Hour* as "Richard Feinman."

4. For further reading on Millan and Dempsey's urban installation and the "one gay city" phenomenon, see Janice Oakley's incisive and thoughtful article "Postcards from the Edge: Decoding Winnipeg's 'One Gay City' Campaign."

5. Though the Manitoba courts dismissed the legality of "Manitoba Script" in late 2007, the ongoing legacy of the Red River Rebellion in Winnipeg culture should not be dismissed. Murals depicting Riel and Gabriel Dumont are regularly displayed all over the city, and "Louis Riel Day" was declared an official holiday in February 2008.

6. Poet and scholar Di Brandt also riffs on the resemblance between Arnason and the Viking statue in Gimli. See Brandt's "The happiest reader in the world: David Arnason's revisionary stories."

7. King is not the only First Nations artist to parody this painting practice. Cree filmmaker and visual artist Kent Monkman works with painting, film, and site-specific performance to insert his image into colonial or exploration landscapes, in a series of projects he calls "Colonial Art Space Interventions." For more on Monkman's provocative and playful reappropriations, see Peter Goddard's "Kent Monkman: Man of Mischief" and Monkman's own *Urban Nation* website.

Works Cited

Barthes, Roland. *Writing Degree Zero*. 1953. Trans. Annette Lavers and Colin Smith. New York: Hill and Wang, 1977.

Brandt, Di. "The happiest reader in the world: David Arnason's revisionary stories." *So this is the world and here I am in it*. Edmonton: NeWest, 2007. 55-71.

Findlay, Len. "Always Indigenize! The Radical Humanities in the Postcolonial Canadian University." *Unhomely States: Theorizing English-Canadian Postcolonialism*. Ed. Cynthia Sugars. Peterborough: Broadview, 2004. 367-382.

Fiorentino, Jon Paul and Robert Kroetsch. "Post-Prairie Poetics: A Dialogue." *Post-Prairie: An Anthology of New Poetry*. Vancouver: Talonbooks, 2005. 9-13.

Goddard, Peter. "Kent Monkman: Man of Mischief." *Toronto Star*. 22 Nov. 2007.

Gunnars, Kristjana. "Avoidance and Confrontation: Excerpts from Notes on a Longpoem Poetics." *Trace: Prairie Writers on Writing*. Ed. Birk Sproxton. Winnipeg: Turnstone, 1986. 179-186.

___. *The Night Workers of Ragnarök*. Victoria: Press Porcépic, 1985.

___. *The Prowler*. Red Deer: Red Deer College P, 1989.

___. *Stranger at the Door: Writers and the Act of Writing* . Waterloo: Wilfrid Laurier UP, 2004.

___. Marilyn Dumont, Hiromi Goto. "Was the West Ever One?" *Open Letter* 10.2 (1998): 101-121.

___. *Zero Hour*. Red Deer: Red Deer College P, 1991.

Keahey, Deborah. *Making It Home: Place in Canadian Prairie Literature*. Winnipeg: U of Manitoba P, 1998.

King, Thomas. *Truth and Bright Water*. Toronto: HarperFlamingo, 1999.

Kroetsch, Robert. "Disunity as Unity: A Canadian Strategy." *The Lovely Treachery of Words*. Toronto: Oxford UP, 1989. 21-33.

Laurence, Margaret. *The Fire-dwellers*. New York: Knopf, 1969.

___. *The Diviners*. Toronto: McClelland and Stewart, 1973.

Lee, Dennis. *Civil Elegies and Other Poems*. 1972. Toronto: House of Anansi, 1994.

Lee, Sky. *Disappearing Moon Café*. Vancouver: Douglas and McIntyre, 1993.

Livesay, Dorothy. "West Coast." *The Self-Completing Tree: Selected Poems*. Victoria: Press Porcépic, 1986. 162-167.

Lowry, Malcolm. *October Ferry to Gabriola*. London: Jonathan Cape, 1970.

"The Manitoba Métis Land Claim: Our Day in Court Has Arrived." *Land Claims History: A Celebration of Métis Rights*, 2007.

Marlatt, Daphne. *Ana Historic*. Toronto: Coach House, 1988.

Monkman, Kent. "Biography." *Urban Nation*. nation.com. June 30, 2008.

Oakley, Janice. "Postcards from the Edge: Decoding Winnipeg's 'One Gay City' Campaign." *Ethnologies* 21.1 (1999): 177-192.

Wah, Fred. *Waiting for Saskatchewan*. Winnipeg: Turnstone, 1985.

Yaying Zhang

What is a Chinese-Canadian Accent? Ideologies of Language and the Construction of Immigrant Identities

A definition of language is always, implicitly or explicitly, a definition of human beings in the world.

Raymond Williams (21)

Like other superficially innocuous "customs," "conventions" and "traditions," rules of language use often contribute to a circle of exclusion and intimidation, as those who have mastered a particular practice use it in turn to intimidate others.

Deborah Cameron (12)

Every time the question of language surfaces, in one way or another, it means that a series of other problems are coming to the fore: the formation and enlargement of the governing class, the need to establish more intimate and secure relationships between the governing groups and the national-popular mass, in other words to reorganise the cultural hegemony.

Antonio Gramsci (183-84)

Scholars from a variety of disciplines have contested the official discourse of multiculturalism in Canada. Instead of accepting at face value the political rhetoric that promises cultural freedom and equality of opportunities for all Canadian "cultural groups" (so defined in the multicultural policy, but commonly read "immigrants" or "racial minorities"), they have engaged in a critical discourse of challenge and resistance, in which cultural complexities are recognized and patterns of power, rules of normalcy, and standards of legitimacy are interrogated (see Bannerji; Li; Fleras and Kunz; Fernando). These scholars have critiqued the fundamentally racist and assimilationist ideologies in Canadian social and cultural institutions that privilege Euro-Canadian values at the expense of racial minorities and immigrants. This paper participates in this critical discourse and studies how immigrants' linguistic abilities, or rather, perceptions and receptions of their linguistic abilities, affect their quality of life in Canada and their sense of cultural proximity to the nation, which, in turn, reflects the extent of Canadian society's commitment to the ideal of multiculturalism. I will examine how, in the context of a Western Canadian city, social norms about linguistic behaviours impact the material and psychological life of those who are not fluent in the dominant official language, affecting access to material benefits such as employment opportunities, as well as shaping perceptions of who belongs in Canada.

Theoretical Context

In discourse studies there has recently developed a body of research that deals explicitly with investigations of language ideologies. This research examines the ways people imagine and define language and the ways these definitions link language to extra-linguistic phenomena such as identity, nation, institution, race, and class (see Cameron; Crowley; Milroy and Milroy; Schiefflin and Doucet; Woolard). As Kathryn Woolard notes,

> ideologies of language are not about language alone.
> Rather, they envision and enact ties of language to
> identity, to aesthetics, to morality, and to epistemology.
> Through such linkages, they underpin not only linguis-
> tic form and use but also the very notion of the person
> and the social group, as well as such fundamental social
> institutions as religious ritual, child socialization, gender
> relations, the nation-state, schooling, and law. (3)

Drawing on Antonio Gramci's and Louis Althusser's work on ideology, research in this area approaches attitudes about language from a range of perspectives, methodological orientations and disciplinary locations. Studies in standardization, for example, investigate the development and maintenance of standard languages and attitudes toward these standards. The works of Tony Crowley, and James Milroy and Lesley Milroy exemplify this concern with the historical development of language standards. Specifically, these researchers focus on the development of Standard English and its links to traditions of complaint, correction, and distinction, variously imagined as personal or national distinction.

Linguistic anthropology, which examines the connections between linguistic and socio-cultural life, between ideas about language and their role in social and cultural reproduction, is exemplified in the work of Bambi B. Schiefflin and Rachelle Charlier Doucet, who maintain that, in Haiti, the sounds of Kreyòl have been invested with "social, symbolic and political values" (287). They observe that in Haiti the stigma that surrounds the sounds of kreyòl and the ambivalence many feel about this variety have resulted in a long-standing orthographic debate, not only about the codification of a written variety of kreyòl, but also about the ways this variety might represent Haitian national identity. In this analysis the confluence of nation, history, identity and epistemology has come to be viewed as a routine aspect of language itself.

Another stream of research in this area, represented by Deborah Cameron, examines how attitudes toward language often embody efforts to impose order or meaning on the social world. In her study of ideologies of language and those regulatory practices that encircle its use, Cameron maintains that language becomes an apparently "fixed and substantive social identity label" (16) that secures anxieties about such things as difference, conflict and social fragmentation. She discovers that in public attitudes toward language in Britain, grammar, virtue and class are so interconnected that grammatical rules are often justified or explained not in terms of how language is used but in terms that reflect a desired type of behaviour, thought process, or social status. According to Cameron, linguistic bigotry is among the last publicly expressible prejudices left to members of the Western world. Individuals who would "find it unthinkable to sneer at a beggar or someone in a wheelchair will sneer without compunction at linguistic 'solecisms'" (12).

Drawing on Judith Butler's work on performativity, Cameron argues that identity is brought into being in part through repeated acts of language-using that are susceptible to a set of cultural codes that define what is publicly intelligible, acceptable and normal. "The reason we perceive ourselves, and are perceived by others, as particular kinds of people," notes Cameron, "is that we repeat the actions that define those kinds of people until in time they come to seem like a fixed and integral part of our nature" (16). These "repeated stylizations" of the voice – its pitch, tone and accent – and of lexical, grammatical and interactional choices can contribute to the production and reproduction of "congealed" social identities for particular language users (16-17).

What these studies have in common is an interest in the ways conceptualizations of language reflect and inform conceptualizations of other things: of nation, society, culture, institution and identity. Inspired by these studies, I wish to investigate the significance of those extra-linguistic factors that shape beliefs about language. Language, in turn, naturalizes hierarchical social relations and the methods by which we perceive these relations. In particular, I would like to think through the ways people make associations between linguistic behaviours and race, place of origin and level of education. In any society, social norms of linguistic behaviours are very much informed by public attitudes toward language and the country's official languages policies. As the above language theorists have implied, public attitudes about language are really about distinction, which contributes to models of language, usage, and accents that variously organize language users and their relationship to the nation along familiar historical, epistemological, class and racial lines. While public attitudes, as reflected in various domains of society such as media, law, education, and the workplace, espouse the importance of both the dominant language and the manner in which it is spoken, in Canada these attitudes may also have a significant impact on those who are not fluent in that language or speak the language with a distinct accent. Since the idea of language as a symbol of the nation is commonplace, knowledge and proficiency in the national language could become a badge of membership, and lack of knowledge or proficiency in the national language could be a marker of outsider status, disloyalty, and bad citizenship. In this regard, prevailing social attitudes towards language could have a profound effect on those who use the dominant language in a non-standard way. For example, Chinese immigrants in Canada are non-native speakers of English: How are they positioned vis-à-vis social norms of linguistic behaviours in Canadian society? How does their particularity as non-native speakers of English enable their identities in defiance of cultural prescriptions? Or how does it expose them as "foreigners" in this country, or ensure their visibility? And what does this regulatory process reveal about the politics of "diversity" and "multiculturalism" in Canada?

Research Approach

While public policies celebrate multiculturalism and diversity, it is perhaps more important to consult immigrants themselves as to how they perceive and represent their own experiences in Canada. Focusing on how ideologies of language organize language users and their relationship to the nation, I will amplify the voices of immigrants about their own experiences in acquiring substantive citizenship in Canada and examine how immigrant voices enter into dialogues with dominant representations of themselves and their experiences. Data for this project come from qualitative interviews and participant observation with 10 immigrants from China who have resided in Kamloops, British Columbia for at least three to five years. Personal in-depth interviews focused on participants' everyday interactions and experiences in the various sectors and institutions of Canadian society. The conversations were centred on how being immigrants combined with their race and linguistic behaviours and mediated their everyday experiences with long-time Canadians and social institutions. Extensive notes taken during the interviews were later collated and analyzed for thematic issues. Since qualitative research methods come closer to the complexities of my research participants' actual experiences, these methods allow me to seek traces of how the ideologies of language operate in the participants' encounter with English, the dominant language in Canada.

It is important to note that the participants in this study do not constitute a homogenous group. Although they all came to Canada with hopes of bettering themselves by starting their lives over again, their socio-economic, educational, professional, and geographic backgrounds in China were different. However, because of their similar experiences with the perceptions and receptions of their Chinese-accented English, these lines of distinction tended to disappear when they arrived in Canada. In very brief descriptions I have given here the most relevant information of my participants. As I discuss the various issues related to their experiences I hope that the complexities of their experiences will unfold and manifest themselves to a certain extent.

As a city that housed one of the earliest Chinatowns in North America, Kamloops is an ideal site for such a study. The Chinese history in Kamloops dates back to the Gold Rush era in the 1850s and the construction of the Canadian Pacific Railway in the 1880s, when Chinese immigrants were victims of overt racism in a white settler society. A study of the quality of life of Chinese immigrants in Kamloops at the beginning of the 21st century not only shows how the position of Chinese immigrants has changed from the past, but also reveals many vestiges of the old racist ideology that remain in our public consciousness, social structures and institutions. As my discussion later shows, my research participants' experiences are different from but parallel to those of earlier Chinese immigrants who came to Canada for a better future, but found themselves confronted with unequal access to employment, with limited chances for social mobility, and with inadequate opportunity to integrate into Canadian society, which was itself stratified and unequal.

This study is also informed by Mary Louise Pratt's theory of "contact zone," which "emphasizes how subjects are constituted in and by their relation among colonizers and colonized ... in terms of copresence, interaction, interlocking understandings and practices, often within radically asymmetrical relations of power" (7). Pratt's theory is expanded by the postcolonial paradigm of "contact zone" as delineated by James Clifford, who suggests ways of looking at culture, tradition, and identity in terms of travel relations, the ways people leave home and return, enacting differently centred worlds. Clifford considers "contact zone" from a critical anthropologist's perspective and raises the question of how a culture, regarded as a centre by its own people, can become a site of travel for others and the question of to what extent one group's core can be another's periphery (64-72).

Since Clifford suggests that one group's centre might be another's periphery, the Chinese immigrant, who has traditionally been pushed to the margin in Canadian society, could be a figure in the centre, observing and questioning the values and practices of Euro-Canadians' attitudes toward language. For the Chinese immigrant as well as the anthropologist, dwelling abroad means living at home; the immigrant seldom relies on the translator, but speaks and listens for herself. This paradoxical centre she occupies seems to subvert the conventional power relations that inhere in a multicultural society and allows researchers to transfer their gaze to examine some fundamental assumptions and values embedded in Euro-Canadians' ideologies about language and culture. Drawing on Clifford's reasoning, my approach privileges and valourizes the voices and perspectives of Chinese immigrants, situating them as central rather than peripheral. Thus, Chinese immigrants' inquiries into their experiences in Canada are valued while Euro-Canadian perceptions and receptions of these immigrants' linguistic behaviors are held up for critical investigation.

In keeping with the critical approach taken here, in the following analysis and discussion I do not claim to have uncovered a social reality independent of my own perceptions and interpretations. Rather, I see any social science descriptions and the descriptions here as inevitably intertwined with the participants' and the researcher's own social positioning and the constantly shifting senses of the social world in which we operate.

Analysis and Discussion

The following pages resound with voices of my participants about their experiences of living in a small city in Western Canada. With their first-hand involvement and insider knowledge as immigrants living in a new country, they speak from a rich and deep lived experience. Their experiences and how they interpret these experiences are insights accessed through in-depth interviews with the participants; these insights cannot be drawn from analysis of government policies on immigration and multiculturalism that we read and hear in public discourse. These insights are valuable in that they may bring not only new understandings of immigrant experience in Canada, but they may also help researchers, educators, and policy makers investigate ideologies of language from fresh perspectives.

Accent as a Marker of "Outsider" Status

The way in which one expresses oneself reflects many crucial aspects of identity, including national or ethnic origin, class, and gender. In a multicultural society it is to be expected that the dominant language is spoken in many different ways. Examining the social norms of linguistic behaviours to which immigrants are held, and the circumstances in which compliance with the norms is privileged and violation of the norms is punished, helps us to assess the extent to which linguistic and cultural diversity are respected.

Linguistic norms are informed by official national language policies and prevailing social attitudes. According to Teresa Scassa, linguistic norms also relate to both "the code of a language and the manner of its speaking" (106). The code can be understood as the rules of grammar and vocabulary of the language. The particular characteristics of the manner of speaking reflect the individuality of different speakers of the same language: they may incorporate cultural conventions, syntax borrowed or adapted from other languages, shifts in stress or accent which alter meaning, and other such features. Thus, compliance with these norms requires the ability to combine a standard language code and a particular set of conventions of speech used by the elite of the dominant language group.

Various communicative problems may exist where linguistic norms are not shared in a multicultural society. However, where the dominant group conceives of its dominance as natural, inevitable and desirable, communicative failure will always be blamed on the non-dominant speaker. The most common responses to "Chinese English" identified by the research participants in my study were being ignored when speaking, and being corrected rather than responding to the content of speech. Comments by Ming illustrate this point:

> It seems that somehow they don't want you to feel good
> about yourself. They want to correct you even though
> they seem to understand what you are saying. It becomes
> very embarrassing when people focus on how you say
> things and not what you say. I have no control of my ac-
> cent, which is really frustrating.[1]

At the time of the interview, Ming had been in Canada for six years.
She has a bachelor's degree from a Canadian university. However,
as her comments suggest, native-born Canadians' perception of her
fluency in "Canadian English" is low, in spite of her educational ac-
complishments and years in Canada.

According to my research participants, they experience language
as a problem in their daily lives not because they have difficulty with
expression or comprehension, but because their "Chinese English"
accents mark them as immigrant, Asian, different, and incompetent.
Hanbin, Lili, and Hong describe in the following their encounters
with local residents at community events shortly after they came to
Canada:

> They first commented on my Chinese accent and my
> "very pretty" Chinese name. Then they asked me about
> the living conditions in China, whether we use cars or
> bicycles as a means of transportation, and why the Chi-
> nese government let so many of us come out to Canada.
> The gist of the conversation was to make me acknowl-
> edge that I had left behind a miserable situation to come
> to this promised land. I saw their attention to me not
> as welcoming me, but as relegating me to my "proper"
> place as a grateful immigrant.

> How can you say you are the owner in this country? And
> everybody says to you, "oh, you are a foreigner." They
> give you some kind of respect. They forgive your poor
> English. They forgive your behaving differently from
> them .... You know, I'm stuck in a very strange position.
> People consider me as a foreigner and ask me when I'll
> go back. But I hope to stay in this country. I'm applying
> for citizenship now.

> I'm a Canadian because I chose to be in this country.
> I could have remained in China or moved to another

country. But I chose Canada because I thought Canada
could provide a better future for me and my family. But
now that you are here, you realize that the people here
consider you a foreigner because you have an accent.

For some people, particularly the speakers, comments and questions
such as "you have an accent," "where are you from?" and "what is
your nationality?" may be regarded as innocent, neutral, and reflective of a genuine desire to engage in conversation or "get to know the
person." For some recipients, however, they are reminders of their
position – reminders of race, and immigrants/minority status – yet
another occasion of "Othering" and a reflection of the speaker's in-
sensitivity. Inherent in the questioning is the view that non-native-
speaking and non-white people are not "Canadians." The experiences detailed here challenge us to think of Canadians as having
different colours and accents, and as speaking different languages.
Long-time residents are not more "Canadian" than immigrants. On
the contrary, as one participant suggested above, some individuals
may be more consciously Canadian because they have made a delib-
erate choice to live in this country, so for them being Canadian is not
simply a matter of an accident of birth.

Another participant, Xing, had been in this country for eight years,
and identified himself as a Canadian. He told me a story about his
encounter with a fellow camper at a local campground.

> A Caucasian man asked me, "Where are you from?"
> "Kamloops," I said. The man seemed a bit confused,
> probably because he had noticed that I had an unfamil-
> iar name, spoke with an accent, and did not look white.
> He shook his head and said, "No, you come from Asia."

Unfortunately, such a question and response represent an all-too-
common occurrence in Canada – the constant need to ask those who
do not fit the mainstream perception of "Canadian" where they are
from. For Xing, his identification of himself as coming from Kamloops represents his desire for a sense of belonging in this country.
Unfortunately he was often reminded that he came from elsewhere.
His motto was "when in Canada, do as the Canadians do." Over
the years he increasingly began to change and mould himself into
the settings around him. He began to follow Canadian politics, learn
about different areas of the country, and took English classes to learn
the correct pronunciations of words. He felt he needed to learn the

standard language, the one legally and socially recognized as being Canadian, the one that carried status and importance. Sadly, he also realized that language was a symbol that acted as a boundary distinguishing between who was and was not seen as Canadian. He gradually came to believe that being Canadian meant that you spoke English fluently and that you were born in Canada.

As indicated by my research participants' experiences, non-standard speech is marginalized, and its speakers are often considered "foreigners" as compared to standard-language speakers. Although one may argue that language standards present a neutral measure of achievement in the dominant language, such standards cannot be considered neutral in a truly multicultural society. Further, by implying that there is a single, correct way of speaking a language and by choosing the style of speech of the dominant group, linguistic norms encourage linguistic and cultural assimilation. In other words, linguistic norms conceal their inherent inclusionary/exclusionary function; i.e., the use of the so-called standard English serves the interests of some better than others. In this sense, standard English can be aligned with "linguicism," which is defined by Skutnabb-Kangas as "ideologies and structures which are used to legitimate, effectuate and reproduce an unequal division of power and resources (both material and non-material) between groups which are defined on the basis of language (on the basis of their mother tongue)" (cited in Phillipson 343).

Accent as a Disadvantage in the Job Market

As the Chinese immigrants in my study made clear, their "outsider" status brought about by their Chinese-accented English persists well beyond an initial period of settlement in Canada. As they venture into the workforce, they often find themselves relegated to peripheral positions of the labour market because of employment practices constructed from concerns about English language proficiency and the speaker's racial origin. They find that very often their credentials and training from their home country are not recognized. Ironically, the very credentials and reasons that enabled these immigrants to be accepted into Canada are disregarded upon their arrival.

When holders of foreign credentials experience differential treatments in the Canadian labour market, it is often not clear whether it is credentials or racial origin or other features that are being disadvantaged. For example, in her study of language law and its impact on the workplace, Teresa Scassa has argued that non-native speakers of English encounter discrimination in employment and in access to services on the basis of their language characteristics. Their lack of fluency, their accents, and their idiosyncratic language use that deviates from the usual practice of native-born Canadians can be used as the basis for unfavourable treatment, as a surrogate for racial discrimination. In other words, in assessing hostility to non-standard language use the source of the divergence from linguistic norms may be as important as the divergence itself. For example, the person's race and national origin may play as important a role in the adverse reaction to the person's speech as does the non-standard form of expression. Thus, one can argue that a "foreign" accent is socially defined, and its definition is related to the cultural norms and expectations of Canadian society in general. For instance, as Gillian Creese and Edith Ngene Kambere point out, British or Australian English accents do not seem to elicit the same treatment as described by immigrants of colour (571). Other studies also point to the intersection between accents and racialization. Researchers have found that, compared to immigrants of European origin, minority immigrants from Asia, Africa, and the Caribbean are more likely to be racialized or stigmatized, because of racial discrimination and a greater reluctance on the part of native-born Canadians to accept them as legitimate Canadians or equals (see Miedema and Nason-Clark; Reitz and Breton). As well, in a field study in Toronto, using matched black and white job seekers to apply for entry positions advertised in a newspaper, Frances Henry and Effie Ginzberg found that white applicants received job offers three times more often than black applicants. Furthermore, telephone callers with Asian or Caribbean accents were often screened out when they called about a job vacancy.

Therefore, accents can be an element of the racial discrimination faced by immigrants, and indeed, in some cases, the elements of discrimination are so intertwined that it is difficult to separate accents from other motivations for discrimination. Accents may serve as a trigger for a range of negative attitudes and stereotypes that have more to do with racism than language ability in immigrants. When embodied by racialized subjects, accents may provide a rationale for entitlement or disentitlement in employment or full participation in civil society without troubling liberal discourses of equality and multiculturalism.

For my research participants, their ability to perform the task is often assessed negatively based on biased assumptions triggered by their manner of speech. Their "foreign accent" is frequently named as a rationale for not being hired in the labour market. Most of the participants who held foreign qualifications as teachers, managers and doctors in China experienced non-recognition of their Chinese qualifications and a lack of equity in access to education, retraining and upgrading of their credentials for employment. Below, comments by Megan, Lin, and Wenxin exemplify this situation:

> I was born in China and have no "Canadian experience" when I apply for work. But I have lots of work experience and credentials from China. When it comes time to look for work, I know my accent will be a problem. In fact I've been told so by many. But there is really nothing I could do about it.

> I find this language requirement has disadvantaged us and it is unfortunate that we are punished because of our accent. I don't speak English in the first place. But since the Canadian government accepts immigrants, Canadian society should also accept my accent. The job ads say applicants should be able to communicate in English fluently, but what can be considered as "fluent" is very arbitrary; it's entirely up to the employer to decide. If they don't like you because you come from a different country and look different from them, they can say that they reject you because you don't speak English well.

> I have an MBA from a Canadian university, but when I apply for positions of receptionist or secretary, I'm told that I have a heavy accent, and that they prefer a native speaker of English to do the job. Over the years, I have come to the conclusion that you have to speak English with a Canadian accent in order to get a decent job in Canada.

To some extent, the discrimination immigrants encounter in the labour market due to their accent is systemic. Job interviews, which measure candidates in a face-to-face context, are a good example of a systemic recruitment practice which might result in the devaluation of candidates who use unfamiliar speech styles or who speak with accents or limited fluency. In this context, language difference may be perceived as a deficiency, a mark of stupidity, or an inability to perform the requisite tasks. Zhu and Lin have encountered such a challenge in their job application process:

I have many years of experience in the welding trade in China and I'm very confident that I have the knowledge and skills to do well in the welding jobs I have applied for in Kamloops. However, I have not received a single job offer because I don't speak as well as other local candidates.

I've gone through many job interviews in Canada. Each time I became more nervous and discouraged than the last time. The interviews I had in China, if they were at all required, were very different from what I experienced here. Here I'm often not sure what to say and how to say it. Each time they seem not to understand me and ask me to repeat what I say, I feel stupid and feel that I'm solely responsible for the communicative problems.

Immigrant candidates often bring with them into situated interviews a major disadvantage based on pre-existing factors outside the interview interaction itself. Conversely, candidates from mainstream middle-class culture who, in the course of their upbringing, normally acquire linguistic and cultural conventions similar to those of the interview genre enter the interview situation with that advantage. In other words, the patterning of interview conventions and systems of learning those conventions according to the cultural norms of one group will surely disadvantage others whose systems of social and cultural reproduction are different. Although it is fair to argue that some jobs do require fluent language skills, not all requirements set by particular employers necessarily have a rational bearing on the nature of the work to be performed and the real skills required for the job. Some might argue that linguistic skills are an asset and therefore people possessing such skills are preferred employees. Yet the result of such hiring practices is discrimination where such language skills bear no relationship to the work to be performed.

Accent and Sense of Belonging

What is important to point out is that for immigrants, it is not only societal expectations and pressures that constrain them, but their own consciousness of the centralizing forces of the standards of Canadian English and their "deviance" from the standards that contributes to their own oppression. The penetration of centralizing forces into the linguistic consciousness of speakers can lead to what Pierre Bourdieu calls "symbolic domination" (cited in Giltrow 365). This domination operates not through physical coercion but through psychological/ social processes. Undergoing these processes, individuals internalize the values that subordinate some members of society to the advantage of others. In fact, symbolic domination recruits people to the service of their own domination. Through social experiences in and out of the labour market, immigrants come to see themselves as the dominant group perceives them. They learn to disparage their own speech, to suspect it of errors, and to feel intimidated by those who speak so-called standard Canadian English, and who do not consider themselves to have an accent. As my participants' comments below demonstrate, symbolic domination has a profound impact on their perception of themselves and their sense of belonging in Canada:

> Many times I felt humiliated because of my poor
> English. Those people feel that they are better than me
> because they can speak English fluently. My self-confi-
> dence slowly dropped to the point I felt like I'm not as
> good as others because of my bad English. Sometimes, I
> even feel scared because I am afraid of making mistakes
> and that people will give me the kind of look saying "you
> don't belong here."
> I do believe that language is part of who I am and only
> those who are immigrants will be able to know the power
> of language. What I mean is that when one has to learn
> English not for pleasure but to just make people hear
> you, see you and recognize that you are a person, not a
> tree or a piece of furniture.
>
> I am always conscious of my accent, of being Chinese,
> to the same extent that white Canadians are not con-
> scious of their whiteness or their accents. Often, when
> people notice my accent and ask me if I'm Chinese or
> Vietnamese, or Korean, I ask them back about their
> origin. "I'm just Canadian," they often say. I doubt that I
> will ever become "just Canadian," whatever that means.

My participants often experienced a connection between their use of language and the sense of belonging—a topic that often came up in my conversations with the participants—and often, their sense of belonging is inextricably connected with their ability to speak English fluently. They feel alienated and devalued within Canadian society because of their lack of English proficiency compared with native speakers.

Language was also the issue that Hui drew upon in contemplating his place of belonging.

> Although I'm confident that I can get a job here, I don't quite view myself as a Canadian, because I don't speak English as well as local people. I hear my own mistakes. And it is also difficult for me to make friends with native speakers, because they may not be interested in listening to me.

Hui suggested that he sometimes felt he was part of the Canadian society, but generally could not see himself as what he termed as a "true Canadian" because of the grammatical mistakes he made in his English. As long as he did not have full command of the language, he could not feel that he fully belonged. He seemed to have a strong incentive to improve his English as he wanted to use English as a means of proving himself. He commented,

> I recognize that the mastery of English to me is not only important in helping get a successful career but also in impressing Canadians and others with my ability with English. As I was not born here, I feel I have something to prove and I can achieve that through the proficient use of the English language.

When the research participants in this study talked about the way their "Chinese accent" underscored their status as outsiders and their anxiety and fear of not belonging, they identified a form of boundary maintenance that prevents crossing from "immigrant" to "Canadian," regardless of formal citizenship processes. Hanbin articulated his frustration in this way:

> I think the fact that you remain an immigrant is the main obstacle because you never become either citizen or Canadian. As soon as you open your mouth to speak English with those Canadians, you are telling them that you are not Canadian. Although I try to pretend that others don't mind my accent, I know deep down that as long as my accent stays with me, and it will, others will look at me differently.

In Hanbin's mind, whatever his legal citizenship status was, he knew he would never be perceived, or perceive himself, as "Canadian."

Some of my participants have adopted English names. They saw an English name as a key that would open the door to success and stability; they associated it with mobility and achievement. They believed that someone hearing or seeing their names, in situations of job applications, for example, would think of them as Canadian, and that being seen as Canadian would deflect discrimination in employment and daily life.

The close connection my participants experienced between their sense of who they are and the perceptions and receptions of their linguistic behaviours is something that I have come across with other immigrants. When immigrants with a tendency to judge themselves very harshly and negatively through the mistakes they make in the language feel that their identity is closely linked to language, and when these anxieties are coupled with social expectations that non-native speakers must meet certain requirements for English proficiency in Canadian society, these concerns will likely hinder and strand their participation in Canadian social and economic life. This hindered and stranded position may therefore become characteristic of immigrants' experience in Canada.

Conclusion

Immigrants' experiences with accented English discussed in this paper beg some serious questions. Who are "Canadians" in this postmodern age of multiple cultures, languages and identities? How big is the Canadian cultural space for linguistic minorities? Can immigrants create an acceptable Canadian identity in a nation where they are held to one standard way of speaking? Although the federal multicultural policy promises cultural freedom and equality of opportunities to immigrants and minority-group members, it is important for us to go beyond the political rhetoric and to explore these questions in order to gain insights into the lives, experiences and well-being of immigrants and other minority-group members. This study suggests the need for more research on how social norms of linguistic behaviour shape perceptions of who belongs in Canada, on how ideologies of language intersect with processes of racialization, and on how this intersection reproduces inequality in our society.

I believe that social change results not only from policy reform and government enactments but also from an awareness of others' experiences and from confronting our very own ideologies, attitudes, and feelings. While public discourses on immigration focus on how immigrants' linguistic, social and economic characteristics influence Canadian society, this study suggests that how immigrants are incorporated into Canadian society also depends on the ideologies and attitudes of long-time Canadians toward immigrants. Through immigrants' experiences, we have seen that accent serves to place an individual in a vulnerable position, that accent is flagged as a fundamental difference that highlights hierarchy and therefore justifies discrimination. As Peter Li argues in his *Destination Canada: Immigration Debates and Issues,* "the manner by which the human capital of immigrants is valued or devalued is a feature of Canadian society and not an attribute of the holders of such capital" (166). In other words, if Canadian society rewards people differentially on the basis of linguistic abilities coupled with racial origins, then linguistic and racial discrimination should be considered a feature of Canadian society, and not that of immigrants, who, in this case, are victimized by societal features of inequality.

That I have placed immigrant experiences at the centre of this study does not mean that I want to limit analysis of the issues to individual experience. Rather it means that I intend to illustrate how, through the understanding of individual experiences, we might gain insight into the ways in which social structures and prevailing ideologies shape and mediate identities, experiences, and interactions: how they include some people and exclude others, and how through our attitudes and actions within those social structures we inscribe difference and maintain inequity. I believe changes on the individual level brought about through increased awareness and knowledge of others' situations can lead to eventual changes in social structures.

Acknowledgement

I am grateful to the Mapping Quality of Life and the Culture of Small Cities CURA for support on this project. I also thank the two anonymous reviewers for their helpful feedback on an earlier version of this article.

Notes

1. The interview excerpts in this essay have been edited for readability. During the interviews, most of my participants spoke in a mixture of English and Mandarin. I have translated the Mandarin expressions into English, as accurately as I could. In editing the interview transcriptions, I have also tried, to the best of my ability, to preserve the emotions embedded in my participants' comments.

Works Cited

Bannerji, Himani. *The Dark Side of the Nation: Essays on Multiculturalism and Gender*. Toronto: Canadian Scholar's Press, 2000.

Cameron, Deborah. *Verbal Hygiene*. New York: Routledge, 1995.

Clifford, James. *Routes: Travel and Translation in the Late Twentieth Century*. Cambridge, Mass.: Harvard UP, 1997.

Creese, Gillian, and Edith Ngene Kambere. "What Colour Is Your English?" *Canadian Review of Sociology and Anthropology*. 45 (2003): 565-573.

Crowley, Tony. *Standard English and the Politics of Language*. 2nd ed. New York: Palgrave, 2003.

Fernando, Shanti. *Race and the City*. Vancouver: UBC Press, 2006.

Fleras, Augie, and Jean Lock Kunz. *Media and Minorities: Representing Diversity in a Multicultural Canada*. Toronto: Thompson Education, 2001.

Giltrow, Janet. "Legends of the Centre: System, Self, and Linguistic Consciousness." *Writing Selves/Writing Societies: Research from Activity Perspectives*. Eds. Charles Bazerman, and D. Russell. Colorado: The WAC Clearinghouse, 2003. 363-392.

Gramsci, Antonio. *Selections from Cultural Writings*. Trans. William Boelhowe. Eds. David Forgacs and Geoffrey Nowell Smith. Cambridge, Mass.: Harvard UP, 1991.

Henry, Frances, and Effie Ginzberg. *Who Gets Work? A Test of Racial Discrimination in Employment*. Toronto: The Urban Alliance on Race Relations and the Social Planning Council of Metropolitan Toronto, 1985.

Li, Peter. *Destination Canada: Immigration Debates and Issues*. Don Mills: Oxford UP, 2003.

Miedema, Baukje, and Nancy Nason-Clark. "Second Class Status: An Analysis of the Lived Experiences of Immigrant Women in Fredericton." *Canadian Ethnic Studies*. 21.2, (1989): 63-73.

Milroy, James, and Leslie Milroy. *Authority in Language: Investigating Standard English*. 3rd ed. London: Routledge, 1999.

Phillipson, Robert. "Linguicism: Structures and Ideologies in Linguistic Imperialism" *Minority Education: From Shame to Struggle.* Eds. T. Skutnabb-Kangas, and J. Cummins. Philadelphia: Multicultural Matters, 1988. 339-358.

Pratt, Mary Louise. "Arts in the Contact Zone." *Profession.* 91 (1991): 33-40.

Rea, Jaclyn. *Ideologies of Language: Authority, Consensus and Commonsense in Canadian Talk about Usage.* Ph.D. Thesis. Simon Fraser University, 2006.

Reitz, Jeffery G., and Raymond Breton. *The Illusion of Difference: Realities of Ethnicity in Canada and United States.* Toronto: C.D. Howe Institute, 1994.

Scassa, Teresa. "Language Standards, Ethnicity and Discrimination." *Canadian Ethnic Studies.* 26 (1994): 105-20.

Schiefflin, Bambi B., and Rachelle Charlier Doucet. "The 'Real' Haitian Creole: Ideology, Metalinguistics, and Orthographic Choice." *Language Ideologies: Practice and Theory.* Ed. Bambi B. Schiefflin, Kathryn A. Woolard, and Paul V. Kroskrity. Oxford: Oxford UP, 1998. 285-316.

Williams, Raymond. *Marxism and Literature.* Oxford: Oxford UP, 1977.

Woolard, Kathryn A. "Introduction: Language Ideology as a Field of Inquiry." *Language Ideologies: Practice and Theory.* Eds. Bambi B. Schiefflin, Kathryn A. Woolard, and Paul V. Kroskrity. Oxford: Oxford UP, 1998. 3-47.

Part II   Peopling West

Kimberley Mair

Subjects of Consumption and the "Alberta Advantage": Representations of Wiebo Ludwig in the Theatre and the Media, 1997-2005

In 1998, Wayne Roberts, who believed his land north of Calgary, Alberta, Canada, was poisoned by an improperly installed oil well, reportedly shot and killed an oil executive during a dispute. Roberts was charged with first-degree murder, convicted of second-degree murder, and sentenced to fifteen years in prison. Outside the immediate area, this event is seemingly forgotten. The name of Wayne Roberts, if once shouted in the press, was soon afterward reduced to a mere whisper.

In contrast to the obscurity of Roberts, Wiebo Ludwig, known nationally as a convicted oil patch vandal, has been the subject of sustained media attention that focused on a rural area known as the "Mighty Peace," situated in the northern part of the oil-rich province of Alberta. Jailed for a year and a half, his release from prison in November 2001 roughly coincided with the release of Andrew Nikiforuk's book entitled *Saboteurs: Wiebo Ludwig's War Against Big Oil*. How is it that the perpetrator of a controversial and unexpected murder is finalized and forgotten so easily and a "vandal" who allegedly blew up one oil well and encased another in cement is remembered and repeatedly constituted and reconstituted in the press and in the public imagination?

This paper argues that the tendency in early news coverage to individualize Ludwig and his struggle undermined possibilities for drawing connections to larger relevant social and economic questions—what Norman Fairclough (1992) calls social practice—and moving toward sustained dialogue. To understand the situation in Alberta, the strong interdependence between the long-standing Conservative government and energy-producing industries needs to be acknowledged.

Ralph Klein's Progressive Conservative government and its policies were supported by the corporate energy sector not only through generous political party contributions (Harrison) but through its contribution to the widespread perception that Alberta's economic health can be attributed to the strength of the governing party, when it is "no secret oil and gas resources, not political leadership, actually fuelled Alberta's long run of prosperity" (Laird 156). The ongoing process of normalization of these institutional power relations in the province of Alberta, which this paper argues is managed largely through narrative practices, was maintained despite the destabilizing potential of Ludwig coverage. Nevertheless, the active participation of Ludwig himself in the construction of self and other representation through these same narrative practices played a role in keeping controversy over industry activities in public discourse, which led to an eventual convergence and identification with debates over Canada's ratification of the Kyoto Accord on Climate Change, opposition to new well development proposals, and conflicts between the oil industry and the beef industry in Alberta. The convergence of public discourses undermined the individualizing process active in early characterizations of Ludwig, allowing for broader identification between social groups and issues. In the long term, Ludwig's use of speech and his public interventions into representational practices posed a more significant destabilizing threat to the process of normalization within the province of Alberta than did his acts of oil well sabotage.

In addition to books, television broadcast reports, articles published in weekly newsmagazines, and two theatrical plays, *Theodore and the Cosmonaut* (subsequently incorporated into *Love Letters from the Unabomber*; see also p.75) and *An Eye for an Eye*, this paper draws extensively from daily newspaper coverage of Wiebo Ludwig, using the database *Canadian Newsstand* for the period between 1997 and August 2005. I am particularly interested in shifts in representations of Ludwig, especially as they relate to social and political changes in the province of Alberta over time. It is vital to emphasize that, at all times, coverage has provided representations of Ludwig that are unstable and paradoxical. In other words, as a subject formed in public discourse, Ludwig has become a site of ideological contestation in broader debates. Thus, while I acknowledge that the ownership structure of media influences coverage towards hegemonic interpretations of events through both interest-based alliances and budget-conscious news production strategies, I found that conflicting representations of Ludwig were produced, circulated, and consumed throughout the period of study. In this paper, I am concerned with broader changes in representational emphasis over the period and their interrelationship with social practices. These social practices include both the Alberta myth within which Ludwig is explicitly situated in media representation and relevant social issues that became tied with the figure of Ludwig in public discourse. Setting, which is caught up in a rural-urban tension, and the proximity of the consuming audience to the events covered are key themes in making sense of the shifts in representational practices.

Act 1: Setting the Stage – Early Ludwig

In his explication of modern life as an experience of paradox and contradiction, Marshall Berman cites the protagonist's move from the country to the city in modern literature as not only "an exploratory move" but as "an archetypal move for millions of young people in the centuries to come" (18). The city, the destination of this characteristic move, is the site of flux, conflict, and turbulence. If the move from the country to the city is the characteristic modern move, and if Berman is correct in drawing this connection in what he refers to as early modernity, then this image is a complicated one. This image is paradoxical because the moment in which the urbanizing move is hailed as the modern one it is disrupted by the desire to bring the countryside back to the fore. But it is not only in late modernity or in the midst of globalizing forces that the countryside returns to occupy the collective imagination. Such a return was represented in the eighteenth century with the popularity of the panorama that began in Britain and quickly spread to other countries. By the twentieth century, the establishment of National and Provincial Parks in Canada as a pseudo commons for the preservation of wilderness responded to urbanization by providing a weekend destination for urban dwellers. But the countryside's promise of *return* is ultimately deferred.

Wiebo Ludwig reverses what Berman refers to as the modern archetypal move. That is, Ludwig moves *away* from the city *to* the country precisely to get away from the chaos of modern life. The result of this reversal is a confrontation with that very chaos again but in hyperbolic terms. For Ludwig, life in rural Alberta brings him into conflict with the oil and gas industry (the economic and political foundation of Alberta), the criminal justice system, and various government departments, as well as places him in the centre of a media spectacle that attempts to represent every aspect of his life.

In 1999, special coverage of Ludwig's life published in *The Edmonton Journal* in two parts under the heading "Of Faith and Fury" reviews Ludwig's arrival in Canada from Holland at the age of ten.

The report describes Ludwig's upbringing in Sylvan Lake and Red Deer in terms of alienated cultural identity: "not wanting to buy into his new Canadian culture, no longer rooted in his old" (Staples, 12 Dec. 1999). In a crude synopsis of this depiction that supports other narratives accounting for Ludwig's history, Ludwig's dissatisfaction with the emphasis on accumulation of personal wealth in the community and his critique of the prevailing morality in the church as superficial and hypocritical lead to his departure, first for work and then to the navy. Later, Ludwig studies for the Christian Reformed ministry and eventually leads his own congregations in Ontario. But Ludwig leaves the Christian Reformed Church when controversies and disagreements over differing Biblical interpretations result in a breakaway congregation, Our Shepherd's King, which consists of Ludwig and other families.

The congregation flees to the United States and makes several major moves to avoid state intervention over their refusal to place the children in school, as the secular curriculum of the public school system clashes with their values and teachings. The tension between Our Shepherd's King and state authorities over the way in which the children are to be educated is of considerable significance in considering Ludwig a modern subject, since it is a reaction to the "ills of society" that the congregation wants to escape. Berman insists that the modern subject is caught in a contradiction that stems from change as a central characteristic of modernity, both as a will to change and as a response to it. After almost a year on the road, the congregation settles in Alberta on some farmland near Hythe and Beaverlodge. They name their farm Trickle Creek. Here, children are educated at home on aspects of subsistence farming, pharmacy, building, and on the Biblical form of the family (*Wiebo's War*). But even a relatively self-sufficient farm in this remote area near the Alberta-British Columbia border does not provide the desired distance from the secular and material world, since this is where for them life in the media spectacle begins.

In the early 1990s the inhabitants of Trickle Creek began drawing connections between gas flares or oil leaks and illnesses, miscarriages, and stillbirths on the farm. And in 1990 Ranchmen Resources Ltd. approached the community to survey the farm to access mineral rights to the property and install an oil well. When the company was not granted permission to survey the property, a struggle ensued. Eventually, the well was placed just outside the property line. While the well was not located directly on the property, it still impacted the land-use potential around the site. This event marked the beginning of Ludwig's acquaintance with the oil and gas industry. He would eventually have to deal with many other companies, including the Alberta Energy Company (AEC), and boards, such as the Alberta Energy and Utilities Board (EUB). While Ludwig actively opposed this process, he later had more urgent concerns than that of land use when inhabitants on the farm started becoming ill. Questions with regard to the effects of oil and gas industry activities on the health of the people and animals on the farm continuously surfaced over the years, and the media began covering it in the latter part of the 1990s. Prior to that time, however, the residents of Trickle Creek had made numerous attempts to address the problems through bureaucratic channels. Since the conventional approach to problem solving failed to bring about any effective response to the health concerns, Ludwig turned to other means.

Nikiforuk's chapter entitled "War" outlines some of Ludwig's most overt interventions into the industry's activities and the asymmetrical treatment of harm as initiated by the Royal Canadian Mounted Police (RCMP). In 1997 Ludwig started implementing a tactic he referred to as "nasal persuasion." In his first attempt he brought a bottle of sour crude into the AEC offices and spilled it in offices and hallways. Then he went to the EUB in Grande Prairie and did the same, but not before the phone lines for the offices had been cut from outside. Ludwig and others from his community also turned to new and individualized technological communication when they made a film called *Home Sour Home*, which included footage of an Edmonton bomb squad's use of explosives to dismantle a blockade of snow with a sign that said "Danger! Buried Explosives" on a road leading up to an industry site (67-71), a reenactment of their evacuation of the farm after one of the leaks that left the family vomiting (90), and video shots of skin rashes and eye infections (95).

Ludwig's approach began with activities that presented a mere nuisance, such as signs on the side of the road, but some of other methods attributed to him (for instance, placing nails on the road, presumably to disrupt industry activities in the area) were considered dangerous, even criminal. In the area, Ludwig had both supporters and detractors. Some neighbours came out to argue that the effects that Ludwig attributed to flaring wells were not experienced by anyone else in the area. In 1999, Rob Everton, spokesperson for West County Concerned Citizens (a group that organized in opposition to Ludwig), suggested that the cattle were unhealthy because Ludwig was an organic farmer. On national television, Everton asked, "Are his livestock getting enough of the proper nutrition?" (*Wiebo's War*). In 2001, after Ludwig's release from prison, Everton mused about the possible connection between Ludwig's intimidating tactics with industry and the loss of a sour gas well site contract on the Everton property. He said, "The well has been cancelled and it cost me a bunch of money, $15,000" (Staples 14 Nov. 2001). Nikiforuk generalizes this concern beyond Everton: "Some failing wheat farmers hailed the new colonizer as their financial saviour. A gas well in the middle of a wheat field looked like hell, but the rent often paid the bills, even kept a farm going. The industry also provided lots of off-farm jobs and paved most of the roads" (Nikiforuk 15).

If the initial move from the city to the farm reversed the archetypal move of modernity, then it is all the more ironic that a second move to Costa Rica took place at the end of December 1993. This move, on a global scale from a semi-core nation to a hinterland in the periphery, found Ludwig and the other members of the Trickle Creek community in the midst of the Zapatista uprising that responded in part to the implementation of the North American Free Trade Agreement. Ludwig had reportedly purchased a patch of rural land in Costa Rica precisely because of his concerns about the oil and gas industry encroaching on his land in Alberta. In this respect, this flight constituted, at least for Ludwig, not only another attempt to situate himself outside of those modern and worldly spaces, but also to evade the globalizing forces that confronted him within the very perimeters of his home. If the promise of Trickle Creek as haven from the whirlwind that is the modern world was false, then the path to Costa Rica failed to offer an alternative. The line between home and globe had perhaps never appeared so blurry. While passing through Chiapas, Mexico, Ludwig came face to face with the chaos of the Zapatista rebellion, characterized by heavily armed soldiers, congested and policed roadways that made passage difficult, and an unbearable heat. Ludwig and the others never made it to Costa Rica. All of these factors contributed to shattering the conception that this move would deliver the pastoral setting the Trickle Creek community sought. Discouraged, they returned to Alberta.

Events peaked in 1999. Among many other occurrences, Ludwig sustained non-life-threatening injuries when his van was bombed. A major impact on the media coverage of Ludwig's challenge to industry activities, however, was the shooting of 16-year-old Karman Willis in June 1999. In the early hours of the morning, after a party, several local teenagers in two pickup trucks allegedly drove recklessly onto the farm property. Willis was a passenger in one of the vehicles. The teenagers reportedly threw beer cans on the Ludwig porch and circled around, nearly hitting a tent in which Ludwig's daughters were sleeping. Someone shot at the vehicles and Ludwig called the emergency service 911. It has still not been determined who shot Willis. After the shooting, members of Trickle Creek were refused services from local businesses and were subjected to harassment if they ventured off of their property into town (Staples 14 Nov. 2001; Nikiforuk 230-239).

The course of Ludwig's experience on his Alberta farm has been characterized in various ways, but all narratives share the same basic structure. Ludwig's is the move from the "Garden of Eden" to the "War Against the Lands," from berry patches to roads (*An Eye for an Eye*). He is the "lightning rod in a province torn between its determination to preserve its wilderness and rugged prairies and a desire to get rich by exploiting North America's largest reserve of natural gas" (Pearlstein 15 Feb. 1999). Hythe, Alberta – a small town near the Ludwig property and the hometown of Willis – is self-described on its welcome sign at the entrance of the community as the "Town of the Flowing Wells," but since has been re-described as a "little town that went from a place of bucolic ease ... to a village populated by angry citizens" (D'Amour 27 Jun. 1999).

In earlier media coverage Ludwig was designated with many different, even conflicting, labels, including criminal, eco-terrorist, cult leader, eccentric, and environmental activist. Criminal designations preceded his conviction for vandalism, despite the claims of some of his neighbours: "Before we could never say Ludwig was a terrorist. Now we can say he's been convicted of vandalizing well sites, and that's a good feeling. It's a fact now, not fiction" (Sheremata 20 Apr. 2000). As reflected in many of the examples here, newspaper coverage of Ludwig frequently took a form in excess of the inverted pyramid convention and often exhibited the "art of storytelling" that John Miller has advocated in journalistic writing. The impacts of these narrative forms cannot be accounted for in any direct causal relationship without severely distorting the richness of the material; however, Ludwig as a public figure cannot be separated out and discussed in isolation of these circulating narratives.

In his work on media coverage of the demonstrations in response to the World Trade Organization meeting in Seattle, Andrew Rojecki emphasizes the importance of legitimacy for activists engaged in post-Cold War social movements. In addition, he argues that participants in social movements already appear to stand outside of political convention. The way in which activists are represented in the media, therefore, is vital to the effective communication of their concerns through media coverage. In particular, he suggests that such activists need to be concerned with being represented as legitimate rather than deviant.

In the context of this study, it is the case that the construction of Ludwig in the media emphasized the ways in which Ludwig could be seen as exceptional in most respects, from worldview to lifestyle, as is documented in the textual examples offered thus far. The struggle over legitimacy and deviance categories, therefore, was a factor in the public communication of Ludwig's concerns. The coverage over time, however, demonstrates that the representational construction of Ludwig's character was not the central dynamic in this process. Rather, significant here were social practices (or broader social context) present in the changes of the surrounding social and political landscapes, and the degree of perceived immediacy the coverage had to the audience that consumed it.

Act 2: Social Practices and the Appropriation of Ludwig

Consistent with Fairclough's insistence that the production and consumption of texts are situated within social practices (the social context of a text's production and/or consumption), it is notable that, while sympathy for Ludwig's concerns declined after the death of Willis, two events interrelated on the environmental theme dominated the media discourses related to Ludwig after his release from prison in November of 2001. The first event was the release of Andrew Nikiforuk's book *Saboteurs*, 2002 winner of a Governor General's Award for non-fiction, which emphasizes and investigates the environmental aspects of Ludwig's struggle with the Alberta oil and gas industry. The second thematically related event was the debate over the Canadian federal government's ratification of the Kyoto Accord on Climate Change, despite the vocal opposition of the Alberta provincial government.

The constitution of Ludwig in media representation is all the more complicated precisely because he is a citizen of the province of Alberta. In the popular imagination, Alberta is Canada's rogue province, which stands in conflict with the federal government on issues such as gun control, same-sex marriage, and public health care, issues widely considered significant to the construction and maintenance of Canada's national identity. In this popular narrative, Alberta is cast as the defiant province that would break with the orientations and objectives of the confederation, but the dominance of this struggle in public discourse obscures volatile tensions within the province. For instance, in her discussion of the moral panic actively produced in the 1990s by sustained attacks on gays and lesbians in the popular news magazine *Alberta Report*, Gloria Filax describes the province as follows:

> Alberta is an oil rich and wealthy province whose domi-
> nant identity and brand of politics includes a frontier
> mentality of rugged individualism entwined with an
> ethos of being misunderstood by an eastern yet cen-
> trist, urbane, large, and biased federal government....
> This struggle is as well a struggle over what constitutes
> a proper, normal Alberta identity and who rightfully
> belongs within the Alberta community/mosaic. (87-88)

Alberta's most successful politicians have promoted themselves not as politicians but as ordinary citizens in opposition to the very notion of the politician. Former Alberta Premier Ralph Klein has never been viewed as a *real* politician, despite having over twenty years of experience in politics that began in Calgary's City Hall. Klein's informal, unpolished speech and rebellious attitude have served well the non-politician myth that surrounds him. When Klein was Alberta's environment minister he was photographed giving the middle finger to environmental and social activist Randy Lawrence, who was arrested and charged with creating a disturbance and resisting arrest. While the famous photo of a provincial minister and his middle finger might have been disastrous for another politician, for Klein it subverted public recognition of the power relations that constituted the situation in the first place. The exchange occurred at a 1990 news conference, during which approval was given to the proposal for an Al-Pac pulp and paper mill in Athabasca, despite the recommendations of a government-appointed panel that emphasized the need for further environmental impact studies (Geddes 21 Dec. 1990).

Among the participants in opposition to the development was the late Tooker Gomberg, whom Klein would meet again later in other contexts, as Gomberg went on to become an Edmonton city councilor during Klein's early years as Premier. In a curious reversal of the Alberta politician as non-politician ideal, Gomberg's tenure as Edmonton city councilor was haunted by unrelenting derisive press that centred not on his performance but on his attire, as Gomberg did not wear a necktie and traveled to municipal engagements via bicycle. Later, while working with Greenpeace, Gomberg became one of Klein's most vocal opponents on the Kyoto Accord issue and uncovered a report regarding the reduction of greenhouse gas emissions,

"Discussion Paper on the Potential for Reducing Carbon Dioxide Emissions in Alberta 1988-2005," which Klein's office had commissioned when he was environment minister. The findings of this report estimated a thirty per-cent return on investment if Alberta reduced emissions by seven per-cent. Such a reduction would have been one percent higher than the six per cent goal of the Kyoto Accord. Despite Gomberg locking himself in Klein's Calgary constituency office vault to attract media attention to the report, Klein's self presentation within much of the province remained intact after the report was made public, just as it did after the pulp mill development hearing.

The careful order imposed upon the pulp mill development meeting began to disintegrate as some began heckling the panel. The famous image of Klein brandishing his middle finger at a public meeting confirmed Klein as the ordinary guy who was willing to take a stand against so-called special interest groups. He was quoted in the papers saying "I mean, I ought not to have done it perhaps. But maybe I was just scratching the back of my neck" and "Well hell, I could get away with it when I was the mayor [of Calgary]" (Cunningham 22 Dec 1990). This image worked for him and lent a legitimacy to the government decision to back the development proposal, in addition to a commitment of public financial assistance totaling $475 million. Nevertheless, to some, the image was objectionable and led to calls for Klein's resignation, but these were dismissed.

Set within Alberta's political and cultural landscape, the constitution of Ludwig is destabilized. Ludwig's story becomes an element in so many other stories, from the Kyoto Accord debate (Avery 21 Feb. 2002; Taylor 25 Oct. 2002), to conspiracy theories (Cairney 27 May 1999), to laments of the erosion of the common law (Mercer 16 Mar. 2000). When hushed conflict between two of the strongest, most symbolically salient Alberta industries – oil and gas and the cattle and dairy – heated up, Ludwig's name was appropriated by the cattle and dairy producers and represented in press coverage (Johnsrude 28 Jan. 2003; Johnsrude 6 Mar. 2004).

The news media's apparent agreement to constitute Ludwig as eco-terrorist after his conviction was made uneasy by artistic representations of Ludwig offered by the plays *Theodore and the Cosmonaut* (2000) and *An Eye for an Eye* (2001), which both invited audiences into the human complexities of the Ludwig case. The news media's designation of Ludwig as an eco-terrorist was subsequently refunctioned to a more neutral label of eco-activist in the coverage of a made-for-television movie entitled *Burn: The Robert Wraight Story* (e.g. Faulder 23 Nov. 2004). The RCMP hired Robert Wraight as their informant who was to get Ludwig to admit to vandalism or to plot a bombing on wiretap. The plan worked against the RCMP, however, when the tape of Wraight's conversations with a reticent Ludwig had Wraight, not Ludwig, proposing a dynamite purchase. The outcome of this muddled and comical undercover project discredited to some extent the prosecution's case when Ludwig was brought to trial. Comments from participants in the movie illustrate a conscious association between the Ludwig/Wraight story and environmental concerns in Alberta. In relation to the project, actor Jonathan Scarfe (Wraight) was quoted in the papers as saying, "When a province in Canada has lower standards than Texas in pollution control, that's pathetic. Hopefully all it takes is a bit of awareness for that to change" (Rankin 25 May 2004). Because of the central role that the oil and gas industries in Alberta play in the Ludwig story, Randy Bradshaw, the film's producer, links the movie to the Kyoto Accord debate in Canada (Wilton 30 Oct. 2002).

Ludwig's image portrayed in late media coverage appears subtly sympathetic. Ludwig is increasingly cited in subsequent struggles with the oil and gas industry. To make the case for more research, 2004 coverage of a laboratory study that would have implications in the debate over neurological effects on humans from exposure to H_2S produced by wells and oil refineries made reference to the stillbirth of Ludwig's grandson (Staples 15 Aug. 2004). A group of young activists was reported to have invoked the name of Ludwig, alongside that of Gandhi and Martin Luther King, in their struggle. The article states, "Ludwig gets little public sympathy, but his genuine grievances against the energy sector and the government run as deep as a sour gas well. Several of the protesters say that they empathize with Ludwig's frustration and, to an extent, his response" (Lazin 14 Aug. 2004). In 2005, the Alberta Energy Utilities Board (EUB) approved Compton Petroleum's proposal to drill several sour gas wells near Calgary neighbourhoods. Coverage of these plans was overwhelmingly critical and frequently made reference to Ludwig to support its message (see, for instance, Nikiforuk 24 Jun. 2005). One business column suggested that the new wells may pose an impetus to, or target for, terrorism on the scale of the 2001 World Trade Center attacks: "These wells are also an invitation to sabotage (remember Wiebo Ludwig?) and even terrorism. Try to imagine an American city allowing a project like this in the post-9/11 world" (Braid 23 Jun. 2005).

The image of Alberta as the rogue and grassroots Canadian province has a long history, but this national image masks dissent internal to the province as well as dissent specific to the rural context. Despite policies that have left grain and livestock producers at the mercy of fluctuations in international markets and, since 1995, cutbacks to social and physical infrastructure in rural Alberta, a conservative electoral base remains faithful. Barry K. Wilson argues that manipulation has played a role in securing support and silencing dissent in rural Alberta. Wilson shows that this manipulation in part has to do with the way in which issues and positions are framed in government organized public consultation meetings, for instance, in terms of "self-sufficiency" (market place) versus "safety nets" (collective programs). It is worth noting that the "self-sufficiency"–"safety nets" binary echoes the central tensions of the cowboy myth. Will Wright describes the mythical cowboy as the free individual on the frontier unhindered by social and economic ties. Through this lens, the Conservative government's rhetorical approach appears to construct rural Alberta as a frontier of equal opportunity for individual producers who are free to compete in the market, without the controls or supports of collective structures, such as the Canadian Wheat Board, that pre-dated the Alberta Conservative government's first election to office in 1971. But Ken Larsen points out that historically Alberta farming was based upon a cooperative tradition, not the free market individualist one advocated by the Alberta Conservatives.

The ideal of the rugged individual that is privileged by Alberta government discourse while in consultation with rural Albertans is consistent with the myth of social origin that Wright shows is key to the narrative figure of the cowboy. That is, the cowboy is a self-sufficient individual precisely because *he* emerges from the wilderness without ties and without support. In this context, the individualist myth is mirrored at the societal level in the myth of the "Alberta Advantage" that boasts low taxes to encourage consumption and makes Alberta attractive for business investment.

Given this broader picture, it may be difficult to see why Wiebo Ludwig has occupied a precarious position in public acceptance, especially given the mythology of the rugged individual and the Alberta Advantage. In some respects, Ludwig fits very well into the Alberta narrative as a potential hero. He is a strong, masculine figure associated with the wilderness. His skills make him self-sufficient enough in terms of his organic farming that he may freely reject the financial income that oil well development on his property would give him. In contrast to those characteristics, however, the organization of Ludwig's life emphasizes communal values that are not only in sharp opposition to dominant, individualist values but are considered suspect. Ludwig would not likely argue that he is self-sufficient but that the commune at Trickle Creek is fairly self-sufficient. Further, Ludwig's criticism of consumer culture and big industry flies in the face of a province so convinced of the value of industry investment that the former Premier could state publicly and repeatedly that he would "not blink" at public outcry in response to the dismantling of Alberta's social programs. Like the province, Ludwig is characterized by the contradictions that mark modern life.

Alberta is simultaneously traditional and innovative. It is at once home to social conservatism and libertarianism. It is both conforming and dissenting. In similar paradoxical character, Ludwig is both a religious conservative and a guerrilla media activist. He lives on an isolated piece of rural land, and yet his home has become the target of a mass media spectacle. His home is nowhere and everywhere. The paradoxical character of the Ludwig story reflects well the inherent contradictions of Alberta that is its setting.

Act 3: Abstractions of Ludwig

Intertwined in the polyphonic monologue of the one-person Edmonton Fringe Festival show *Love Letters from the Unabomber* (produced at the festival in 2000) are the voices of Ted Kaczinski, the Unabomber; Sergei Krikalev, the cosmonaut who left the Soviet Union but returned to Russia (although not before he was left stranded in space station Mir in the confusion caused by the sudden geo-political shift that ended the Cold War); and Wiebo Ludwig, among many others. Significant to the addition of Ludwig to the script—this play was produced originally at the 1998 Edmonton Fringe Festival as *Theodore and the Cosmonaut* and did not include the representation of Ludwig—is that, like Ludwig, Kaczinski moves from the city to the country, and there rails against the perils of technological advancement by sending letterbombs to scientists and attracting the attention not only of the media but the FBI as well. For Kaczinski, as for Ludwig, the attempt to exit the modern world becomes the realization of that very world.

Later shifts in media representation of Ludwig, then, reflect numerous factors entering into the active, multi-directional shaping of Ludwig as a public figure, including social practices, constituted in part by the contexts of the national Kyoto Accord debate; industry tensions within the province of Alberta between cattle and oil producers; and the approval of new well developments near neighbourhoods in a politically powerful urban centre such as Calgary. On the other hand, representations of Ludwig also changed the limits of public dialogue. For instance, some observers have suggested that Ludwig-related events sparked reviews of industry and tightened regulations

(Avery 21 Feb. 2002 and Avery 10 Jul. 2002).

Such reflection demands that the impact of the urban-rural dynamic not be underplayed. The structure of media production, consumption, and circulation, in fact, focuses coverage on a predominantly urban audience in a perceived external position in relation to the events. Over the period between 1997 and August 2005, coverage tended toward an increasingly deviant representation of Ludwig, but only when his industry complaints were both individualized and confined to the well activities in his local area. By individualized, I mean that Ludwig increasingly became singled out as an anomaly within criticism of the industry. This individualization occurred in spite of indications that Ludwig was not alone in his opposition to industry activity in the area. First, many area residents shared his concerns. Residents at a meeting spoke of sit-ins and marches to get government response on health issues related to environment and the oil and gas industry, but they were referred to as anarchists by the then environment minister (Struzik and Sadava 1 Dec. 1998). Subsequently, generalized efforts to get political or media attention appear to have dissipated. Second, there had long been problems with industry sabotage: as early as 1998 Premier Klein announced funds to investigate oil patch vandalism (Martin 29 Oct. 1998). Third, there was ample reason to question the efficacy of public consultation on local industry activity when Wayne Roberts shot an oil executive over a well dispute regarding his property, but, as noted earlier, this related event quickly succumbed to mass media amnesia.

The lack of symbolic proximity of the largely urban audience to the wells at issue, along with the tendency to individualize Ludwig's opposition, contributed to the deviant designations attached to Ludwig. This is not to say that Ludwig, as constructed in public discourse, is ordinary. In several respects, Ludwig's lifestyle and worldview, as represented in the media, appear to be counter-cultural. It is important to note, however, that some of these very practices do more to restore and support dominant discourse than to challenge it. For instance, Ludwig was often derided in media coverage for the treatment of women on the farm. In particular, the practice of headship, which places women under the direction of men, was frequently cited as an example of his difference. It is not enough, however, to carry out a crude analysis of the power relations between genders at Trickle Creek. A broader gender analysis is required, especially given that the perspective that Ludwig reportedly adheres to is merely a fundamentalist reading of gender relations rooted in the same Judeo-Christian tradition that provides the moral underpinnings of the province and

the nation. At the cultural level, this influence normalized the down-
loading of responsibility of care to women in the form of unpaid
labour during the years of deficit and debt elimination that under the
Klein government saw cutbacks to social sectors in Alberta (Dacks,
Green, and Trimble). Moreover, this is the same tradition cited in the
anti-gay rhetoric Alberta was well known for in the recent struggles
over same-sex marriage legislation at the federal level, when Premier
Klein threatened to use the notwithstanding clause to defend the definition of so-called traditional marriage. In other words, Ludwig takes
a restorative, albeit somewhat extremist, view of hegemonic views on
gender relations in Alberta.

In addition to the lack of symbolic proximity to the events by
urban dwellers, who constitute the consumer base of the print and
other media sources, there is the concrete advantage that the threat
of such development is not a reality for most urban communities.
This fact renders these disputes as extraordinary, unrelatable, and
even strangely close to fictional western cowboy narratives. This di-
minished threat is coupled with the perception that urban residents
have more power to be heard in political contexts, as illustrated by the
following comments made by a resident angered by Ludwig's actions
against well sites:

> Those bombs had a huge impact on people. If they had
> been exploding in Edmonton or Calgary, we'd have the
> military out here. There was probably less bombing dur-
> ing the FLQ crisis. But it was out here in the hinterland,
> so this was a great place to fit into the political agenda.
> (Brian Peterson quoted in Sharpe 52)

The lack of immediacy between the consuming audience, the
events reported, and the lifestyle represented marked early coverage
as reporting something external or other. The alienation between
audiences and Ludwig was heightened following the death of Willis in 1999, which further emphasized the individualization process
that separated Ludwig from others engaged in quiet opposition to
oilpatch activities. Not until 2001 and later – in the face of the Kyoto
Accord debates, tensions between the oil industry and the beef industry, and sour gas well proposals in urban settings – did this alienation abate in media representation. Particularly in the cases of the
Kyoto Accord ratification and the development proposals in Calgary,
the immediacy of the consuming audiences to the events reported
appears to have contributed to the legitimacy, even coherence, at-

tributed to Ludwig's struggles. Thereafter, Ludwig was increasingly appropriated by and for other social groups. Still, this more gentle representation was not universal. For instance, the Alberta Centennial edition of the *Edmonton Journal* ran a piece entitled "Crimes of the Century" (28 Aug. 2005) in which Ludwig's sabotage of a couple of oil wells ran alongside sensationally brutal crimes committed over the past 100 years, including an act of necrophilia and dismemberment, and an insurance fraud murder scheme.

Denouement

Despite the acclaim and recognition that it has received, Ghost River Theatre's *An Eye for an Eye* with each run has faced criticism in the press for its parodic handling of the death of Willis and the tensions between Wiebo Ludwig and the Alberta oil and gas industry. Significantly, the play attempts to present events from several viewpoints, although this is structurally limited to the characters represented: Ludwig, an oil executive, Willis, an RCMP officer, and the headline-writing media. The play erases the lines between spectator and spectacle, between consumer and producer. When the vilified oil executive turns to the audience and says that there is nothing evil about the principle of supply and demand—"We supply, you demand, you consume"—the audience can no longer maintain distance from him, since they must recognize themselves not only as consumers of the conflict but of the oil and gas at the centre of it. Because the play utilizes no backstage, not only the script's words but the set itself conflates the spatial representation of the narrative. The backgrounded characters thus remain visible to the audience throughout the performance, allowing for the unfolding of a choreographed proximity between them. This opportunity is embraced by the play's production, which creates a powerful yet unspeakable text that has all characters in frequent physical closeness, such as a hand resting on the other's shoulder, which connotes a logic of proximity—of chance and circumstance—that reflects some aspect of the social context and political interdependencies not articulated in other representations of these events.

This proximity was repeated on the steps outside of the theatre after the August 24, 2002 Edmonton Fringe Theatre Festival performance of *An Eye for an Eye*, which was attended by the Ludwig family and protested by friends and family members of Karman Willis. As the audience left the theatre after the play, the Ludwigs and the protesters were corralled into a tight space on the street, surrounded by media journalists and cameras, so that real life mirrored the non-textual aspects of the drama performed by actors only moments before.

An Eye for an Eye won the Betty Mitchell Award for Outstanding Musical in 2001, and its script was adapted into a radio play for the CBC. Further, the play was selected for production at the Alberta Scene Festival at the National Arts Centre in Ottawa in 2005 in celebration of Alberta's 100th anniversary. The curatorial mandate of the festival to present the "sights, sounds, and flavours of Alberta" puts a sardonic twist on the selection of a work subtitled as "An Oil & Gas, Piss & Vinegar Cabaret."

Ludwig's story captures the popular imagination in part because it expresses immediate but unspoken aspects of the social situation in which it is embedded. The discursive constitution of Wayne Roberts as the soon-to-be-forgotten killer of an oil executive stands in contrast to the popular evolving conception of Ludwig. Ludwig is at once saboteur and concerned citizen. Perhaps Ludwig's act of sabotage was to elucidate the invisible aspects of the industry, denaturalizing what is central to the maintenance and coherence of the Alberta identity and civil religion.

Notes

The author gratefully acknowledges support from the Social Sciences and Humanities Research Council of Canada and thanks the editorial committee and readers for their comments. A special thank you to Gloria Filax for generous suggestions on a previous version.

Works Cited

Berman, Marshall. *All That Is Solid Melts Into Air: The Experience of Modernity*. New York: Penguin Books, 1988.

Dacks, Gurston, Joyce Green, and Linda Trimble. "Road Kill: Women in Alberta's Drive Toward Deficit Elimination." *The Trojan Horse: Alberta and the Future of Canada*. Eds. Trevor Harrison and Gordon Laxer. Montréal: Black Rose Books, 1995.

Fairclough, Norman. *Discourse and Social Change*. Cambridge, UK: Polity Press, 1992.

Filax, Gloria. "Producing Homophobia in Alberta, Canada in the 1990s." *Journal of Historical Sociology* 17.1 (2004): 87-120.

Harrison, Trevor W. "The Best Government Money Can Buy? Political Contributions in Alberta." *The Return of the Trojan Horse: Alberta and the New World (Dis)Order*. Ed. Trevor W. Harrison. Montréal: Black Rose Books, 2005.

Laird, Gordon. "Spent Energy: Re-fueling the Alberta Advantage." *The Return of the Trojan Horse: Alberta and the New World (Dis)Order.* Ed. Trevor W. Harrison. Montréal: Black Rose Books, 2005.

Larsen, Ken. "Alberta's Thirty Years War Against the Family Farm." *The Return of the Trojan Horse: Alberta and the New World (Dis)Order.* Ed. Trevor W. Harrison. Montréal: Black Rose Books, 2005.

Miller, John. *Yesterday's News: Why Canada's Daily Newspapers are Failing Us.* Halifax: Fernwood Publishing, 1998.

Nikiforuk, Andrew. *Saboteurs: Wiebo Ludwig's War Against Big Oil.* Toronto: Macfarlane Walter & Ross, 2001.

Rojecki, Andrew. "Media and the New Post-Cold War Movements." *Media and Conflict: Framing Issues, Making Policy, Shaping Opinions.* Ardsley, NY: Transnational Publishers, 2002.

Sharpe, Sydney. *A Patch of Green: Canada's Oilpatch Makes Peace with the Environment.* Toronto: Key Porter Books, 2002.

Wilson, Barry K. "Cultivating the Tory Electoral Base: Rural Politics in Ralph Klein's Alberta." *The Trojan Horse: Alberta and the Future of Canada.* Eds. Trevor Harrison and Gordon Laxer. Montréal, New York, and London: Black Rose Books, 1995.

Wright, Will. *The Wild West: The Mythical Cowboy & Social Theory.* London, Thousand Oaks, New Delhi: Sage Publications, 2001.

Internet source
Wiebo's War. CBC The National. 6 November 2001. <http://tv.cbc.ca/national/pgminfo/ludwig/ludwig5.html>.

Newspapers and Periodicals
Avery, Bryant. "Kyoto jitters unwarranted, author insists: Alberta has already made great strides." *Edmonton Journal* 21 Feb. 2002.

__. "Group sticks nose into gas well monitoring: The Gas Rush: A Special Report." *Edmonton Journal* 10 Jul. 2002

Braid, Don. "The danger is all too apparent." *Calgary Herald* 23 Jun. 2005.

Cairney, Richard. "Who bombed Ludwig's van? Theories point to everyone from 'dark forces' of industry to rogue activists." *See Magazine* 27 May 1999.

Cunningham, Jim. "Klein succumbed to 'an urge'; Middle-finger routine may not be a good act, minister says." *Edmonton Journal* 22 Dec. 1990.

D'Amour, Mike. "A Small Town's Outrage." *Calgary Sun* 27 Jun. 1999.

Faulder, Liane. "Wrong or Wraight? Movie takes odd focus on an explosive story." *Edmonton Journal* 23 Nov. 2004.

Geddes, Ashley. "Pulp mill OK sparks ugly scene." *Calgary Herald* 21 Dec. 1990.

Johnsrude, Larry. "Sour gas has few effects on cattle." *Edmonton Journal* 28 Jan. 2003.

___. "Beef producers, gas industry reach truce over emissions." *Edmonton Journal* 6 Mar. 2004.

Lazin, Dan. "Action & Tree-Action." *Edmonton Journal* 14 Aug. 2004.

Leonard, Ed. "My one hundred days as a rebel's hostage." *Edmonton Journal* 19 Sept. 1999.

Martin, Don. "Klein acts to halt oilpatch terrorism: Funds approved for crime strategy." *Calgary Herald* 29 Oct. 1998.

Mercer, Ilana. "Common law has been defanged." *Calgary Herald* 16 Mar. 2000.

Nikiforuk, Andrew. "EUB assaults our sovereignty." *Calgary Herald* 24 Jun. 2005.

Pearlstein, Steven. "Gas Emissions Blamed for Health Problems in Humans, Cattle." *Washington Post* 15 Feb. 1999.

Purdy, Chris. "Crimes of the Century." *Edmonton Journal Alberta Centennial Edition* 28 Aug. 2005.

Rankin, Bill. "Bit player in Ludwig saga burns up prime-time TV: CTV movie focuses on RCMP informant." *Edmonton Journal* 25 May 2004.

Sadava, Mike. "The case of Klein's disappearing finger: Athabasca woman has exclusive rights to photo of premier." *Edmonton Journal* 11 May 2000.

Sheremata, Davis. "Neighbours breathe easier." *Edmonton Sun* 20 Apr. 2000.

Staples, David. "Of Faith and Fury Part One: A harsh shepherd." *Edmonton Journal* 11 Dec. 1999.

___. "Of Faith and Fury Part Two: Trouble at Trickle Creek." *Edmonton Journal* 12 Dec. 1999.

___. "Ludwig free; neighbours see no peace until slaying solved." *Edmonton Journal* 14 Nov. 2001.

___. "A poison in our midst?" *Calgary Herald* 15 Aug. 2004.

Struzik, Ed and Mike Sadava. "Don't label pollution foes 'eco-terrorists,' prof. warns; Sabotage in the Oil Patch." *Edmonton Journal* 1 Dec. 1998.

Taylor, Lorne. "Klein 'scaremongering,' Ludwig says." *Calgary Herald* 25 Oct. 2002.

Thomas, Don. "South Edmonton residents want stricter oilpatch rules."*Edmonton Journal* 31 Oct. 1998.

Wilton, Lisa. "Film set to ignite Ludwig tale." *Calgary Sun* 30 Oct. 2002.

Plays – Performances and Scripts

Curtis, Doug (dir.). *An Eye for an Eye*. Ghost River Theatre. Edmonton Fringe Festival performance 24 Aug. 2002.

Curtis, Doug (dir.). *An Eye for an Eye*. Ghost River Theatre. Theatre Network performance at the Roxy Theatre, Edmonton 15 Feb. 2003.

Page, Jeff and Wes Borg. *Love Letters from the Unabomber*. Unpublished script 2000.

Gloria Filax

Unruly Alberta: Queering the "Last Best West"

It is not a question here of either/or, but rather of both/and; of intractable paradoxes, not contradictions resolvable by Hegelian sleight of hand.

Sayer (148)

T he goal of this edited collection is to provoke and advance thinking about Canada's West, to take definitive steps towards developing "thesis of the west." This theorizing would capture what Castells refers to as the "space of places" as the "historically rooted spatial organization of common experience; in essence the nation-state, the workplace, the home," or a region like Alberta. Each of these is located in a fixed territorial area with which people form a bond, a sense of identity and culture. This paper argues that developing a "thesis of the west" must recognize that positing a unified notion of the west, the place and/or the people, risks overlooking struggles about who counts as a legitimate member of a region or, in the words of Toby Miller, who counts as "well-tempered" and who counts as unruly.

A notion that there is a distinct regional identity—the last best west—is raised through cultural representation[1] and histories of "the west," provincial or territorial governance that has the care of a region and people as its mandate, and political restlessness against federal government restrictions and incursions that ferment a quest for separatism. This paper discusses how "the west" and its people, specifically in the province of Alberta, are represented in popular, official, and historical accounts. I am especially interested in representations of unruly citizens, those who resist gender and sexuality norms, who disrupt unified notions of a place and its people.

Alberta is a modern, urbanized province, deeply integrated with national, continental, and international commercial and political networks. In popular accounts Alberta is "represented as a maverick agrarian region that is distinct, politically, socially and economically, from the rest of Canada" (Blue 74). Sydney Sharpe represents Albertans, on the one hand, as contrarians and doubters, "the wealthy westerners who question national habits and search for other paths," but who, on the other hand, are proud Canadians who want to take a central role in Canada's affairs. She reiterates the notion that there is an Alberta spirit that springs from a well of independence and self sufficiency: we want to control our own destiny and march to our own beat. On the other hand, Sharpe also portrays Albertans as having communal pride of place and a deep-rooted sense of responsibility. Governor General Michaëlle Jean built on this characterization of Alberta in her 2006 address to the Alberta legislative assembly when she proclaimed

> The pioneer spirit of independence and resourcefulness in the province is legendary, yet your deserved reputation for fierce individualism and economic self-reliance belie another, lesser known aspect of Alberta: your people are the most generous of Canadians. Eighty five percent of you make financial contributions to charitable and non-profit organizations. (Jean 19)

Albertans are represented as different from people residing in other provinces, but less attention is given to how differences between and among regions of Alberta and between and among people who identify as Albertans complicate what is understood as Alberta and its people. By noticing that there are important differences among those who live in the West, it is possible to bring a critical reading to representations of who is to count in accounts of the "last best west." This paper highlights representations of sexuality and gender differences in Alberta as one set of differences that also include, for example, ethnicity, region, race, age, and ability, each of which, when highlighted, alter popular depictions of Alberta identity. This work is informed by research that attempts to understand Canadian places and people by including sexual minorities. This research includes Gary Kinsman's *The Regulation of Desire: Homo and Hetero Sexualities*, Mary Louise Adams's *The Trouble With Normal: Postwar Youth and the Making of Heterosexuality*, Miriam Smith's *Lesbian and Gay Rights in Canada: Social Movement and Equality-Seeking, 1971-1995*, and Debra Shogan's essay, "Queering Pervert City." Before turning attention to how a thesis of the west is complicated by representations of sexual difference, this paper must address the split subject.

The Split Subject

The idea of a natural, essential, unified and coherent human subject[2] is a legacy of modernism that continues to inform how individuals think of themselves. Examples in this paper show instead that identity is continually in process, incomplete, and indeterminate. Toby Miller describes this incompleteness or indeterminacy in terms of split subjectivity. Split subjectivity is a consequence of engagement with competing discourses as these materialize through representations of legitimate cultural participation, while also questing for completeness. A quest to become a "well-tempered" or harmonious human is compared by Miller to Bach's well-tempered clavier/keyboard, from which Bach banished unruly notes through his musical compositions. Likewise a quest by human subjects for harmony or completeness is reflected in attempts to adhere to dominant depictions of what counts as, for example, legitimate engagement with popular culture, citizenship, gender norms, or sexuality.

Unlike Bach's well-tempered keyboard, a quest to live harmoniously with the dominant representations of a culture is undermined because it is not possible to banish all the contradictions, ambiguities, and paradoxes with which one lives. As people negotiate the dominant stories and discourses of a culture, they take up multiple subject positions, some of which are contradictory. Judith Butler captures the inevitability of this incompleteness when she writes of expectations of femininity that "to be a good mother, to be a heterosexually desirable object, to be a fit worker, in sum to signify a multiplicity of guarantees in response to a variety of demands all at once" (145) necessarily results in failure. Split subjectivity or incompleteness in relation to the codes or expectations of a culture, in turn, leads to multiple ways to engage with one's culture, producing yet more indeterminacy.

Miller's starting point for the well-tempered subject is "the ways in which formations of persons as individual subjects and collective publics may be seen to operate with relative autonomy from each other" (xxi). Alberta-ness is paradoxically both a collectivizing subject position and an individualizing subject position. What is often represented as a good community member in the province of Alberta is someone who is a rugged individual. The collective or public culture that is "Alberta" is contradictorily made up of a community of rugged individuals, whose very sense of self-interest contradicts the idea and well being of the collective. An effect of representations of Albertans as individuals negotiating life in a collective is that they produce well-tempered and unruly subjects (those who conform to a notion of rugged individuality and those who do not) but also unruly well-tempered subjects (those who identify with a collective notion of the independent Albertan) and well-tempered unruly subjects (those who reject a common Alberta identity while working for the collective good).

Aggravating, Awful Albertans

Albertans are often portrayed as an alienated bunch of rednecks, entrepreneurial and self-reliant as well as uniformly in support of a narrow sense of family values, business and free enterprise, unfettered economic growth, small-g government with shrinking social responsibilities as the provincial government continues the process of underfunding or withdrawing from fiscal and ethical responsibility towards, for example, public education, affordable housing, health and welfare, the environment, non-human life forms, and infrastructure funding for cities and towns.[3] In the words of Alberta writer Aritha van Herk, Albertans are "aggravating, awful, awkward, and awesome."

The importance of cowboys to Alberta narratives began with "Alberta's golden age of ranching," located in the south of the province. Ranching grew with an influx of cattle from Montana, but it began with a small herd of eleven cows and a bull in Fort Edmonton in 1873 (van Herk 162-163). Possibilities for white settler communities to ranch cattle burgeoned side by side with the dispersal and demise of Aboriginal inhabitants and their cultures. Non-human inhabitants suffered massive loss of habitat, and some species were driven to the brink of extinction.

The cowboy is often mobilized as a symbol of Alberta-ness that gestures to a common past. The cowboy as symbolic of Alberta-ness is taken up in and outside the province. A standing exhibit at the Glenbow Museum in Calgary celebrates the important place of the cowboy in Alberta's short history, and the Calgary Stampede is a world famous festival celebrating cowboy culture. Festivals celebrating cowboy poetry proliferate in towns and communities across the prairies, including the Alberta prairies, and the image is consumed through products and services like hair styling, car care, beef, blue jeans and other clothing, trucks, bars, bumper stickers, and beer.

Cowboys are depicted as ranging over wide-open spaces – the ranch and beyond – spaces of unfettered possibility, representing an unfettered freedom. Van Herk writes of this time as "before barbed wire," a time prior to fences and forms of governance that closed off possibility. According to this familiar story, cowboys were free in their isolated lives; often "a cowboy's only company was the soft ballad he sang to lull the animals." Cowboys had to be self-reliant and independent; they had to think on their horses. Cowboys are represented as hard workers, quintessential red-necks, earning their red necks from physical work under a strong Alberta sun. Cowboys were a tough breed, yet with a restless charm, known for their "determined bachelorhood...the cowboy code of neighborliness, loyalty, independence, and uncomplaining." Van Herk notes that their "persistence became a part of the West's code....[although] now pickup trucks have replaced horses" (162-164).

The trope of the cowboy is important to a newer narrative as well. In today's Alberta, the importance of cattle ranching has become eclipsed by oil. This is an evolving story of success gushing forward from the discovery of Leduc Number 1 in 1947. The continuing importance of oil is visible in the cathedral-like oilrigs dotting the Alberta landscape. Adding to these smaller eruptions, larger cathedral-like fortresses have been built in the service of extracting Alberta's famed tar sands in the northern part of the province, the Fort McMurray area. Economically, oil has made Alberta into a "have province," not only in Canada but within the global economy as well. In 2003 the *New Internationalist* reported that Canada has the second largest reserves of oil in the world, next only to the Middle East. Economic growth related to resource extraction in the province has been astronomical. Oil extraction and production across the province, but especially in the tar sands, has led to intense human activity, leading to air pollution and enormous pools of poisonous tailings. Environmental degradation, massive water contamination, local habitat and species loss thus accompany economic wealth. Alberta's oil patch is also home and workplace to the new Alberta cowboy–the pipeline cowboy. Oil extraction in the province links Alberta to a larger global economic and world gender order in which masculinity is dominant (Connell).[4]

Sarah Carter argues that frontier values, including independence and individualism, only partially capture prairie development in the settler period of Alberta, which also affirmed bourgeois values of work and economy and lifelong, monogamous marriage between ethnically identical individuals.[5] Van Herk's history of rugged, singular cowboys seems at odds with Carter's history about an emerging social norm of heterosexual, nuclear family. Yet, both existed side by side in Alberta in contrary and contradictory ways and continue to do so. The rugged liberal individual frontier identity has morphed into a neo-liberal entrepreneurial individual, along with notions of the importance of the nuclear, monogamous family for regional and state

Fig. 1. Redneck Beer Carton

formation and stability. Both narratives of Alberta and prairie history cleave to social norms about sexuality and gender.

Queering or Splitting the Subject of Alberta: No Queer Beer Here

Much of the idealism associated with the cowboy has been achieved through exclusions, even while the cowboy has come to represent a homogenizing Alberta-ness. Cowboys are men and cowboy virtue is a white man's virtue. Cowboys, like all good male Albertans, are heterosexual.

In an article "No Queer Beer Here," the *Alberta Report (AR)*[6] was effusive in its praise of Redneck Beer, a beer targeted at westerners: at Albertans proud to stick out their red necks. Molson beer, on the other hand, was depicted as the "official beer of gender ambiguity" (Milke 12). The Molson Canadian commercials from this time period depicted men and women in a range of activities and often in homosocial settings. The label on Alley Kats Redneck Beer, on the other hand, features a cowboy dressed in traditional denim shirt and a large western style cowboy hat, and sporting a large handle-bar mustache (see Fig. 1). He is white, and, in *AR*'s reading of the Redneck cowboy juxtaposed with Molson's gender-ambiguous Canadians, decidedly straight.

To the *AR*, Molson beer commercials represented the worst of central Canadian-ness: hyper-urbane, self-centred, and decadent. Albertans, on the other hand, as represented by *AR* and often echoed in provincial pronouncements, were alienated, right-thinking individuals, in support of a particular sense of family values, business and free enterprise, unfettered economic growth, and small g-government (Filax 2006). Not only were these characteristics represented as distinguishing Albertans from other Canadians, anyone living in Alberta not matching these characteristics was cast as an outsider—as not a true Albertan. What is at stake here, and in so much of what the *AR* published, especially in the 1990s, is what counts as a true Albertan in the context of Canada. *AR* was committed during this time to distinguishing Alberta and its interests from the rest of Canada, particularly central Canada (Filax 2004).

Writers for *AR* apparently fail to recognize their reification of Alberta-ness. In a column after the praise of Redneck beer, editor Paul Bunner wrote that he had since discovered that Alley Kat Brewery, described without irony as "proud makers of Redneck Beer," hosted a fund-raiser for Gay Pride Week in Edmonton. Rather than recognize that the *AR's* representation of rednecks and, by implication, Albertans as heterosexual might be problematic, Bunner's editorial response was "memo to real rednecks: choose your beverages carefully." Absent from their account was an appreciation that an Albertan might be both redneck and a sexual minority, or heterosexual and open to difference. Absent was recognition that it is possible for Alley Kat brewery to both produce Redneck Beer and support sexual minorities in the province; that it is possible to be a successful Alberta business with expertise from a sexual minority friend and consultant, Roxxie, an award-winning brew-master. Rather than see a straight, redneck cowboy on the Redneck Beer label, one might see a subject who both values the allure of the freedom of the cowboy and the campiness and gender ambiguity of a sexual minority.

In 2003 the United States banned the import of Alberta cows and beef because of a case of bovine spongiform encephalopathy (BSE). In response to the U.S. boycott, millions of dollars were made available by governments to support beef producers, and in Alberta thousands of I LOVE ALBERTA BEEF bumper stickers appeared on cars around the province (see Fig. 2). Those associated with the beef industry were shocked that the entire export of cattle and beef to the

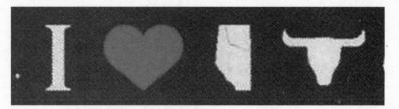

Fig. 2. Bumper Sticker

United States had been shut down. People in Alberta were encouraged to continue to eat beef to show the rest of the world that there was not a problem with this emblem of Alberta-ness. BSE could have provided an opportunity for a public discussion about beef production in Alberta (Blue 82), which in turn might have drawn attention to the association of the province with the cowboy. However, with the BSE crisis, identification of beef with Alberta identity was strengthened (Blue 71) because it was linked with a discourse rooted in a folk tradition of "wholesome cowboys, wide open spaces, and 'natural' modes of beef production" (Blue 82).

Significantly, Alberta beef is not "Canadian," or beef produced in the "last best west"; it is "Alberta" beef. Alberta beef is mobilized in these ads to represent a regional identity in much the same way that "Alberta oil" stands for values, beliefs, and norms of a people contained within the geographic space of the province of Alberta. The association of Alberta values with Alberta Beef is captured in the Alberta Beef Producers' (ABP) 1988-2001 marketing campaign: "If it ain't Alberta, it ain't Beef" (see Fig. 3). ABP launched this campaign as world attention was being paid to the 1988 Olympic Winter Games in Calgary. Through the imagery of three cowboys on a ranch, the public was given a face to associate with the Alberta Beef industry (Alberta Beef Producers: Marketing Campaign) as well as a public face for Alberta.

This image of Alberta cowboys is confounded by the image of international singing star from Alberta, k.d. lang, who, in a 1990 television ad produced by People for the Ethical Treatment of Animals (PETA), urged a boycott of the beef industry. Her "Meat Stinks" ad, which was never aired but was reported to exist by *Entertainment Tonite* (Alberta Beef Producers 80), riled the cattle ranchers of Alberta as well as the immediate community of Consort, where her mother still lived. Yet, lang's PETA ad makes apparent that it is possible to be both an Albertan and a vegetarian.

In January 1993, attention was again on lang, who had been named

Fig. 3. If it ain't Alberta, it ain't Beef[7]

a third-time recipient of a Grammy award. It was usual for the Alberta government to honour outstanding achievements by extending congratulations in the legislature. In lang's case, public acknowledgement was withheld for a month while politicians debated whether she should receive official recognition from the province. Accounts varied whether the delay was because lang is a lesbian or because she is a vegetarian. The *AR*'s take was that the singer was using her prodigious talent and fame to mess with youths' "impressionable minds" ("Editors Notes" August 26, 1993). To the dismay of many, however, lang's lesbianism made apparent that it is possible to be all three: an Albertan, a vegetarian, and a sexual minority.

lang began her career as a country music artist, but she was controversial in Nashville circles because of the close ties between country music and cattle ranching. Nashville tolerated her lesbianism but not her animal rights advocacy. Not only did lang not look like a female country music singer, her music had an edge to it that suggested to some that she was not entirely serious about country music. With albums such as *Absolute Torch and Twang* and lyrics such as "She was a big boned gal from southern Alberta," for some this androgynous female wearing femme clothing and cowboy boots was playing with cowboy culture. In Alberta, "questioning the consumption and production of beef is akin to being a traitor to the region" (Blue 80). For some, lang's sense of cowboy culture suggested multiple ways of being gendered, sexual or Albertan. For others, k.d. lang was confirmed as "queer," and therefore outside what counts as a true Albertan.

In 2001 ABP re-launched its "If it ain't Alberta, it ain't Beef" campaign. This time three women were featured that all people could re-

Fig. 4. If it ain't Alberta, it ain't Beef, 2001

late to…a young mother, a mother and producer, and a grandmother (Alberta Beef Producers: Marketing Campaign, see Fig. 4). Each reflected the contribution made by women to Alberta's ranching legacy as well as women's role as primary household food purchasers (Blue 76).

While there is a suggestion of split subjectivity between the cowboy and the women in traditional male cowboy gear, this split does little to disrupt the notion of open range ranching under the watchful eye of the cowboy. While opening up questions about gender expectations, these "RancHers" reaffirm gender categories. They do not evoke gender ambiguity as do the images of k.d. lang in her cut off cowboy boots, wedding dress, and short hair, singing her "Big Boned Gal" and espousing vegetarianism.

In January, 2007 a drag king group, Alberta Beef,[8] formed in conjunction with a talk by Judith Halberstam, author of a number of books and articles on female masculinity and transgender identity. Alberta Beef uses cabaret to take up ideas of female masculinity, performativity and gender.[9] The unofficial theme song of Alberta Beef is "Save a Horse, Ride a Cowboy," which is also the name of their first public performance. In each of their performances, which also included Alberta Beef … Rebranded! and Alberta Beef Overexposed, they play up Alberta cowboy masculinity (see Fig. 5).

Founding Alberta Beef member, Laura "Lawrence" Crawford, argues that transgender people – those who move between genders – offer a site to investigate gender demarcation and the regulation of public space. Ironically, Crawford is a recipient of a Trudeau Scholarship, named for former Prime Minister Pierre Trudeau, who promoted unification of regional identities under the umbrella of the Canadian

ALBERTA BEEF

DRAG KING CABARET

THURSDAY, JANUARY 25TH | 10 PM SHARP

PRISM BAR & GRILL | 10524 101ST STREET

NO COVER CHARGE | 18+

SPECIAL INTRODUCTION BY JUDITH 'JACK' HALBERSTAM

Fig. 5. Alberta Beef Drag King Cabaret

federation. Crawford's performance as swaggering drag king cowboy makes apparent the split subjectivity of sexuality and Alberta identity. As Crawford says, "questioning ... can be rewarding, fun, and change your life .... [I]ts hard to let things remain in question, yet those moments I didn't know lead me to some of my greatest moments of understanding" (Kerrsted).

Dominant representations about ranching cowboys as emblematic of Alberta and Albertans is disrupted by "queer beer," k.d. lang, and the Alberta Beef drag king group. So too are stories about those linked to the oil industry, oil barons and pipeline cowboys as the new Alberta cowboys. *The Globe and Mail* headline "Lord Browne's Champagne Chaperone: BP Scandal, The Oil Baron and His Boyfriend" (Alphonso A3) is one such disruption. Lord Browne is the former head of British Petroleum PLC, one of the top oil corporations in the world ("Pipeline Cowboys: Rustling For Oil"). Canadian Jeff Chevalier and British Lord Browne were involved together in a four-year affair that emerged as a scandal, exposing the continuing presence of a dominant gender and sexuality order that produces scandals out of non-conforming behaviours. Exposed as well, is that pipeline cowboys, indeed oil barons, can align with the culture of oil and be a sexual minority and that, by implication, someone might both reject the values associated with oil and identify as Albertan and heterosexual.

Alberta Beef and k.d. lang have the potential to expose the limits of regional, gender and sexual identity in a province whose identity is often represented in the figure of the straight, masculine cowboy. Challenging cultural norms of sexual or gender appropriateness as well as what counts as regional identity through alternate representations and readings of cultural stories produces the possibility of understanding the split subjectivity of Alberta identity. Whether this will open up dominant stories about Alberta and Alberta identity is not predictable. It "depends upon a context and reception in which subversive confusions can be fostered" (Butler 139). Shogan underscores this point when she writes of a photograph of the wild drag race at the Calgary Gay Rodeo:

> He is dragging what appears to be a full-grown steer
> while wearing a chiffon dress, gloves, a crown, and
> sneakers.... It is possible for the man in drag participat-
> ing in the gay rodeo to be "read" as a spoof on rodeo, as
> an insult to women, a spoof on the artifice of gender, or
> as a consolidation of gayness as perverse and of a notion
> of what rodeo "really" looks like when "real" men par-
> ticipate. Only some of these readings have the potential
> to create new ways of understanding. (97)

The Making of a Radical Thesis of a Split "West"

Our argument has been that the subject of the "last best west" is both split and unified as these are articulated in representations of the west and its inhabitants. Stories about the subject of the "last best west" are simultaneously split (through competing and contradictory stories about the place and its people) and unified (through dominant stories). As the examples in this paper illustrate, the cowboy and the places cowboys wander are subjects of both popular and well-known representations about Alberta and Albertans, and subjects of alternative ways of living in the province. Cowboys are depicted both as rugged individuals and players in a collective story about Alberta and Albertans. The cowboy is masculine, often female, and at times campy or transgendered.

The trope of the cowboy allows us to recognize that unruly subjects inhabit the place that is Alberta and consequently that a unified notion of Alberta or Albertan fails. A thesis of any place and people, including that of the "last best west," or even the "west of Canada," must flesh out and ground multiple stories, histories, and how these are located in place. This makes for a thesis of the "west" that insists on ambiguity and paradox, that includes both the "well-tempered" and the unruly.

Notes

1. See the work of Stuart Hall on representation as "one of the key practices which produce culture and a 'key' moment in what has been called the 'circuit of culture'" (1). Hall writes further, "representation, here, is closely tied up with both identity and knowledge. Indeed, it is difficult to know what being English, or indeed French, German, South African or Japanese [Canadian, Albertan, or 'last best western' or west-ness], *means* outside of all the ways in which our ideas and images of national [regional] identity or national [regional] cultures have been represented" (5). With Hall, this paper questions "what, then, is the status, the 'truth-claims'" (7) made when representations are mobilized to support, for example, Frenchness, Canadian-ness, Alberta-ness, or "west-ness"?

2. See Nick Mansfield's *Subjectivity: Theories of the Self from Freud to Haraway* on the human subject. See as well the work of Michel Foucault, *Power/Knowledge*, which theorizes a definition of subjectivity as the product of culture and power, as these pulse for example, in the confluence of power/knowledge inherent in representational systems.

3. See, for example, work on Alberta and the idea of a unified Albertan in the following: Doreen Barrie, Catherine Ford, Mark Lisac, William Marsden, Sydney Sharpe, *Edmonton Journal, The Calgary Herald,* and the *Alberta Report* (now defunct). Calling up an identity category calls up an assumed set of characteristics, pulsed through representational systems that define what is and is not included within the category. Each of these works calls up, variously, something called Alberta, Albertan, Alberta-ness, assuming a definition, even if the definition is not spelled out.

4. Robert Connell (1997, 2000) describes a global gender order that is dominated by men in suits. See the composition of the World Trade Organization, most political regimes, the United Nations, as well as top administration in business and universities for ample evidence of this point. Connell's work looks as well at the legacy of colonialism in the production of this gendered order.

5. Monogamous marriage, as described by most historical narratives, assumes a heterosexual subject. Queer relationships in Canada

reveal that it is possible, prior to recent legislation that conferred the right for same-sex partners to marry in Canada, for one to be lesbian, gay, transgender, transsexual, and be married to a straight partner. The debate about historical identity categories regarding queer subjectivity will not be taken up in this paper. In Canada, the right to marry for same-sex partners is recent.

6. While the *Alberta Report* is often regarded as unimportant in cultural narratives about the province of Alberta, this is simply not true. See the work of Filax (2004, 2006) analyzing the co-dependence of the provincial government during the 1990s and the *Alberta Report* in producing widespread moral panic about queer Albertans. As well, the *Alberta Report* was a significant print news magazine for rural Albertans. Regardless of how one views the ideological sensibility of much of the reporting of the *Alberta Report*, it was a significant voice and publication in Alberta.

7. Permission has been granted by the Alberta Beef Producers Association to use this image and the image of the RancHers.

8. In keeping with recent demographic trends in Alberta, most of the members of *Alberta Beef* now live in Alberta but are originally from elsewhere in Canada.

9. See http://mise-en-abyme.blogspot.com/2007/01/save-horse-ride-cowboy. Retrieved January 29, 2008.

Works Cited

Alberta Beef Producers: Marketing Campaigns. <http://www.albertabeef.org/consumers/marketing-campaigns/>.

Adams, Mary Louise. *The Trouble With Normal: Postwar Youth and the Making of Heterosexuality.* Toronto: U of Toronto P, 1997.

Alphonso, Caroline. "Lord Browne's Champagne Chaperone: BP Scandal, The Oil Baron and His Boyfriend." *The Globe and Mail* 7 May 2007: A3.

Barrie, Doreen. *The Other Alberta: Decoding a Political Enigma*. Regina: Canadian Plains Research Center, 2006.

Blue, Gwendolyn. "'If It Ain't Alberta, It Ain't Beef'": Local Food, Regional Identity, (Inter)National Politics. *Food, Culture & Society* 11.1 (2008): 69-85.

Bunner, Paul. 1998. "Editor's Notes." *Alberta Report*, 25 May 1998: 4.

__. 1998. "Editor's Notes." *Alberta Report*, 26 Aug 1993: 4.

Butler, Judith. *Gender Trouble: Feminism and the Subversion of Identity.* New York: Routledge, 1990.

Cairney, Richard. 2007. Trudeau Scholar Examines Gender Demarcation. Express News. Faculty of Arts News, University of Alberta. <http://www.uofaweb.ualberta.ca/arts/news.cfm?story-6263>.

Carter, Sarah. *The Importance of Being Monogamous: Marriage and Nation-Building in Western Canada to 1915.* Athabasca: Athabasca UP and Edmonton: U of Alberta P, 2008.

Castells, Manuel. *The Rise of the Network Society.* Oxford: Blackwell, 2000.

Connell, R. W. "Sex in the World." *A Dangerous Knowing: Sexuality, Pedagogy & Popular Culture.* Eds. Debbie Epstein and James Sears. London: Cassell, 1999.

Connell, R. W. "Masculinities and Globalization." *Gender Through the Prism of Difference.* 2nd Edition. Eds. M. Baca Zinn, P. Hondag-neu-Sotelo, and Michael Messner. Boston: Allyn & Bacon, 2000, 1997.

Crawford, Laura. Blog. <http://mise-en-abyme.blogspot.com/2007/01/save-horse-ride-cowboy>.

Filax, Gloria. "Producing Homophobia in Alberta, Canada in the 1990s." *Journal of Historical Sociology* 17.1 (2004): 87-120.

___. *Queer Youth in the Province of the Severely Normal.* Vancouver: UBC Press, 2006.

Flohil, Richard. "Voice from the West: The k.d. lang Success Story Involves Much More Than Luck." *The Canadian Composer* 206.985 (1985): 4-11, 34.

Ford, Catherine. *Against the Grain: An Irreverent View of Alberta.* Toronto: McClelland & Stewart, 2006.

Foucault, Michel. *Power/Knowledge: Selected Interviews and Other Writings 1972-1977.* Ed. Colin Gordon. New York: Pantheon, 1989.

Gregg, A. "The True West, Strong and Free." *The Walrus* 3.7 (2006): 39-45.

Halberstam, Judith. *Female Masculinity.* Durham, NC: Duke UP, 1998.

___. *Skin Shows: Gothic Horror and the Technology of Monsters*. Durham, NC: Duke UP, 1999.

___. *In a Queer Time and Place: Transgender Bodies, Subcultural Lives*. New York: New York UP, 2005.

Hall, Stuart. "Introduction." *Representation: Cultural Representations and Signifying Practices*. Ed. Stuart Hall. London: Sage, 1997.

Jean, Michaëlle. *Alberta Views* July/August 2006: 19.

Kerrsted, Ted. 2007. QueerMonton. *VueWeekly* 2007.19. <http://www.vueweekly.com/article.php?id=7021>.

Kinsman, Gary. *The Regulation of Desire: Homo and Hetero Sexualities*. Montreal: Black Rose, 1996.

Lisac, Mark. *Alberta Politics Uncovered: Taking Back Our Province*. Edmonton: NeWest, 2004.

Mansfield, Nick. *Subjectivity: Theories of the Self from Freud to Haraway*. New York: New York UP, 2000.

Marsden, William. *Stupid to the Last Drop: How Alberta is Bringing Environmental Armageddon to Canada (And Doesn't Seem to Care)*. Toronto: Knopf, 2007.

Milke, Mark. "No Queer Beer Here: Alley Kat Targets Alberta's Redneck Market." *Alberta Report* 30 Jun. 1997: 12.

Miller, Toby. *The Well-tempered Self: Citizenship, Culture, and the Postmodern Subject*. Baltimore: Johns Hopkins UP, 1993.

Nikiforuk, Andrew. "Saudi Alberta: No Place Like It." *The Globe and Mail*, 1 Jul. 2006: A15.

"Pipeline Cowboys: Rustling For Oil." *New Internationalist* 361 Oct. 2003.

Sayer, Derek. *Going Down for Air: A Memoir In Search of a Subject*. Boulder: Paradigm, 2004.

Sharpe, Sydney. "Introduction." *Alberta: A State of Mind*. Eds. Sydney Sharpe, R. Gibbins, J. Marsh, and H. Bala Edwards. Toronto: Key Porter, 2005. 19-24.

Shogan, Debra. *The Making of High Performance Athletes: Discipline, Diversity and Ethics*. Toronto: U of Toronto P, 1999.

Shogan, Debra. "Queering Pervert City." *Torquere* 4-5 (2002-2003): 110-124.

Smith, Miriam. *Lesbian and Gay Rights in Canada: Social Movements and Equality-Seeking, 1971-1995*. Toronto: U of Toronto P, 1999.

Van Herk, Aritha. *Mavericks: An Incorrigible History of Alberta*. Hammondsworth: Penguin, 2001.

Pamela Cairns

Teaching Adventures in Seymour Arm: A Case Study of Rural Education

Well, personally I was after a "real" job, but when I had a real job and I was driving to work, I thought, "Where is the adventure?" Even getting to work was an adventure at Seymour Arm and all day-to-day things – the custodian work, the maintenance – were missing in the regular school system ... you just felt like one part of the wheel. In a small community you feel more special ....

Eleni Morris, June 2007

British Columbia's landscape was once dotted with one-teacher schools. The Ministry of Education's Annual Reports present a great deal of information about these schools: where the schools were located, when they were established, the number of students, the subjects and levels taught and even if the school started the day with the Lord's Prayer. However, other than the teachers' names and qualifications, they do not describe the teachers' experiences that deepen our knowledge of rural education. Education is a relatively new field of historical study, only gaining momentum in the last decades of the twentieth century as Canadian historiography expanded to include social issues (Wilson & Jones 7-10). The focus is often on urban schooling and school leadership, perhaps because of an unspoken hierarchical structure that places rural issues behind these urban matters.[1] This is particularly true in the study of schools in British Columbia.[2] A review of the articles in *BC Historical News* for the last twenty years yields fourteen articles about rural education, the majority of which are two- or three-page memoirs or bibliographies about teachers in these schools. (See also Appendices I, II, III.)

The study of rural education is important because it was the mode of schooling for many students in British Columbia and the means of employment for over a quarter of its teachers in the early part of the twentieth century.[3] Also, the issue of how best to educate students in rural communities continues to be an ongoing topic for debate. An investigation into the nature of the teachers' experiences adds depth to our knowledge of the past and guides us in our future endeavours. Seymour Arm, which experienced one-room schools from 1910-1937 and again from 1986-1997, presents an optimal opportunity to investigate the nature of rural teaching. Though the eras were almost fifty years apart, despite some improvements in the conditions, there are significant similarities in teachers' experiences in both periods.

Information from the first era comes mainly from the Ministry of Education Annual Reports, the Teachers' Bureau Surveys and local newspapers, as well as some secondary sources. Data from the second period is largely from interviews. Five of seven teachers at the school were contacted: all those located consented to either an interview or a questionnaire. Their responses were corroborated by interviewing parents, a teacher's aide and the assistant superintendent responsible for opening the school and hiring for it. Pseudonyms have been used to maintain confidentiality. Using memoirs or interviews as historical data sometimes is a mistrusted practice since critics question the reliability and veracity of the data. However, traditional sources are also subject to errors. For example, the 1918 Annual Report for the Ministry of Education records the average attendance at Seymour Arm School as 10.65 but the number of students enrolled was only ten. Another example is the transcription of names: various written sources, including government documents, list a family of settlers in the area as Allison, Alison and Alyson. It is unlikely such a small community had three families with similar names and much more likely the error is in the recording of data. In the absence of diaries or correspondence written during the era under study, interviews and memoirs are the only methods of developing a more complete history of rural schooling.

Located in the interior of British Columbia, Seymour Arm is nestled against mountains at the tip of the northeast arm of Shuswap Lake. It is not easy to drive to as it is over an hour away from the nearest settlement by radio-controlled dirt logging roads, but if you are willing to land on a grass strip it is also accessible by single-engine plane or by boat. Residents do not enjoy the benefits of hydro electricity or cable television, but Seymour Arm citizens take pleasure in their distinctive lifestyle and the area's unique environment. The heavy precipitation allows a dense forest of cedar, fir, the occasional pine and a variety of deciduous trees. In the summer and fall the area is a virtual pantry of berries, mushrooms, and edible plants. It is home to the second largest salmon run in the Shuswap system. Historically, the Secwepemc regularly took advantage of the bounty in the summer and fall. They occasionally defended the area against raiding parties from the Blackfoot and Okanagan. Pictographs remain to document the resulting skirmishes. The raiding tribes travelled a trail through the mountains that would later become the prospectors' conduit to the Big Bend gold fields in the 1860s (Bradley 1).

Although traders and explorers began moving through the area around 1811, not until the Big Bend Gold Rush (1865) did Seymour become a boomtown. The town was called Ogden City, or Ogden-ville, after Peter Skene Ogden, who had served as joint Hudson's Bay Company Chief Factor in the 1850s. On March 6, 1866, the town officially became Seymour Arm City, named after Frederick Seymour, Governor of the Crown Colony of British Columbia (Abercrombie 33). The town grew rapidly, but during this era there was no schooling in Seymour, for several reasons. First, the colonial government had no mandate to provide schooling for the population. Second, the town attracted adventurers, mostly men and not families, so no community identity emerged from a population that was largely transient.[4] Finally, the city did not prosper; by late 1866 the gold rush dwindled and the population of the town declined. Late in the decade, a fire destroyed the remnants of the boomtown (Bauer 17). By 1877, the Geological Survey of Canada reported "The settlement of Seymour is now entirely abandoned, not a single building remaining intact" (NSHS 22b).

At the turn of the century, Seymour Arm attracted the attention of Ontario investors who created Seymour Arm Fruit Lands Limited. The corporation purchased 7000 acres just north and northeast of the original town site and subdivided 440 acres into five-acre blocks (see Fig. 1 below). The five-acre blocks were advertised at $100 - $125 an acre and were promoted as far away as England. The terms were promising. The company estimated the total outlay at $2312 for a ten-acre orchard, which included clearing and preparing the land, planting and the first year's cultivation. The settlers could sign up by putting down one fifth and paying the balance in four annual payments (Bradley 7). The company also promised to carry, interest-free, the debt of anyone unable to work because of illness or weather, and it offered jobs in the construction of public buildings and other infrastructures. In return for purchasing land, the company promised to provide amenities, such as a school and regular transportation to Salmon Arm (Abercrombie 83-84).

The company lived up to its promise of providing a community

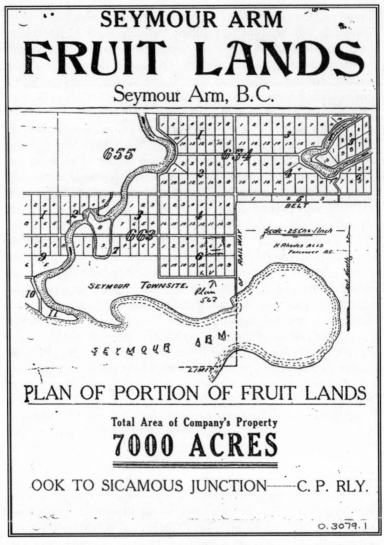

Fig. 1. A Seymour Arm Fruit Lands' advertisement, 1910. (Original from the Collings' mansion; photocopy available at the North Shuswap Historical Society)

school. The directors began by inviting Thomas Leith, Inspector of Schools, to visit the town in 1910. He "found a sufficient number of children to warrant the establishment of an assisted school" (1910 Annual Report 30). The company paid for the school building and supplies. Annual discretionary grants from the provincial government

were to compensate the teacher. The community was to be responsible for forming a three-person Board of School Trustees to hire
teachers, maintain the schoolhouse, and provide school materials
(Wright 26-27; 1909-1938 Annual Report). The creation of schools
in this era was largely due to the organizing influence of the company, but schools could not have been opened without community or
government support.

In late 1910, Adelaide Graham travelled to Seymour Arm to become the town's first teacher. She conducted school in temporary
quarters in the hotel. The first year she had only nine pupils, but the
average attendance was over six, so the school was in no danger of
closing. Graham's students ranged from the First Primer to the Third
Reader. All the students studied writing, dictation, spelling, composition, arithmetic, and drawing. They also had lessons in Nature and
Hygiene. Older students also studied Geography, History (British and
Canadian), English Grammar and Literature (1911 Annual Report).
Graham would have needed a detailed timetable and plan to teach
thirteen subjects to nine students at five different levels. Writing lessons on the blackboard to keep the other levels busy, Graham would
hear lessons or teach one group at a time. A few subjects were taught
in larger groups. In the 1911-1912 school year, in keeping with the
provincial focus on fitness, Physical Science/Exercise was added to
the curriculum for all the students. Graham also added music studies
that year. Over the course of the school's history, music was taught
only occasionally, probably based on the teacher's ability and confidence in teaching the subject (1911-1938 Annual Reports).

The teachers' abilities varied. In the twenty-six years the school
was open between 1910 and 1937, at least sixteen different educators
taught in Seymour Arm. Existing records show that of the sixteen,
six held Third Class Certificates, six held Second, two held Firsts and
two held Academic Degrees.[5] Teachers with higher-level certificates
had more options and rural assisted schools were low in desirability.
A teacher with a First Class Certificate might apply for a rural job for
experience until a better job became available, but few planned to
stay in the community; most wanted jobs with better pay, increased
social opportunities, or less work (Johnson 161). Teachers with Third
Class Certificates were far more likely to stay for more than one year
in Seymour Arm, so teachers with a Third Class Certificate taught
for fifteen out of the twenty-six years (1911-1938 Annual Reports; see
also Appendix II).

Teaching in a rural one-room school was a great deal of work.
Aside from the lessons to be planned and taught, many teachers

were responsible for other duties, which might include cleaning and beautifying the school, cooking hot lunches for the students, planning community events such as Christmas Recitals or Spelling Bees, and making sure the schoolroom was warm, with water available. All this might mean chopping kindling, starting the wood stove and pumping water. Sometimes older students were paid to take on these responsibilities, but all the students would help maintain the school in some way, usually on a rotating basis. As well, teachers corresponded with the trustees and the superintendents and documented visits to the school (McGuffey; Charyk; Cochrane). In 1911-1912 Graham recorded thirty-eight visits from inspectors, trustees and others. Finally, teachers were required to complete administrative duties to document students' progress. In the first two full years of school, Graham wrote 237 reports to parents, the equivalent of a report every second month for each student enrolled (1912-1913 Annual Reports).

As the community grew, so did the number of pupils. Soon a new schoolhouse was built just up the hill from Daniels' store (Abercrombie 85). By 1913, the number of pupils peaked at twenty-three, with the teacher's salary reflected in this growth. Graham, who started at a salary of sixty-five dollars a month, was paid seventy-five dollars a month in 1913. This was also Graham's last year in Seymour Arm as her Third Class Certificate expired in December. After travelling to Victoria to obtain a permanent Third Class Certificate, Graham found work in Carlin Siding, a rural community close to Salmon Arm, the largest town on the opposite (southwest) side of Shuswap Lake (1912-1914 Annual Reports). Graham exemplifies several qualities commonly found in rural teachers, not only in British Columbia, but also across Canada: she was female, young, single and mobile. She would have faced the common problem of local politics, but in her short tenure she would not have felt other widespread difficulties, such as community impoverishment or settler transience (Wilson & Stortz. 239-240). Seymour Arm was once again a boomtown.

By 1911, Seymour Arm boasted a population of two hundred, making it the second largest town on the Shuswap, after Salmon Arm. During this decade a semi-regular column called "Seymour Arm News" in the *Salmon Arm Observer* documented a lively social life in the town. It described weekly dances, held first at the hotel and then the schoolhouse. The schoolhouse was also home to numerous meetings, from the Conservatives to the Farmer's Institute. By 1913, the community even boasted oil standard lamps to light some of the intersections and wood piping to supply water to the community (Bauer 21). The town suffered its first misfortune with the outbreak of the

Great War, when many settlers joined the forces. Seymour Arm Fruit Lands Limited dissolved in 1914, but many of the immigrants to the area stayed. Most families were homesteading farmers or trappers or logged in a small way. The community faced another tragedy during the winter of 1916, when a heavy black frost destroyed many of the young fruit trees and berry plants. The frost was so heavy that cattle froze where they were standing in fields near Seymour (Abercrombie 85). More settlers left to seek work in the larger centres, but others still came to homestead.

Teachers at the school came and went swiftly for the next decade, reflecting the transience of the community. Not one stayed for more than a year; some even less. Hermie Fraser was eighteen when she went to Seymour Arm to teach for a fall semester. She remembers being "all skin and bones, weighing ninety-eight pounds." She wore "a second-hand fawn suit, high buttoned boots and a dilly of a sailor hat." On her way to the village on the steamer she met an old-timer, who warned her about the local "war" over a cauliflower-tramping cow. He cautioned her to stay out of the local politics and advised her of the families to avoid. He finished by telling her, she would not last in the community because no one stays in Seymour Arm. He told her the First Nations' name for the area was She-whun-i-men, meaning "they go away" (Fraser in Abercrombie 440).

The problem of retaining teachers was far from unique to Seymour Arm. Inspectors were increasingly commenting on the inferior quality of rural education, a problem partly related to teacher retention. To combat this problem, the government formed a Teacher's Bureau (TB) to help place teachers in suitable jobs and to help communities find suitable teachers. The TB, therefore, surveyed rural teachers about their working conditions in 1923 and 1928. Additionally in 1928, Lottie Bowron was appointed to help rural teachers, the majority of whom were young and female, deal with the reality of teaching in small communities. Bowron acted as a spokesperson for teachers and negotiated settlements for local disputes. Bowron was fired in 1934 when the government changed, but while at her post she worked hard to alleviate her charges' troubles despite having no authentic power to effect large-scale changes (Wilson 259-279).

Fraser remembers some of the problems she faced as a young teacher in a small community. The local men were disgruntled that she was engaged, because "new school teachers were expected to be unattached, so that the young men of the village could 'pick their choose' [sic]." Her potential suitors decided to "Let her light her own durned [sic] fires in the schoolhouse and chop her own durned [sic] wood." She changed her lodgings several times, since each place had drawbacks, until she had nowhere else to go. One of the "drawbacks" included being chased by "a young demon brandishing an axe." At least Fraser got along well with most of her students: she was not much older than some of them. She enjoyed the fact that she commanded respect as teacher, saying, "At home I was only the middle one, a mere child, but in Seymour I was treated as an adult." She ends her reminiscence with a tale of returning to Seymour Arm to visit, only to find all her friends had left (Fraser in Abercrombie 440-5). Seymour Arm's population was in transition in the early 'twenties, with only a few of the original families such as the Daniels, Collings and Hoopers remaining.

Around 1919 the Schwab Land Development Company, registered in Winnipeg, began developing an area near Gilman's Bay. Schwab promoted Seymour Arm as an excellent farming opportunity with a pleasing, moderate climate, convincing many Ukrainian settlers from the prairies to sell their homesteads and move. The company paid twenty-five dollars an acre for the prairie homesteads and charged two hundred dollars an acre for land in Seymour Arm. Fifty families moved into the area and rejuvenated the population. Since many of the Fruit Lands' settlers had departed, more children lived near Gillman's Bay than by the old school site. In 1920, therefore, the community built a new schoolhouse closer to Gillman's Bay. However, the Ukrainian settlers soon realized the land was not as specified, with the climate hardly what they had been promised. When they demanded restitution, eventually the Schwab Company relocated the immigrants to Grindrod, so by the summer of 1922 the Ukrainian influx was merely a memory (Baron).

The school remained at Gillman's Bay, but the new setting was less than ideal, partly because it was not easily accessible for all the students. For example, the Daniels children had to walk around the bay, row across the water or traverse the ice to go to school, but they persevered (Benson -NSHS; Hucul 22).[6] Teachers found the setting inconvenient as well. In March 1923, the teacher Lydia Hayes wrote in her Teacher's Bureau Survey (TBS), "Since Christmas holidays we have had school in part of the cottage. The school building is too airy for winter." Although the school building was an important gathering point for the community, the fluidity of the community meant the location and type of building often changed. By 1928, again in response to the TBS, teacher Ella McPhee replied, "School is accommodated in an empty house, to suit convenience of pupils, who are all on the south side of the lake." Teachers were expected to be flexible and capable enough to teach in many different situations. Most coped, but it took its toll, as demonstrated by the high turnover rates in rural schools.

Schools and communities have a symbiotic relationship: each needs to thrive for the other to succeed. However, when a community suffers economically, as Seymour did in the 1930s, people leave and the school struggles. By 1935, school was held again in the hotel, since most of the residents of Gillman's Bay had left. By 1936, only members of the Daniels and Hooper families were attending school in Seymour Arm. The father, Alf Hooper, was also the schoolteacher and had been for seven of the twenty-six years the school was open. He first taught in 1915 and appears to have supplemented his income by teaching occasionally for the next two decades. As a male with a family, Hooper probably avoided many of the problems that the single female teachers faced, such as loneliness and lack of social opportunities. If female teachers found social opportunities, such as marriage, and developed ties in the community, such as a homestead and a family, they were not expected to teach. However, Hooper still faced the problems of small town politics and lack of advancement possibilities. When Hooper moved out of Seymour Arm and withdrew his children from school in 1937, the school was forced to close (*Seymour Arm Elementary*; Hucul 22).

The Seymour Arm school remained closed for the next few decades for several reasons. First, while transportation systems in most of the province had improved, Seymour remained dependant on water access, making it less attractive for potential settlers. There were also changes in the school system as consolidation gained favour. Larger schools offered benefits such as increased opportunities for students, reduced workloads for teachers and reduced administration costs. As well, the improved provincial infrastructure, lower vehicle cost and greater vehicle reliability made travelling in the interior much easier and consolidation feasible. Of course, consolidation also had drawbacks, such as reduced local control and the need to transport the students to the school, but these were deemed insignificant beside the benefits of increased efficiency (Adams and Thomas 9; Johnson 110-115). It seemed only a matter of time before one-room schools were forsaken. Nonetheless, they never completely disappeared. British Columbia still has one-room schools today.

Seymour Arm was never completely abandoned either, but during the 1940s its population continued to decline. In 1947 the lack of inhabitants resulted in the post office closure, making the area even less attractive to potential settlement. Nonetheless, small-scale farming,

Fig. 2. The Seymour Arm Hotel as it looked in the 'seventies.
(http://www.milligan.ab.ca/seymourarm/hotel.jpg)

logging and trapping continued. People visited the area to fish, hunt and picnic; and some bought land (Abercrombie 331). By the end of the next decade, several families were living in the area year-round again, and the 'sixties saw the return of schooling to Seymour Arm, when three families had their children enrolled in correspondence courses (Hucul 23).[7]

However, by the late 'seventies, Seymour was a busy place again. With the 1974 completion of Mica Dam, approximately one hundred kilometres to the north-east, came the need to build power lines over the mountains. The power lines were several kilometres inland from Seymour Arm, but the British Columbia Hydro crews and their supplies travelled through the town. This necessitated a regular ferry service and an airstrip, which then also accommodated tourists wanting a taste of British Columbia's natural beauty (*Eagle Valley News* 1970-1984). The 1970s thus saw a building boom and economic growth in the community. This did not immediately result in a new school, but the foundations were laid early during this period when the Seymour Arm Resident Ratepayers Association (SARRA), with the help of a Local Initiatives Project Grant, undertook the building of a community hall over the fall and winter of 1974-1975. The hall was an important step in the strengthening of the community, but it also played an important part in bringing a school to Seymour Arm. (Winters interview; *Eagle Valley News* 1974-1975).

In 1986, parents of correspondence students petitioned the school district under Section 19 of the School Act, which concerns "schools that provide tutorial services or other supplemental educational services to school age children." The parents successfully petitioned for a part-time teacher in the community to help their children with their correspondence classes. The school was located in the community hall and operated one week a month, providing the students with assistance and giving them an opportunity to socialize and work with other children (McKee, Morris and Winters interviews). The first teacher of the second era of school in Seymour Arm, Lee Hansen, arrived in September 1986. She taught for the fall term before being replaced by Eleni Morris (*Seymour Arm Elementary*).

Morris knew the Seymour Arm job would be perfect for her despite having husband and children in Salmon Arm. She had grown up in a rural setting in the Kootenays in a "very homestead kind of lifestyle" and would be able to handle the frontier-style duties required like "starting up the generator so I could show educational videos and starting up wood fires and hauling water." She realized that it would be more than a teaching job. She would have to bring drinking water to the school, be her own custodian, and work with few supplies. She looked forward to the experience as an adventure. As well, teaching jobs were hard to acquire in the 1980s and Seymour Arm would allow her to gain experience and credentials to teach closer to home.

In her first year, Morris was paid by her students' completed assignments: if the assignments were not mailed to the correspondence teacher, Morris's paycheck dropped. Morris remembers the first place she stayed in as a little log cabin where "the chinking was falling out…and the water froze in the buckets, because they didn't have running water." She soon moved to one of the cabins behind the hotel, where she had heat, electricity and running water for at least part of the day when the generator was on. Neither facility had a shower or bath, but parents would often invite her to dinner and offer her the use of their bathing facilities. In her second year, Morris negotiated for and received a salary based on her time and travel expenses rather than her students' work. She also began working in Seymour Arm two weeks out of every month. She boarded with two families who had children in the school and found the arrangement "worked better because you'd come home and the house would be warm, because even the motel room would be cold, and they would cook for me, so that was really nice."

The community hall lacked the amenities of a school. The first year students did not even have desks, so they worked together on

Fig. 3. The Seymour Arm Community Hall as it looked in 2007
(Pam Cairns photo, July 15, 2007)

shaky folding tables that would vibrate whenever a child used his or her eraser. However, Morris found a district school with "obsolete" desks and piled them on the barge to solve the problem. The school also received donations from the community and other district schools, including a piano, a set of chipped recorders, and mats for gymnastics. When someone donated an old slide, Morris used her construction background to build a playground for the children. As Morris dealt with the problems and put in extra time to make up for the lack of amenities, the school once again became a focal point for the community. Musicals, demonstrations and exhibits helped fill the community calendar (McKee, Morris and Winters interviews).

The community was also an integral part of the school. Members of the community worked in the school as the secretary, custodian and teachers' aide. Morris remembers asking a geologist to talk to the children about minerals and rocks. He took them on hikes to see samples in their natural settings, and he played matching games with the children by putting out samples of the raw materials as well as some finished products and asking the children to pair them. Morris also asked a European trained gymnast to help teach the children gymnastics and a member of a band to help with music. The enrichment activities combined learning with social interaction in a way that correspondence school alone could not approach.

The part-time school provided a combination of individualized learning and group activities that was ideal for many families. However, by 1988 circumstances conspired to change the face of schooling in Seymour Arm again. A Royal Commission, directed by Barry M. Sullivan, published "A Legacy for Learners," which stressed the equality of the rights of all learners, as well as the need for equal access to learning resources to fit individual situations. Specifically, the Sullivan Report commented on the benefits of multi-age groups and changed the funding formula, giving the school district a financial incentive to open a full-time school in Seymour Arm (261). The Correspondence Branch was undergoing reorganization as well, with Section 19 support being withdrawn. Concerned citizens thus petitioned School District #83, North Okanagan/Shuswap, hoping to obtain a school for the community (McKee and Winters interviews). When an exploratory committee for School District #83 went to Seymour Arm to investigate, the Seymour Arm citizens offered convincing arguments. They quoted the School Act, which still stated that wherever ten or more children were found within 4.8 kilometers along local roads from the schoolhouse, a school might be established. Bussing the students to the nearest school was out of the question since the nearest school was approximately an hour and a half away over primarily radio-controlled logging roads. The spring of 1989 saw sixteen children between the ages of six and twelve living in Seymour Arm. If a school had over fifteen students, the district would be fully compensated by the provincial government, so in spite of a half century of closing one-room schools and consolidation, a one-room school was officially opened in the community hall in October of 1989 (SD 83).

Anders O'Reilly was the first teacher hired for the new school. Like Morris, he had a family who could not move to Seymour Arm because of ties to the community, so he returned to Salmon Arm each weekend. However, O'Reilly had been working as a teacher-on-call in the district for five years after graduation, so he was looking for a stable, full-time job. His experience with Outward Bound and adventure training with the cadets in Whitehorse helped him to obtain the position in Seymour Arm and the Seymour Arm experience would help him find the work he sought. He enjoyed his time in the community: "Basically the part that I really enjoyed about it was you had a full time of teaching out there. There were no interruptions ... no telephone calls to worry about, no people coming into the school ... so we could concentrate on the business of teaching and learning." He also took pleasure in his surroundings, commenting several times on the environment. For example, "The fall was just gorgeous, absolutely golden. Partially wood smoke, because everybody used wood out there, but trees were all birches and aspen and there was larch out there, so everything was golden. It just had a hue to it that was lovely."

The novelty of the surroundings impressed many of the teachers. Commenting on isolation, Sean Richardson allowed that "the first year was kind of an adventure." When asked about drawbacks, Natasha Yeltsin wrote, "I really can't think of any. If I had stayed another year and worked with the same children, perhaps I would have seen some." Yeltsin also saw other positive factors: "The freedom to do whatever you want whenever you want is another benefit. If the sun is shining, go outside. Flip the whole schedule, go for a hike." O'Reilly seconded the opinion with his comment, "The great thing was that if things weren't going well and you wanted to break for recess and you wanted recess to be half an hour—it was half an hour. You didn't have to worry about timetables, or bells, or anyone causing a problem." However, Richardson warned, "You do have a tremendous amount of autonomy, and that is a good thing and a bad thing. It's a good thing if you know what you're doing ... if you can utilize the local environment.... It's a bad thing if you can't, if you're not creative enough to utilize those things." Most of the teachers seemed well able to utilize their environment and Caitlin March even saw the lack of immediate access to resources as a benefit, because she found she was using things that connected with the students better by using examples and items from their "other life, the life out of school." According to Richardson, another benefit was getting "to know the individuals, your students and the community at a real intimate level. And so you develop an empathy for them, not even empathy but a relationship which is important because it is a growth experience for a teacher .... You have a totally different awareness of what kids' needs are." All the teachers interviewed agreed that teaching in Seymour Arm was a memorable experience.

During the summer of 1989 news of the school spread. The school opened to twenty-four students that fall, eight more than had been on the application (SD 83 file). It was an optimistic time. A second teacher, March, was added to teach the primary students, and the Shuswap School Board submitted an application to the Ministry of Education to build an actual school in the community (SD 83 file). Writing for Okanagan History, Hucul quotes O'Reilly as saying, "[T]he school may go to Grade Ten in future years, as development brings more families into the area . Road improvement, electricity and telephones are all in future plans for Seymour Arm." Hucul concludes, "The school is a positive attraction and an important addition to the growing community" (23).

The school was definitely a benefit to the community: it attracted people to the area, provided a community focal point, and increased cash flow. It is reasonable to assume that the presence of the school added to the year-round population. The community supported numerous events throughout the year, even for members without direct links to the school. As Amanda McKee remembers, "It was a central point, using the hall meant that it was warm all winter so other functions could occur, the social calendar was full with school events. It pulled the community together." The school also added money to the local economy, paying the community association rent for use of the hall, hiring support staff from the community, and paying to keep the road ploughed in the winter. The school district also helped the community with capital improvements to the hall to bring the structure to area standards.

But the hall in which Section 19 teachers worked for three years strained the teachers' resources. O'Reilly remembers struggling with the original generator and wood heater. He would "start the generator up in the morning for electricity but it was so noisy that by, certainly noon, we'd turn it off, because [the sound] was unbearable." He would tussle with the central wood heater, but it would never put heat out. In the first few weeks he would "throw the doors and windows open to let the heat in, because it was warmer outside than it was inside." Eventually the school district subsidized the cost of a new generator and an oil/wood furnace, and a two-way radiotelephone; septic tank and flush toilets were also added to bring the school up to acceptable standards. By 1991, when Yeltsin taught at the school she noted, "We had all the facilities of a modern town school."[8] Throughout the life of the school, the district and parents continued to look for ways to improve the schooling the children received, thereby also increasing the community's appeal.

By the 1990s most teachers found the renovated community hall more than adequate. Yeltsin noted that the hall had "a partial basement under the stage which housed a large wood furnace and two washrooms. We had a caretaker who looked after maintenance, snow removal and daily started the furnace and the generator capable of supplying our needs." The teachers in the 'nineties had much more support than their predecessors: they had custodians, part-time secretaries and teacher's aides. The teacher's aides also substituted for the teachers attending meetings in town or staying home when they were sick. Using a district teacher-on-call was not possible because of the distance. The modern teachers also had superior supplies compared to the earlier ones. Yeltsin described the community library with "rotating books being supplied by the Okanagan Regional Library" as very useful, and believed "our School District Resource department was also very helpful and I would say our budget was more than adequate." Richardson agreed: "I had access to whatever supplies I might need," and elaborated, "I could order resources from the resource centre and they would be sent up on the barge once a week, or maybe twice a week … so there was lots of support there."

But the arrival of a full-time school in Seymour Arm was not all positive. The stricter guidelines and increased bureaucracy complicated some aspects of the school. The playground that Morris had built was destroyed "because it wasn't regulation equipment … not that it was unsafe in any manner." Further, the new school was an elementary school from which students were supposed to graduate after grade seven. Most went back to correspondence, but many would visit the school to do their work there, especially if they wanted to take part in the music or social activities of the school day. As more students "graduated" the number of children attending school increased but the official roster did not. The teachers understandably did not want the additional responsibility added to their already heavy workload, but it did not make sense to prohibit the students from at least the social aspect of the school. Eventually a compromise was reached and a support worker was hired for the correspondence students (McKee and Morris interviews).

The school changed the lives of many people in Seymour Arm. Some of the parents in earlier years had chosen to live in Seymour Arm because they liked the idea of quality time with their children and correspondence lessons. One parent remembers that her children would usually finish their schoolwork a month early on correspondence because they were efficient workers. The full-time school changed that: the students were required to attend for the entire school year. As well, the school brought more uniformity and regimentation to the children and their lives and not everyone saw that as a benefit. When a child died in a tragic suicide soon after the school opened, one teacher wondered if the event had been precipitated because the child was overwhelmed by the thought of school every day. Although such drawbacks should not be ignored, of course, overall the teachers felt that the school resulted in positive changes for the community (McKee, Morris and O'Reilly interviews).

Although all the teachers gave glowing reports of teaching in Seymour Arm, four of the five teachers interviewed did not return for a second year. They gave a variety of reasons for leaving, the most common being hardship for the family, another job offer, and lack of social opportunity. While not stated as a reason for leaving, most also commented on the confining nature of the community. Morris remembers feeling "as if I were in a goldfish bowl. Every activity I felt I was watched. Whereas here if you drive to town no one cares, but there everyone knew every movement I took." She admits to occasionally taking the circuitous back route to school just to escape the scrutiny. Even when the scrutiny was not judgmental, the feeling of having every move watched could be hard. O'Reilly made the cryptic comment, "You did have to be careful about your middle class values, because they didn't always mix with everyone else's values out there." Richardson echoed a similar sentiment when he commented, "There was some politics. At times, I think people would have liked me to voice an opinion. I tended not to get involved with that too much. But occasionally somebody would get upset with me." One parent stated that "each [teacher] had hard stuff up here…a lot of the parents were really hard on the teachers. I was never surprised when I heard a teacher wasn't coming back." (For teacher turnover rates from 1987-1997, see Appendix III).

Schooling in Seymour Arm underwent new difficulties toward the end of the decade. Provincial declines in enrolment meant less money was available for education, and community economics and politics compounded the difficulties. When the British Columbia Hydro crews finished work on the power lines, the ferry service became less profitable so runs were dropped, which led to fewer tourists as well. The school itself was not enough to attract new families to the area, so its enrolment declined as students graduated. The school remained open until 1997, but when the projected enrolment for the following fall dropped to only three, the school district withdrew its support. In his official termination letter, the Secretary-Treasurer wrote, "Seymour Arm School provided a unique learning situation that would be reconsidered should enrolment stabilize to again require a school situation" (Griswold 89; Doggerton letter in SD 83 files).

An overview of the Seymour Arm school thus reflects that teachers in the first era were often young, female and ill prepared to cope with the isolation, social scrutiny and hard work demanded from them. While school trustees, the superintendent and others visited the school, teachers lacked support. Their jobs were made difficult by the lack of resources, the need to maintain the schoolhouse, deficits in social support and isolation. Because of these shortages, Seymour Arm, like many rural communities, was plagued by high teacher turnover.

The part-time teachers in the second period faced many of the same challenges. They also had to make do with less than ideal living situations and resources. Their job included many extras that urban teachers did not have to manage, such as carting water to the school, starting wood stoves and generators, and custodial duties. However, unlike their earlier counterparts, they were better equipped to cope with these problems because they were hired based on their ability to deal with them. While Seymour Arm was not a desirable teaching position for most people, care seems to have been taken to ensure that teachers had the necessary experience, social support and maturity. Also, these teachers' isolation was less pronounced because they were not in the community fulltime and had access to radiophones.

As the school became more formalized, the teaching environment gradually evolved to match urban teaching situations. In addition to the regular barge service ensuring timely delivery of teaching resources, by the 'nineties the school had running water, an oil/wood heater and a powerful generator. This allowed teachers to use technology such as computers, tape recorders, televisions and videos. The teachers even had access to a radiophone, although they were still limited in their ability to contact parents, since many residents did not have phones. Custodians, secretaries and teacher's aides were added to the school payroll, allowing teachers to focus on teaching.

However, no matter when they taught in Seymour Arm, teachers faced many of the same difficulties. Each teacher had multilevel classrooms and the challenge of finding time to help each child succeed in his or her individual course of studies. While isolation was less pronounced in the latter era, all teachers interviewed mentioned feeling cut off from the rest of the world at some point in their tenure. Although teachers in the latter era had more maturity and social support, they still felt scrutiny, and sometimes judgement, from the small community. Despite the fact that the interviewed teachers had fond memories of their experiences in Seymour Arm, none stayed for more than a year and a half. It appears that, like their earlier counterparts, teachers saw the small community as a springboard to teaching in more desirable areas rather than a calling. While the physical experience of rural teaching may have improved with time, social-emotional well-being and career opportunities were still hampered by the size and location of the school.

Notes

1. For instance, Thomas Fleming's *School Leadership*; Nancy M. Sheehan, J. Donald Wilson & David C. Jones' *Schools in the West*.; F. Henry Johnson, *History of Public Education in British Columbia* .

2. In general there is more historical education literature available for central Canada: a search on ERIC for rural, Ontario education yielded 291 entries compared to 170 for British Columbia. Many of the articles deal with administration of or teacher preparation for rural schools rather than the nature of education in these institutions. A cross-Canada review of literature reveals several books from across Canada, including Jean Cochrane's *The One Room School in Canada*; John Charyk's *The Little White Schoolhouse, The Pulse of the Community*, and *Syrup Pails and Gopher Tails* (all with a prairie focus); Myrtle Fair's *I Remember the One-Room School* (Ontario); Joan Adams & Becky Thomas's *Floating Schools and Frozen Inkwells* (British Columbia). Another view of rural schooling is from the viewpoint of Women's Studies, since most rural teachers were (and are) female; for example, Rebecca Priegert Coulter and Helen Harper's *History is Hers*.

3. For example, in the 1932-1933 school year 1002 teachers were employed in rural districts (not including rural municipalities) and 3912 teachers were employed overall (Ministry of Education Annual Report 1932-1933 M10 –M11).

4. While no census numbers exist for Seymour Arm in the 1860s, numbers for similar communities in the 1870 Census show the population was predominately male, with low rates of marriages and births in the community. (Statistics Canada. BC Table I – "Statement of the Population, 1870, British Columbia" [table 1870] and BC Table II–"Occupations, Marriages and Births, 1870, British Columbia" [table 1870] - Census of British Columbia (database). Using E-STAT (distributor). <http://estat.statcan.ca/cgi-win/cnsmcgi.exe?Lang=E&ESTATFile=EStat\English\SC_RR-eng.htm>.

5. With the start of the Public Schools Act, which required all teachers to be certified by the Superintendent of Education, teacher certification began in 1872. Candidates were required to write an examination, with different certificates awarded, depending on the results of the candidate's exam: Academic Certificates, which were permanent, were given to graduates of British Empire universities; First Class Certificates, also permanent, were granted to candidates who scored over 70 percent; Second Class Certificates, valid for three years, were awarded to candidates scoring

over 50 percent; Third Class Certificates, valid for specified terms and renewable, were issued to those who scored above 30 percent; and occasionally Temporary Certificates were issued for special circumstances. The details, such as percentages, terms and testing authority changed over time, but the basics remained constant until 1921, when normal school graduation replaced the testing system to assign certificate levels.

6. The Daniels family arrived in 1908 and the children were plentiful. The first generation born in Seymour Arm numbered thirteen, and two of the brothers, Clarence and Vern, remained in Seymour Arm. Clarence had three children and Vern had seven. All the children attended school in Seymour Arm.

7. British Columbia's correspondence courses for elementary students began in 1919 in an effort to help children of lighthouse keepers (1919 Annual Report C87). Lessons were assigned by mail and students were expected to complete and return them to their correspondence teacher, who would grade them and make suggestions, again by mail. The system was highly dependant on the postal system and the ability of the parents to help their children, but it allowed children across British Columbia to complete their schooling in isolated areas such as Seymour Arm.

8. The appliances were run on generator power: BG remembers this causing the computer to "sometimes ebb and flow." As well, the television and computer were isolated, that is, not connected to the outside world: there was no cable or Internet service. In 1992 the school district looked at the feasibility of erecting a satellite dish so the students could "access education television programs such as the Knowledge Network" (SD 83 file, Letter from Dawn Benson, Director of Instruction, to Paul Montgomery, Correspondence Branch. October 14, 1992).

Appendix I
Students in Rural Districts During Peak Period

Year Ending	Number of Students*	% total Student Population in B.C.
1930	19,980	22.00%
1931	20,744	22.80%
1932	21,168	23.20%
1933	21,526	21.70%

*Number of students in rural districts, not including rural municipalities. The majority of these schools were assisted. For example, in 1932 there were 773 schools in rural districts: of those assisted one-room schools. Assisted schools were funded by the community and the provincial government. The ministry would pay a base salary for the teacher and the community would be responsible for building and maintaining the schoolhouse and for providing supplies, such as desks, slates, paper etc.
(Source: Annual Public School Reports of British Columbia, 1930-1933.)

Pamela Cairns

Appendix II
Teacher Information 1910-1937

Year ending	Teacher	Certificate	Salary (*indicates monthly)	Amount paid by Government	Amount paid by district
1911	Adelaide R. Graham	3rd (Dec/13)	65*	323.85	
1912	Adelaide R. Graham	3rd (Dec/13)	70*	795	63.45
1913	Adelaide R. Graham	3rd (Dec/13)	75*	855	25.9
1914	Margaret Ella Murray	1st	75*	900	51.33
1915	Alfred H. Hooper	3rd(Lifetime)	75*	900	175.49
1916	R.E. Bunt	2nd	75*	861.3	43.46
1917	Mrs. C.G. Lister	1st	75*	900	43
1918	Miss S O'Neil	3rd	75*	450	15.7
1919	Miss E.M. James	3rd	960	918	74.57
1920	Miss J.E. Reid	Academic	1080	974.3	
1921	Alfred H. Hooper	3rd	1080	1074.6	83.76
1922	Mr. S. Moore	Academic	1080	891	
1923	Miss L. Hayes	3rd	1080	1057.25	
1924	Miss L.W. Abrahamson	2nd	1080	1074.3	51.96
1925	Miss Alberta M Hobson	2nd	1080	1080	50
1926	no school 1926				
1927	Miss Louise M Parisian	2nd	1020	359.2	
1928	Miss E.I. McPhee	2nd	1020	1014.65	
1929	Miss J.M. Richards	3rd	1020	1020	
1930	Miss J.M. Richards	3rd	1020	1020	
1931	Miss E.E. Abriel	2nd	1020	1020	100
1932	Miss E.E. Abriel	2nd	953	994.9	125
1933	Alfred H. Hooper	3rd	900	675	310
1934	Alfred H. Hooper	3rd	800	683	166.16
1935	Alfred H. Hooper	3rd	800	719	188.13
1936	Alfred H. Hooper	3rd	780	723	178.12
1937	Alfred H. Hooper	3rd	780	724	151.02

(Source: British Columbia Ministry of Education. Victoria: King/Queen's Printer, 1911-1937)

Appendix III
Teacher Information 1987-1997

Year Ending	Teacher	Situation
Fall 1987	Female 1	Taught part-time under Section 19 of the School Act. Quit due to pregnancy.
1988-1989	Female2	**Married with children, teaching as a second career, Seymour Arm a starting position, lived in Salmon Arm. Taught part-time under Section 19 of the School Act. Left because part-time job ended.**
1990	Male 1	**Married with children, teaching as a second career, working as a substitute teacher in Salmon Arm, Seymour Arm as first full-time position, lived in Salmon Arm. Left for job at Carlin.**
1990	Female 3 (hired mid-fall)	**Single, newly moved to BC and looking for permission to teach. Had worked overseas teaching. Left for job in Vancouver.**
1991	Male 2	**Married with children, teacher from Lower Mainland looking to teach in the interior. Left for personal reasons/job elsewhere in the district.**
1992	Female 4	**Divorced with one child, newly moved to BC and trying to get back into teaching after taking some time off. Left for a job elsewhere in the district.**
1993-1994	Female 5	Single parent with three children (2 adults, 1 nine year old)
1995-1997	Male 3	Still has a residence in the community.

*Information in bold is from interviews.
(Source: Seymour Arm School Five Year Annual and interviews done in 2007)

Works Cited

Abercrombie, A.D. *Sicamous: Mara to Three Valley. Gateway to the Oka-nagan: Land of the Shimmering Sunset Waters.* Cloverdale, B.C.: D.W. Friesen, 1985.

Adams, Joan and Becky Thomas. *Floating Schools and Frozen Inkwells: The One Room Schools of British Columbia.* Madeira Park, B.C.: Harbour Publishing, 1985.

Baron, Leonard. "Letter to Carol Milligan, September 2005." *Seymour Arm: Top of the Shuswap Lake.* <http://www.milligan.ab.ca/seymourarm/ukrainian%20families%201920.htm 2005>.

Bauer, Gwen. *History of Seymour Arm.* Salmon Arm: Shopper's Quick Printing, 1980.

Bradley Family, *Historical Outline of Seymour Arm Area, 1860-1970.* 2nd ed. Handset in Sicamous, B.C., 1978. Also partially posted at <www.milligan.ab.ca/seymourarm/history_of_seymour_arm.htm>.

British Columbia. "Inspector's Designation for Section 19." <http://www.bced.gov.bc.ca/legislation/schoollaw/k/i2-98.pdf>.

British Columbia Ministry of Education. *Annual Public School Reports of British Columbia.* Victoria: King/Queen's Printer, 1872, 1909-1938 and 1986-1998.

British Columbia Ministry of Education. *Royal Commission on Education: A Legacy for Learners.* Victoria: Queen's Printer, 1988.

British Columbia Ministry of Education. *Year 2000: A Framework for Learning.* Victoria: Queen's Printer, 1991.

Charyk, John C. *The Little White Schoolhouse.* Saskatoon: Western Producer Prairie Books, 1968.

___. *The Pulse of the Community.* Saskatoon: Western Producer Prairie Books, 1970.

___. *Syrup Pails and Gopher Tails: Memories of the One- Room School.* Saskatoon: Western Producer Prairie Books, 1984.

Cochrane, Jean. *The One-Room School in Canada.* Canada: Fitzhenry & Whiteside, 1981.

Coulter, Rebecca Priegert and Helen Harper, eds. *History is Hers: Women Educators in Twentieth Century Ontario.* Calgary: Detselig, 2005.

Eagle Valley News [Revelstoke, B.C.]: Selections from the "News from Seymour Arm" column. 1974-1980.

Fair, Myrtle. *I Remember the One-Room School.* Cheltenham, Ont.: Boston Mills Press, 1979.

Fleming, Thomas, ed. *School Leadership: Essays on the British Columbia Experience, 1872-1995.* Mill Bay: Bendall Books, 2001.

Fraser, Hermie. "A Change in the 'Rootin.'" *The Family Herald,* May 15, 1958. Quoted from Abercrombie, *Gateway.* 404-405.

Griswold, June. "Seymour Arm School Faces Long Recess." *Okanagan History* 62(1998): 88-89.

Hucul, Alice. "Seymour Arm School Opens." *Okanagan History* 54 (1990): 21-23.

Johnson, F. Henry. *A History of Public Education in British Columbia.* Victoria: Morris, 1964.

McGuffey, Verne. *The Differences in the Activities of Teachers in Rural One Room Schools and of Grade Teachers in Cities.* New York City: Bureau of Publications, Teachers' College, Columbia University, 1929

NSHS North Shuswap Historical Society. Archival file. "Seymour Arm."*Salmon Arm Observer.* Selections from the "Seymour Arm News" column, 1910-1937.

SD83 School District 83, North Okanagan - Shuswap, archival file "Seymour Arm Elementary."

Sheehan, Nancy M. and J. Donald Wilson, David C. Jones, eds. *Schools in the West: Essays in Canadian Educational History.* Calgary: Detselig, 1986.

Seymour Arm Elementary: The First Five Years. Seymour Arm: Yearbook Committee, 1995.

Teacher's Bureau Surveys (TBS) for Seymour Arm School, 1923 and 1928. Courtesy of the B.C.Archives.

Wilson, J. Donald. "'I am Ready to be of Assistance When I Can': Lottie Bowron and Rural Women Teachers in British Columbia." *Children, Teachers and School in the History of British Columbia.* Eds. Jean Barman and Mona Gleason, 2nd ed. Calgary: Detselig, 2003. 259-279.

Wilson, J. Donald and David C. Jones, eds. *Schooling and Society in 20th Century British Columbia.* Calgary: Detselig, 1980.

Wilson, J. Donald and Paul J. Stortz, "'May the Lord have Mercy on You': The Rural School Problem in British Columbia in the 1920s." *Children, Teachers and School in the History of British Columbia.* Eds. Jean Barman and Mona Gleason, 2nd ed. Calgary: Detselig, 2003): 233-258.

Wright, Robert. "The Plight of Rural Women Teachers in the 1920s." *B.C. Historical News.* 28:1 (1994): 26-29.

Interviews
Pseudonyms were used for all subjects.

Ajhar, Angelica. Parent. Questionnaire June 20, 2007.

Carter, Joseph. Former Assistant Superintendent. Phone interview July 4, 2007.

March, Caitlin. Teacher. Interview May 23, 2007.

McKee, Amanda. Parent/teacher's aide. Interview July 13, 2007.

Morris, Eleni. Teacher. Interview May 24, 2007.

O'Reilly, Anders. Teacher. Interview May 24, 2007.

Richardson, Sean. Teacher. Interview May 24, 2007.

Winters, Mona. Resident. Interview May 23, 2007.

Yeltsin, Natasha. Teacher. Questionnaire July 20, 2007.

Roundtable on Defining Quality of Life & Cultural Indicators For Small Cities

Friday, September 14, 2007 (13:45 - 15:15 PST)

Paul Stacey (Moderator), Gilles Viaud (Thompson Rivers University), Douglas Worts (Art Gallery of Ontario), Alex Michalos (University of Northern British Columbia), Nancy Duxbury (Centre of Expertise on Culture and Communities, Simon Fraser University), Ron McColl (City of Kamloops), Andrew Tucker (City of Nanaimo), Mark Seasons (University of Waterloo).

Panel Participant Biographies

Paul Stacey (Moderator)

Paul Stacey is Director of Development for BCcampus, where he is responsible for educational technology and online learning development and professional services for BC's public post-secondary system. Paul's work focuses on collaborative program and course development initiatives, shareable online learning resources, online communities of practice, and educational technology professional development for educators across all of BC's public post-secondary institutions.

Douglas Worts

Douglas Worts is a culture and sustainability specialist and his research and writing over the past ten years has been focused on the cultural roots of our increasingly unsustainable society. For Doug, museums have tremendous potential to become catalysts of public engagement and change that leads to more sustainable lifestyles. A key focus for Doug now is the development of indicators that can help museums and cultural policy-makers improve the role and impact of cultural operations in urban centres. Doug also has 25 years of experience with the Art Gallery of Ontario as an Interpretive Planner, where he was involved with the public dimension of the museum's activities. Specifically, his work included exhibition development, preparing interpretive policies and strategies, facilitating community consultation and carrying out audience research projects.

Alex Michalos

Alex Michalos is the Director of the Institute for Social Research and Evaluation and Chancellor at the University of Northern British Columbia. He has been working with the quality of life measurement for many years. Alex started a journal called *Social Indicators Research* in 1974. In 2004, Alex was awarded the Gold Medal for Achievement in Research from the Social Sciences and Humanities Research Council of Canada (the Council's highest honour) for his research on quality of life and community-based solutions to problems around the world, from Britain and Spain to Hong Kong and the US, to Prince George, BC, where he contributed to the founding of the Prince George Community Planning Council and the University of Northern British Columbia.

Nancy Duxbury

Nancy Duxbury is the Executive Director of the Centre of Expertise on Culture and Communities (CECC) at Simon Fraser University. For the past ten years, Nancy has been involved in launching and developing the Creative City Network of Canada, which operates as a knowledge-sharing network and research hub and links municipal staff across the country (in about 140 municipalities) who have responsibilities for arts, culture and heritage development. The Centre of Expertise on Culture and Communities emerged as a project of the Creative City Network in collaboration with SFU, and as part of her work at the Centre Nancy has conducted research on cultural indicators. This work began by investigating the emergence of community quality of life projects that didn't include culture (or where culture would be mentioned initially and then dropped) and over the years the inclusion of culture in these projects has grown. In 2006, CECC conducted an international scan of cultural indicator projects and identified some common themes among them. CECC also conducted a national workshop in Ottawa in 2006, which brought together federal and provincial staff with municipal staff and some other agents who are actively working at creating cultural indicators at the local level.

Ron McColl

Ron McColl is the former Manager of Corporate Programs and Projects for the City of Kamloops. His interest in quality of life and cultural indicators stems from the issue that there are very few defined cultural and quality of life indicator projects that cut across a number of different cities, particularly small cities. As large cities move forward with indicator projects, the City of Kamloops is therefore unable to participate or to get involved. The City of Kamloops is very interested to work with the university to ensure that this type of indicator project continues to improve the opportunities for small cities and to be able to use it as a planning tool to move forward, but also as an indicator of where we have been and where we are going in the future, so that over time there will be a good, solid base, which twenty years from now we will be able to look back on. Ron and his colleagues in other government planning divisions and departments work with various planning tools that cities have used to make changes in their communities as they have the responsibility of moving social, cultural, and economic indicators forward for a number of purposes in our communities.

Andrew Tucker

Andrew Tucker is the Director of Planning with the City of Nanaimo, Development Services Department. Andrew's responsibilities are primarily in the area of land use, but he increasingly views the social agenda as part of the municipal area of responsibility as local governments struggle with social issues. Indicators can be of help in this area. In relation to the quality of life, Andrew's interest is in how municipalities respond and where the cultural discussion fits within other, more pressing and basic social needs on a municipal agenda, particularly the political agenda.

Gilles Viaud

Gilles Viaud is an Assistant Professor in Geography at Thompson Rivers University, where he leads the Quality of Life Indicators Projects for the Small Cities CURA. Working in concert with the Federation of Canadian Municipalities and other partner groups, he is developing a quality of life reporting system sensitive to the reality of small cities.

———⟨ℰℰℰ⟩———

Paul Stacey: Thanks very much. I'm Paul Stacey. I'm from BCCampus in Vancouver and a proud partner with the Small Cities CURA initiative; and we have an online moderator who's my colleague–Dan O'Reilly. The two of us are handling the webcast side and the management of the panel. In terms of the format for the panel, we will begin with two presentations. Gilles Viaud will go first. He's going to give us a short presentation, ten to twelve minutes or so, on quality of life indicators and public policy and "Does Community Size Matter?" And then following him will be Douglas Worts, who will present a critical assessment framework, looking at culture and sustainability–and again, it's a short presentation. Then the remaining members of the panel will each be given five minutes or so to speak to some of the points that they've seen presented, to identify the key points that they think are particularly core to this area–and then maybe talk a little bit about quality of life indicators and the work they do: how they think that quality of life indicators should be constructed and, in particular, highlight the research that they are doing in this particular field. Mark Seasons, our seventh panelist, has not been able to join us this afternoon, but he will be contributing a written response piece for the published version of this dialogue.

After all our panelists have had a chance to present their thoughts and work, we are going to turn it over and make it into a big audience panel–a question and answer discussion forum–and engage everybody and again invite some dialogue on this particular topic.

Just before we go to Gilles' presentation, I want to mention very briefly a few words about the actual environment that we are in. We are in a webcast environment and you are seeing here some of the participants that are online. This is a webcam. It's actually stuck on the top of my laptop here so you are all being webcast as we do this. The whole thing is being recorded, as was mentioned, and will be available as an archive via the Small Cities website. All the presentation materials that the presenters have created we have brought up into this webcast environment, and we are actually showing you what people are really seeing in real time on the web. With that, let me turn it over to Gilles and we'll have his presentation first.

Gilles Viaud: I'd like to first thank the organizers for inviting me here to talk to you today about the research I'm currently conducting.

In a nutshell, my presentation addresses the necessity of developing analytical tools suitable for capturing the reality of those populations that live in smaller communities.

The research I would like to present considers the quality of life studies produced by one particular CURA community partner, the Federation of Canadian Municipalities (FCM). What I'm particularly interested in is how FCM uses the quality of life studies it produces, studies which are based on a sample of large and medium-sized Canadian cities. I'm interested in how it uses results from these studies in order to establish what I call the "overall Canadian urban agenda."

That particular agenda identifies a list of urban priorities that have become the centrepiece of the Federation's political lobby effort as it tries to encourage the reallocation of public resources – and also as it tries to become a very strong partner in the development of national public policies.

Basically the question that I'm asking in that context is, "Does the urban agenda that is identified by the FCM speak to the priorities of all Canadian municipalities?" What about the quality of life in smaller cities? What about their priorities? Their agenda? Does size matter in our interpretation of, and in our views about, quality of life indicators?

I'm just going to briefly talk to you about the FCM and its quality of life reporting system, and then outline the Canadian agenda that has emerged from their analysis of that reporting system. I'll review quickly some key indicators and policy changes that contrast the reality of small and large cities in Canada and after that, I'll try to project what a future small city agenda, an urban agenda, might look like.

Very quickly, then, the FCM is a professional association that has been acting as the national voice of municipal governments in Canada for over one hundred years. So it's very well established. It represents the interests of over 1,400 municipalities and those municipalities can be small, medium or large and can be located in rural areas, urban areas, or in Northern settings. But the main mandate of the FCM is to advocate on the behalf of all municipalities in Canada and also to lobby the Federal Government to make sure that the many voices of municipal governments are heard – and also that municipalities become very strong partners in public policy debates of national importance.

Now, in order to meet that very lofty mandate and also in order to establish the foundation of a common urban agenda, the FCM has been very busy developing and fine-tuning (since around the mid-1990s) a very sophisticated quality of life reporting system. I won't have time to describe to you exactly the ins and outs of that reporting system for today's roundtable, but suffice to say that it follows trends

Fig. 1. Federation of Canadian Municipalities Quality of Life Reporting System domains and indicators

Demographic and Background Information

Population Growth
Household & Family Composition
Average Income
Renters & Owners
Population Mobility
Foreign Born
New Immigrant Groups
Language Spoken at Home
Visible Minorities
Aboriginal Population

Affordable, Appropriate Housing

30%+ Income on Shelter
50%+ Income on Shelter
Core Housing Need
Substandard Units
Changing Face of Homelessness
Vacancy Rates
Rental Housing Starts
Monthly Rent

Civic Engagement

Voter Turnout
Women in Municipal Government
Newspaper Circulation
Volunteering
Charitable Donations

Community and Social Infrastructure

Social Housing Waiting Lists
Rent- Geared-to- Income Housing
Social Assistance Allowance
Subsidized Child Care Spaces
Public Transit Costs
Social Service Professionals
Private Health Care Expenditures
Spending on Private Education

Education

Education Levels
Literacy Levels
Adult Learning
Education Expenditures
Classroom Size
Student / Teacher Ratio
Post- Secondary Tuition

Employment

Unemployment/ Employment Rates
Quality of Employment
Long-Term Unemployment
Labour Force Replacement

Local Economy

Business Bankruptcies
Consumer Bankruptcies
Hourly Wages
Change in Family Income
Building Permits
Solid Waste
Ecological Footprint

Natural Environment

Air Quality
Urban Transportation
Population Density
Water Consumption
Wastewater Treatment
Infant Mortality

Personal and Community Health

Low Birth Weight Babies
Teen Births
Premature Mortality
Work Hours Lost
Suicides

Personal Financial Security

Community Affordability
Families Receiving EI/ Social Assistance
Economic Dependency Ratio
Lone-Parent Families
Incidence of Low Income Families
Children Living in Poverty
Income Gap

Personal Safety

Young Offenders
Violent Crimes
Property Crimes
Injuries and Poisonings

Source: FCM (2008) Quality of Life in Canadian Communities: Trends and Issues in Affordable Housing and Homelessness – Theme Report #4. The FCM Quality of Life Reporting System, Ottawa, Ontario.p.27.

on eleven key quality of life domains, which are listed in Figure 1.

The FCM indicated at a meeting in January 2006 that they were talking about developing a cultural series of indicators. But right now the focus is on eleven quality of life domains that are indexed by seventy-two indicators. Altogether we are talking about hundreds of census variables; also, some of the information gathered comes from municipal surveys that are distributed to city administrators.

This is the basis of the quality of life reporting system. What's most important for those of us interested in the study of small cities is the sample of cities that are used in that research.

Now in the last report in 2004, twenty cities and regional municipalities that accounted for about forty percent of the Canadian populations were part of the research (Figure 2).

Fig. 2. Federation of Canadian Municipalities Quality of Life Reporting System Member Municipalities - 2004

Municipality	Population	Municipality	Population
Toronto	2,481,495	Waterloo	438,515
Peel (Ont)	988,945	Niagara	410,575
Calgary	878,870	Halton (Ont)	375,230
Ottawa	774,405	Halifax	359,185
York (Ont)	729,255	London	336,540
Quebec	674,075	Windsor	208,405
Edmonton	666,105	Saskatoon	196,810
Winnipeg	619,545	Regina	178,225
Vancouver	545,670	Sudbury	155,220
Hamilton	490,265	Kingston	114,195

Source: FCM (2004) Highlights Report 2004: Quality of Life in Canadian Communities. The FCM Quality of Life Reporting System, Ottawa, Ontario, p.5.

The sample ranges from the minimum of 114,000 for Kingston to a maximum of 2.5 million in Toronto. So as we can see, the sample of cities is clearly made up of essentially large and medium-sized cities and regional municipalities.

And it's from the results gathered through those cities that the FCM and its partner municipalities have to date identified many of Canada's key urban priorities – those priorities that they see requiring response and action from the provinces and the federal government.

So according to the last series of studies, the FCM identifies air pollution, public transportation, affordable housing, homelessness, issues dealing with the social inclusion and the social integration of an increasingly socially and ethnically diverse population, and community safety and security issues as being some of Canada's key urban priorities.

And then, having identified those priorities, FCM has been actively involved in trying to lobby governments and policy makers to influence public spending to try to resolve some of those issues that they've identified through their research.

Of course everyone will agree that these are very, very significant issues. They are all very relevant and they warrant public attention by our governments and our policy makers.

But considering the process by which these issues or this agenda was created and generated, I'm left wondering whether they are a fair and just reflection of the priorities of all municipal governments in Canada, especially whether they are a fair and just reflection of smaller communities. We need to consider whether population size matters in our understanding of factors that may impact on the quality of life of a community or region. Would a study on the quality of life of small cities generate a list of urban priorities significantly different from the accepted urban agenda currently promoted by the FCM?

These I think are legitimate questions. So what I want to do, very quickly, is to look at some key indicators, contrast the reality in both small and large cities, and see the general policies that would need to be considered in order to resolve issues that will become evident in the following table (Figure 3).

When we contrast the demographic characteristics of large and small cities—this is a key set of indicators—we see that both types of cities are definitely on different demographic paths. In large cities, the population still grows at a rate that is higher than the national average, and they tend to benefit greatly from immigration. As a rule, international immigrants and visible minorities in Canada tend to locate in larger cities. And because of this, the population structure in large cities is much more youthful and ethnically heterogeneous than what we find in smaller cities. In small cities, the population is growing at a slower rate and is aging at a faster rate than the Canadian average. So the policy challenge in large cities is one of managing population growth—a growth that is increasingly socially complex because it is mostly fuelled by younger, international immigrants. The policy challenge in small cities, on the other hand, is one of managing slow growth and even population decline because the population is aging fast and there are too few new immigrants moving to those communities. Large and small cities face divergent demographic realities, which have to be addressed by different sets of policy responses.

The population in large cities is not only more culturally heterogeneous than in small cities, but it also shows a high level of social

Fig. 3. A sample of key indicators and policy challenges in large and small Canadian cities

Indicator	Large cities(> 450,000)	Small cities(< 100,000 and > 5,000)
Demographic Characteristics (1996 - 2001)		
Natural increase	Declines slower than the national average	Declines faster than the national average
Death Rate	Declining	Increasing
Aging of the population	Ages slower than the national average	Ages faster than the national average
Immigration	Increases much faster than the national average	Negative growth
Visible minorities	Increases much faster than the national average	Increases much slower than the national average
Population growth	Grows faster than the national average	Grows slower than the national average
Policy challenge	Managing growth	Managing slow growth or decline
Social Characteristics		
Cultural diversity	High (heterogeneity)	Low (homogeneity)
Life styles diversity	High and visible	Low and less visible
Social segregation	High and visible	Low and less visible
Policy challenge	**Social inclusion and integration**	**Attracting immigrants and intra-provincial and inter-provincial migrants**
Urban issues		
Housing cost	Much higher than the national average	Much lower than the national average
Population and job decentralization (sprawl)	Very pronounced	Less pronounced
Traffic congestion	Major concern	Minor concern
Public transit	Major concern	Minor concern
Problems due to pollution	High to moderate	Moderate to low
Policy challenge	Complex, issues are of high magnitude and are faced in the aggregate form	Less complex, issues are of low magnitude and are generally faced one at a time
Economic characteristics		
Profile of economic activities	Diversified	Heavy reliance on a limited number of sectors
Capacity to attract investments and developers	High	Low
Capacity to attract and retain competent, skilled professionals	High	Low
Policy challenge	**Global competitiveness**	**Diversification, attraction and retention of investment and skilled professionals**

Sources: Statistics Canada 1996 and 2001; Simmons, J., and Bourne, L. S. (2003). New fault lines? Recent trends in the Canadian urban system and their implications for planning and public policy. Canadian Journal of Urban Research, 12 (1), 22-47.; Roberts, K., and Gibbins, R. (2005). Apples and oranges? Urban size and the municipal-provincial relationship. Alberta: Canada West Foundation Discussion Paper.

segregation. Visible minorities are very present in our large cities and the public policy issue here becomes one of creating an environment where everyone feels included—where everyone feels integrated socially, culturally and economically. In small cities, again, when we look at these types of issues, the picture we get is very different. We are looking at environments that are much more homogenous, where cultural and life style diversity are much less present and visible. And at the end, the big issue is, because they are not the location of choice for new immigrants, how can we design policies that would help small, urban communities attract more international immigrants and internal migrants in order to counteract the aging of the population and allow smaller cities to grow rather than decline, if this is the outcome sought by municipal leaders.

When we look at the urban issues listed in the table, the policy challenges faced by large cities are very, very complex and of high magnitude. That's a reflection of the very high population counts found in these places, but also of the high population densities. And the complex and high magnitude issues usually all need individual attention by municipalities to prevent the urban and social infrastructures from collapsing. In small cities what we are looking at are much less complex issues. Their magnitude is much less pronounced, due, of course, to lower population densities and lower population counts and these issues can usually be faced one at a time.

Finally, because of large cities' capacity to attract investments, developers, and skilled professionals, their main policy challenge in these economic matters is how to remain globally competitive. The challenge for small cities is totally different. Because their economy is usually very dependent on a limited number of economic sectors only, they have a hard time attracting what it takes to grow and strengthen their economy. Among other things, they need to find ways to diversify by attracting investment and skilled workers.

What I am suggesting, then, is that there are major contrasts between large and small cities on many issues. When we start focusing on certain key indicators, our response to try to address these issues should be adapted to the context. So it's clear that the use that we make and the interpretation that we derive from the analysis of the quality of life indicators should and must be adjusted to reflect the size of the cities under study, but also the demographic, social, urban and economic realities that they face.

Overall, priorities that are of greater concern to smaller cities revolve around, in many cases, addressing the slow rate of population growth and even decline and also issues that pertain to economic development and the lack of economic diversification.

So when we look at trying to establish a small city urban agenda, policies more relevant to the overall reality of smaller cities should focus on fostering conditions for economic development and economic diversification because their economies still rely heavily on a very small number of economic sectors. Also those policies should address the limited fiscal capacity of smaller cities to attract and retain investment in the public and private sectors. Policies should also focus on trying to foster investment in social and cultural infrastructure. It should try also to divert part of the flow of immigrants away from larger cities and more towards smaller cities. And finally, try to design policies to attract and retain skilled labour within a small city environment.

These are just ideas that I am putting on the table here, but I believe that the implementation of such an agenda would provide opportunities to improve the quality of life of small communities and would improve their attractiveness as well as their regional, provincial and global competitiveness.

In conclusion, the point I'm am trying to highlight is that there exists a disconnect, a clear break between the urban agenda derived from the FCM quality of life research—which is based on the reality of large and medium-sized cities only—and the agenda needed to represent small city interests. One of the objectives of the research project I'm conducting is to determine whether quality of life indicators specific to small cities do exist, the goal being to develop a parallel and simplified system of indicators that could be used by small city administrators in order to help them monitor the evolution of key quality of life indicators in their own communities. And the hope is to generate interest in a dialogue that would lead towards the development of a national standard to better monitor the quality of life in small cities. We need to objectively define an urban agenda specific to small cities, for only by doing so can we give small cities an effective voice on the national stage—something which they don't seem to have at the moment.

Paul Stacey: Thank you very much, Gilles. And now we are going to turn to another perspective from Douglas Worts.

Douglas Worts: Thank you. I enjoyed Gilles' presentation and am fascinated to hear about how FCM is creating a research agenda and how research related to large cities may not in fact be meeting the needs of smaller cities within Canada.

My take now is going to be a little bit different. Because of my background within the cultural sector, and because of my work over the past decade in sustainability, I tend to think of quality of life as being something that has to be positioned within the larger sustainability framework. We can't continue to raise quality of life if the cost of doing so is far greater than the capacity of the planet to actually support it.

Traditionally, the sustainability image is that of a balance between economic, social and environmental spheres and I think we heard this morning that increasingly that model is being expanded to include a fourth leg of the stool, which is culture. I think that's even a little bit wrong. I think culture is actually the foundation upon which all the legs are resting. But I don't mean that in the sense of the way culture has become commodified and institutionalized, but rather, culture in the sense of our deep values, our behaviours, our attitudes and our consciousness of how we live in the world.

Canadian culture has many attributes. By international standards, Canadians enjoy a relatively high quality of life and I think that's pretty evident by almost all measures. We do have democratic governance, which seems essential to current notions of "quality of life." Ours is a representative democracy. I think it's important to point out that democracy takes many different forms, ranging from participatory models to representative models. For the most part, Canadians have access to an abundance of food and water, superior education systems, health care systems and employment opportunities. Certainly not all Canadians enjoy the same quality of life and these exceptions warrant further analysis. And yet, as good as life is in Canada, Canadian culture is completely and utterly unsustainable. And I say that within the context of the wider global reality. In this graph you can see the green bars illustrate the decreasing biological carrying capacity of the planet, while the purple bars illustrate tremendous global population increases. And so, the point of equilibrium between biological carrying capacity and global population was actually achieved somewhere in the 1970s. Since then we have been in a position of ecological overshoot. We have been extracting more resources from the planet than the planet is able to replenish. This is a pretty important factor in how we understand our culture, because we live now in a globalized world and our lives are all linked to global systems. But we are largely unconscious of the impacts of the decisions we make, whether it's buying things, flying in jets, using automobiles or what have you. These "normal" activities have global impacts that we don't feel very responsible for. I think the level of consciousness that's required to rebalance global human consumption and global natural resources is a critical goal that must be achieved, particularly in a world that already has exceeded its carrying capacity.

It's probably good to go back to the question: "What do we mean by culture?" I like a definition that Edgar Sheen, a psychologist from the United States, came up with: "Culture is a basic pattern of assumptions that are invented, discovered or developed by a given group as it learns to cope with its problems of external adaptation and internal integration."

So, in a word, I think that it's pretty interesting to think about culture as an *adaptive function* and this differs dramatically from a lot of definitions of culture, which measure museum visits, theatre tickets sold and other leisure-time activities.

But to see culture as an adaptive and integrative function for individuals and groups is a powerful notion. Our world is certainly changing in many, many ways very quickly and we need to adapt and to integrate this reality into our own personal value systems and collective value systems. But along the way, I think there are a few significant questions that are worth asking.

One such question: "Is our culture resilient?" And this really leads to another question: "How much disturbance can our cultural system tolerate without altering its controls and structures?" I don't know the answer to that question, but we will certainly find out in due course.

The next question is, "Is our culture capable of adaptive renewal?" That essentially means, can we change how our culture is structured and functions in ways that will address our changing needs and ultimately make the culture stronger?

So what is culture made up of? And again, just a partial list to give you a sense of how I'm using the word "culture": what are a culture's values, behaviours, systems, memory, rituals, spirituality, symbols, creativity, language, beliefs and much more?

What I might say about this list is that these components are neither static nor mutually exclusive. They are constantly in a state of interaction and therefore are dynamically related. And these dynamic relationships exist at both individual and collective levels. Relationship is critical.

In the PowerPoint version, this is an animated slide, but it basically shows at least one way of looking at culture, which is through the lens of the individual. Individuals have relationships to themselves – their own thought patterns, their own unconscious – how they develop a sense of the world, including how they relate to family and communities. Society, global humanity, the environment and ultimately "the unknown" are all levels of relationship that are rooted in each of us, as individuals. Museums are situated at the community level, but function as a facilitating agent between individuals and all levels of relationship. I think one of the interesting things about our culture, Western culture, is that it's less inclined than some other cultures to deal with those issues of "How do you relate to the unknown?" Whereas in a lot of traditional cultures, how you relate to the unknown is absolutely at the core of the notion of one's culture. But in a civil society a lot of the focus on the unknown is simply pushed to the side, often because it cannot be controlled. Western cultures focus on what is pragmatic. Perhaps that is why much of the cultural sector focuses on the economics of operating leisure-time and tourist-based facilities, rather than focusing on the dynamics of adaptive processes at individual and collective levels.

What are the indicators of success and well-being in our culture? That's a big question that we have yet to answer. But one thing is pretty clear – that the wrong indicators are dangerous and misleading. As you see here, in the case of this poor fellow who has found himself in a fairly calamitous situation, bandaged from head to toe, the attending "expert" is looking at a vial of blood as an indicator of the patient's well-being. The expert completely misses the obvious – that this poor guy has been battered and bruised – and pompously declares, "Your blood is fine. What are you complaining about?" The parallel is being made between how an 'expert' can seriously misunderstand an individual's well-being, and how the GDP is frequently used as an indicator of societal and economic well-being.

This brings me to the Critical Assessment Framework, which was developed by nine people who make up the Working Group on Museums and Sustainable Communities, of which I've been a part for seven years now. Two other members of the group, Linda Liboiron and Glenn Sutter, are also attending this conference. The Working Group has been delivering workshops and developing resources that engage the museum community and promote action around some of these issues of sustainability. In an attempt to develop cultural indicators, the Working Group needs to think about it in a stratified way, giving emphasis to experiences of the individual, the community and the institution (as a facilitating agent). Now there's an obvious fourth, which involves global well-being, which we haven't put into the model yet, primarily to avoid overwhelming people. The important thing is that it's a stratified approach and we are proposing it here as a planning framework for museums and other cultural organizations.

I will give you a little sense of what's involved in the Critical Assessment Framework. For any given project proposal, questions related to anticipated outcomes are posed to the planning team. At the individual level one might ask such questions as "Does this project really contribute new insights?" or "Does it capture imaginations?" or "Does it stimulate curiosity?" It is important for the team to answer these questions, as well as the related question of "How do you know if your project was successful?" What would be the indicators you would use to actually prove it? These are questions that museums have failed to answer. Cultural institutions are much more inclined to do their public planning based on an outputs model (i.e. to produce an exhibit) than to develop an exhibit as a mechanism to achieve cultural goals, at individual or collective levels. So this is a very challenging set of questions for them.

At the community level, questions like "Does the proposed program address vital and relevant needs and issues within the community?" and "How do you know?" rarely direct the work of program designers. I'm not sure that I have ever heard of a cultural organization that asks "Is there a set of prioritized needs and issues within a community that we, as a cultural organization, should be responding to?" How many museums ask questions like "Will our exhibit generate information and connection at the personal, community, provincial, territorial and national and global level?" or "Does it engage a diverse public?" So a number of questions are being asked here.

At the museum level, the Critical Assessment Framework asks, "Are museums operating as 'learning organizations'? Do these organizations actually grow and change as the world around them changes?" Or do our cultural organizations simply continue to do the same old thing they have always done? And we heard this morning that the Kamloops Art Gallery is in the process of deep reflection about what it's doing and how it's responding to the community. I think it's wonderful to see that kind of leadership.

The last slide is simply a quote I like about culture, and that is, "Development divorced from its human or cultural context is growth without a soul." And it comes from *Our Creative Diversity: Report of the World Commission on Culture and Development*, which is a UNESCO publication from 1995.

Paul Stacey: Thanks very much Douglas. That's another fascinating view of quality of life indicators and the importance of culture. And now I'd like to take the time to engage the rest of our panel in some response to these two presentations. I will rotate the microphone to the remaining members of the panel and ask them to take five minutes or so to either pull from those presentations' key points, or perhaps add some additional points from their own research that they think shed additional light—and maybe speak to some of their own views on quality of life indicators and how those might be constructed.

And we will start with you, Alex.

Alex Michalos: I have some copies of a couple of papers that I wrote. If you didn't get one on the table there or for the people with us via webcast that won't be able to see the diagrams, send me an email and I'll send you the papers [amichalos@unbc.ca].

And it just so happens that some points in each of the papers are related to what Gilles said and what Doug said. I won't go through the papers. I will touch on those points.

With respect to the FCM system, when I first studied the FCM system a few years ago, it had something like fifty-four indicators. They still had the eleven key indicators and it was all on one page and you could see what they were going to measure. I had no problem with the stuff that they were going to measure, but I did have a problem at the time: there were no indicators indicating that they had asked anybody how they felt about anything. They were all what we call objective indicators. I think, as do many people working in the trade, that the quality of life for people or communities is a function mainly of two key variables. It's a function of the actual conditions that they are living in and what they make out of those conditions. And then what they make out of those conditions depends on how they perceive them to be: What they think about what they perceive them to be and how they feel about what they think and they perceive their conditions to be. There is also the question of what they do—their actions—and then the consequence of their actions. So there's a good deal of complexity with the variable of what people make out of their lives that doesn't come out in any clear way if you want me to talk about objective indicators.

So I guess that's the first point. You really have to take seriously that people are agents. They are not just cogs in a wheel. I don't know if they have absolutely free wills, but they have enough free will to make them miserable to be around or delightful to be around, and they can engage in the environment that they are in and transform it sometimes. That's the first point.

The second point is that I remember years ago some geographers did some studies of—I don't remember what the exact variables were—but with respect to Gilles' paper, they looked at an array of indicators related to settlements of different sizes and the thing that I remember was that communities of a size about 50,000 to 100,000 have, according to this study, the highest quality of life, which I liked at the time, as I was living in Guelph and now I'm living in Prince George. Here in Kamloops, we are all in that ballpark. I don't know that there's anything in that because it depends what indicators you use and what countries you are looking at.

I just wanted to mention that somebody did that kind of a study and it worked for people living in our size of communities.

The other thing is related to city size. Some people had at least hypothesized that the big cities have all these problems as a function of density. Other people did studies of neighbourhoods within big cities where there were equal sized densities but there were not those problems. It depends on if you are living in high-rise condos with Tom Cruise next door to you or somebody or Joe Schmo who is just barely getting by, but with the same population density. So density doesn't seem to be an important variable in itself.

The other thing, the main question that Gilles asked is, "Would you expect to see the same array of important indicators for cities of any size?" In my paper "Connecting Communities With Community Indicators" there was a conference in Istanbul sponsored by the OECD in June 2007 and I was asked to talk about the relation of local community indicators to the national and international indicators. And so I drew a picture in there, which starts with individuals as the smallest units of analysis and then the individuals lived within dwellings. If you go to Statistics Canada information, it starts with households because they do their surveys based on a random selection of households. And inside households you have some families, but families can be defined in different ways and different kinds of families have different kinds of benefits and costs. And then individual dwellings are inside neighbourhoods generally and neighbourhoods, if you were in a big city, could be in contiguous streets. If you lived in Prince George your neighbour might be ten or twenty-five acres away. But people in rural areas do talk about neighbours, even though the area that they are talking about is much bigger.

Neighbourhoods are inside villages, towns or cities and those are inside metropolitan areas, and metropolitan areas are nested in provinces or counties and they are also nested in different kinds of ecological sheds. Here in British Columbia, we have something called the Fraser Basin Council, which looks at the watershed of the whole basin, which takes up two-thirds of the population of the province and is divided into five regions. But you have all the richness in those five regions that you would have practically in the country, only it's squeezed into one province. So you have the provincial level and the ecological level and those are imbedded within countries, and the countries are imbedded within regions like North America or something like the NAFTA region. And then you have world communities and different kinds of international communities. But the point of the story is that these things are related and very few people have ever looked at how they are related, but we know that at the simplest level, individuals are not just Descartes's "thinking substance." They really are individuals, typically are related to people and most often they are related to people in families. So if you don't understand families, it's going to be hard to understand individuals in the families.

And then the dwellings themselves, the houses typically, certainly in cities, are not just in the abstract in the environment. There are houses next to other houses, so you do have to understand neighbourhoods, and neighbourhoods are within cities. The point of that story is that although it's true that there is a core set of indicators that would measure things that are important to people, in any kind of those different sized agglomerations, there are also relations among the agglomerations that we don't understand and it takes some really sophisticated statistical modeling to know how the neighbourhoods impact on the city, but the city is also impacted by what happens in Ottawa (and for us, also what happens in Victoria).

There's a fine quote in the paper. No it's not a quote. I just mentioned it there. But if you go back, I said this somewhere else today, if you got back to roughly the 7th century BC and the Ancient Greeks and you read the poems of Hesiod, you'll find him talking about the good things. The good things for Ancient Greeks were things like good health. Aristotle talked about the goods of the body, primarily good health, but he also meant being physically attractive. And goods of mind – things like wisdom and moral virtue and then there were bodily pleasures, which were goods of the body and there were mental pleasures, which were goods of the mind. And then he talked about external pleasures, external goods, which were things like having wealth and having a good community to live in and having good friends. That core set of ideas is there from the 7th century BC. It may go back further with Chinese history. Around the world, when you go looking in communities of any size, you'll find that core of things, which, in a sense, define our humanity.

It's true that there will be differences and it's unclear exactly what the differences are but it's also true that there will be a core of similarities no matter how big the city agglomeration is or how small it is.

I haven't mentioned Doug. I won't touch culture. I remember reading one paper with fifty-seven definitions of cultures.

Let's start with a definition. My view about the defining of quality of life is, that's what we get at the end of our exercise, not at the beginning. I think that individuals and people in different communities have to negotiate the idea of quality of life for their own community. Because we are all the same species, you know that there's got to be this core of quality of life that we are looking at. In any particular community I think you really do have to let the community find their own way. When you look at a whole bunch of different menus that are allegedly capturing quality of life in various communities, you will find a lot of similarities but you'll also find a lot of differences. I think the main thing about the exercise of measuring quality of life is the exercise of pursuing the quality of life because that makes you talk to your neighbours and makes you think about your own life, about what's important. And in that exercise, you build communities and I would never think of a measure of quality of life—no matter how many indicators you had—as an endpoint. It's the endpoint on your journey as you are crafting a good life for yourself. That's the way I think of it.

Paul Stacey: Thanks folks. And now we'll turn to Nancy.

Nancy Duxbury: In the work that I've done recently, I've observed that there are a lot of groups across Canada doing work around cultural indicators—it's actually quite surprising how many people are thinking about, if not developing, indicators.

Today, I want to touch on two things: First, a growing consideration of applicability/relevance, process, and use; and second, a cluster of trends I've observed in Canadian cultural indicator development practice.

One of the influencing factors in the development of this emergent field is the use or the applicability of the indicators, or, in other words, the relevance of the indicators. The description for this session mentions advancing the relevance of cultural indicators for small cities and, to this end, it's quite key to having the buy-in and making them relevant for the community that will be using them.

Increasingly, as I've observed this field, it's become clearer and clearer that it's more than an academic field and that it's really an integrated relationship between the knowledge of the conceptual frameworks and the measurability and the communities that are interested in working to develop something that's relevant for them—and this speaks to process and inclusion. The important connecting thread of this cycle is use or applicability, so that the knowledge that's created by the community is used by the community. Indicator development and application is an interrelated knowledge project.

At the front end, there's growing attention to the purpose as to why are we developing indicators. But the flip side of that–how they are actually used and their applicability–seems to receive a lot less attention. It might just be a matter of *purpose* being one of the concerns that really hits us at the front end of these processes. Once they are underway, it's just out there. Oftentimes the use is unanticipated and sometimes inappropriate. But this dimension is definitely influencing indicator development and the emergent field because those that are interested in having indicators exist are actively involved in (some) discussions to make them applicable.

It was well illustrated in the earlier session today that it's a very complex field. In discussions of the quality of life and cultural indicators, there are multiple interests and the issue involves parties with diverse perspectives and multiple uses and use-contexts. Reflecting on Doug's presentation, considering the purposes of this exchange of practices and the thinking of institutions, on the other end of the spectrum, is indicator usage tied to resources and funding and evaluation. Together this spectrum of uses raises a series of questions around: What do we want to know? Why? For whom? What processes and purposes? What's the most persuasive in these processes and the implications of these persuasive bits?

In conversations recently with some arts organizations, there still seems to be a disconnect between arts organizations and individuals who approach this whole question from the perspective of "What do I value in practice and in my life and how can that broad spectrum of value be reflected in these indicators?" versus more policy-interested individuals or projects who come at it from "What are the key outcomes of policy or indicators of those outcomes?" And, of course, these are going to be much narrower than a broad definition and a feeling of value that a person has living his or her life.

The two sides often don't communicate all that much on this topic and because the indicators within government may be linked to evaluating its own staff and programs, indicators are often tied up with evaluation and funding. A sort of fear plays into that, fueled by the lack of a bridge, or an understanding specifically about the use of the indicators. There need to be discussions about how these indicators are going to be used or why do you need them, but often the discussions don't take place. That's the general context that I've observed, but it's not always an either-or sort of thing. It may not be quite so fraught with distinct division when there's an academic component to it to act as a mediator or facilitator in the middle of it all.

Within this overarching context, I've observed four trends in terms of "clusters of cultural indicators" being developed. These are brought forth as initial observations – I'm sure there are others. The first area, I guess it's usually characterized as the *making the case* indicators, focus on impacts. It focuses on linking culture to other domains or to other communities, considerations and concerns, and quality of life does come into that. Its focus is on how this culture contributes to urban regeneration or quality of life generally, or social advancement or whatever, but it's making those linkages.

The second area that emerges, at least in thinking about cultural indicators if not in further development, involves *improving practice*. Municipalities and cultural communities need a better understanding or documentation using indicators as a tool to understand the dynamics of the cultural vitality of a community. What entails a healthy cultural environment, or the health of the cultural sector itself, and how do you gauge that over time?

Making the case to improving practice – these are connected in a knowledge process where indicators serve as one of the important tools in the process. Yet the connections and the indicators are not always as clearly embedded in these overarching frameworks as they need to be.

The third area, which is highlighted by Gilles' discussion and in the Ottawa workshop we conducted, is *inter-municipal comparability*. This is a huge issue among communities and municipalities. The FCM has a working group looking at cultural indicators, a group which involves municipal staff from a number of (larger) cities. The working group is discussing general areas it wants to look at, but is also finding that it is very difficult to find a nexus on indicators.

At the provincial level, the province of Ontario has a series of inter-municipal comparisons that are being developed as a benchmarking project, and culture has been added to the list. However, the process has not been driven by the cultural workers themselves – the city managers are deciding what they want to compare across communities. At a local level with a national scope, community foundations are also involved in cultural indicators, within their Vital Links project. They've recently added culture to the project and interest seems to be taking off. The issue of inter-municipality comparability is a consideration as the project evolves.

Finally, I think an overarching force in this area is the rising perceived importance of *including culture within a recognized or influential quality of life or well-being index or a sustainability framework* such as the four-dimension model of sustainability–something that is seen as a broader, credible reference point. This also serves as an important piece to support the inclusion of culture in broader community planning processes by building some conceptual frameworks on how culture should be included in community planning processes and by thinking about planning through a cultural lens.

Paul Stacey: Alright, now we'll move on to Ron.

Ron McColl: Thank you. The point of crafting a good community for a good life: how do we take this information and put it to use so that we can craft a community in which individuals can thrive and develop and grow and achieve some of those deep values that they need to achieve in order to be complete?

We suffer from a huge problem with thousands of quality of life indicator projects throughout the country and throughout the region. We are always struggling with the numbers as one particular quality of life indicator holds our community up as a good example and another one absolutely trashes it. That's an issue. It's an issue for us. It's an issue for most small communities. The information that you need or the time and money you need to spend in developing some good quality of life indicators for your community presents a costly endeavour, and therefore presents a problem. It is also difficult if you have those quality indicators developed for yourself–people look at it with a little bit of hesitance and say, "Well who paid for this and is it really a true reflection of my community as opposed to your community? Your community is great, mine is bad, but you paid for that, therefore we don't quite trust your quality of life indicators." The engagement of a university in this process is almost as a third party that helps us in that process of trying to define the complex field of quality of life indicators in which we are not necessarily experts.

The addition of not just the quantitative statements but the quality statements of life that add to that, as well as looking at some of the culture's deep values and the progression or key values continuing to be reinforced through community–these are very, very important to cities and city survival, so those things and those approaches are very key to us. We also see it as an economical way out for small municipalities that cannot engage in the depth that they need to define either cultural quality or just the empirical quality of life, which is something that most small communities can't afford to buy into.

With having this established as being a base set, we believe that it's going to make a huge difference for our city. It really excites me to see that there is a difference between small communities and large communities and the agendas we want to push forward. We've always been sort of sitting in the back saying to FCM and the big city forums and the big city mayors, "No, that's not what we feel and that's not what we look like," but we haven't had the ability of being a voice to be able to put that piece forward.

I'm glad we started with the culture piece as well, up front, because that adds to the roundness and fullness of the indicators for us.

Andrew Tucker: As a community partner in the CURA and as a community partner who comes from outside the cultural field, I feel I've sort of wandered in to the wrong room and I'm wondering how I fit into this whole discussion and equation. My background is land use, development approvals, and the planning of infrastructure.

I'm going to spend a couple of minutes giving you a bit of a lens into my world, the world of local government, and how this question of indicators and culture fits on a small city agenda.

I'm going to go to a specific event: It was a Monday night. I'm going to take you through a five-hour City Council meeting and I'm going to try to do it in two minutes.

The meeting started with four presentations. The first one was the Mayor giving a decoration to a citizen who helped evacuate elderly people from a building in a fire. The citizen received an award for bravery. There was recognition of a city staff member who completed a certificate in local government professional development. The Chief Medical Health Officer for Vancouver Island made a presentation on harm reduction and, specifically, on the distribution of crack pipes for safe crack smoking, which went over really well.

There were also three delegations. One on a rezoning application was on that night's agenda. One was regarding an Official Community Plan amendment application, which the speaker felt would destroy the neighbourhood. There were residents voicing their concerns in response to the harm reduction strategy that was presented by the Chief Medical Health Officer.

There were three proclamations issued that evening: Mahatma Gandhi Day, Raise a Reader Day, and Waste Reduction Week.

The next section of the agenda was staff reports. There were, well I won't do the math, but I'll run through them quickly:
- Two reports on parking issues (one related to increasing parking rates and one related to a strategy for parking);

- A huge report on the corporate climate change strategy, which is part of the FCM Partners for Climate Protection;
- Five development permits;
- One liquor license;
- Three official community plan applications;
- Two leases for city owned property, one of them was for a yacht club, the other was an affordable housing project;
- Minutes of a public hearing;
- Fourteen nuisance property reports including a grow-op, building without a building permit, unsightly premises and building deficiencies;
- A report on twin city relationships; and
- Four information-only reports (which I won't go into).
  [Laughter]

There were ten bylaws introduced for third reading and adoption that had completed their public hearing process. There were two by-laws that were brand new to the process and were being introduced for the first time.

Then at the end of the meeting, and for those of you who have been watching the clock, this is now about 10:00 or 10:15 p.m. and we've been going since 6 p.m. in the evening. So at 10 p.m. we had five delegations for items not related to matters on the agenda. Two of them were related to selecting a site for a community soup kitchen for the homeless and street people. The proposed location was in the speakers' neighbourhood and they were concerned about the impact that the soup kitchen would have on their neighbourhood. There were two delegations related to a development proposal, which was considered at a public hearing and there was one related to a goat. Now the last one concerned a woman who had brought a goat onto her property in order to keep the blackberries down. And that presentation actually took about twenty minutes, so, I'm not doing it due justice here. You can see details of the meeting on the Nanaimo City Council Agenda for last Monday (September 10, 2007).

The point of that lengthy description is that a municipal council's agenda is very full. There are a myriad of issues that they are faced with on a weekly basis. Well, okay, my example was an exceptional list, that's a really heavy agenda and particularly diverse, but that level of complexity, of diverse issues and that number of conflicting agendas, from neighbourhood residents to developers to property owners who are standing in front of council because their property has been listed as unsightly, is not uncommon.

So the question becomes, "Where do cultural indicators fit within it?" Within that mass of information coming before municipal council, how does a cultural indicator, in a realm of the types of issues that a City Council typically would discuss, how do you get "space at the table," if you will? And how do you make those indicators important so that the council will sit up and say "Yes, culture is important to our community. And culture is one of our economic drivers and culture does have quality of life implications and speaks to the values of the community"?

What you end up with is a very crowded agenda with a lot of noise that is constantly in front of municipal council. So this is where the CURA is providing us, as municipal employees, what we need to take to that crowded agenda, which are tools with credibility because its based on the research that you as academics are doing. You are doing the necessary research.

We haven't got the time or the resources. Ron mentioned the difficulty of trying to get the resources and the budgets to do this sort of work. We don't have it. So when a program like CURA steps forward and says that "We're interested in this and we're going to help you out with this" – great!

So how does CURA research have an impact on the cultural agenda at the municipal level? To use the City of Nanaimo as an example, we were taking community contributions as part of development project approvals, which went into a public art fund. Because the social agenda has increased in importance, due to homelessness and the impacts that it's having, the community contributions are now being shifted over into an affordable housing fund and taken out of the public art fund. So there's a direct impact on the cultural agenda, where one set of values has moved forward on the municipal agenda, and another set of values is suppressed. It does have a direct effect on those of you who are working in the cultural field.

Implications for CURA? The word that I most liked about Gilles' presentation was the need for a simple set of cultural indicators. And I'd like to say, specifically, simple in terms that can be easily understood by municipal politicians. Those are the types of indicators we are looking for.

As for the type of information, Nancy touched on this in her presentation with the question, "What is it you are trying to collect the indicators for?" If you are doing it as a community development exercise and doing things like community mapping and getting the community involved in those sorts of exercises, where you are working with a community, the comparability across communities isn't really that important. For those exercises, indicators that are specific to that community are totally appropriate.

But municipal politicians like comparison. They like looking at similar communities to see how their community compares. Nanaimo will look at Kamloops and say, "Gee Kamloops – look at the sports facilities they've got. How do we measure up?" There is that comparing and the title of Gilles' presentation, "Does size matter to the municipal politician?" is fitting because, well, yes, size does matter.

Objective indicators serve a different purpose than what I would call community development indicators and if you know your purpose going into identifying those indicators and you know how they are going to be used, then you are going to be much further ahead in their application.

Are the indicators there to provide community learning? By that, I mean, is it that the community is learning about itself and self-realizing, or are the communities there to learn in terms of their place in the world? How do we stack up against the Kelownas, the Prince Georges, the other communities of similar size?

There's that side, but the other side of it is, are the indicators there to create or inform an agenda? I think that the risk is there and I think it came out in Gilles' talk, in particular. The large cities, in recognizing that they do have forty-five percent of our population, they have taken hold of that quality of life agenda. The small cities have different needs and the kind of work that Gilles is doing is something we need. I hope small cities are not ignored in setting Canada's municipal agenda. I don't know. It remains to be seen.

Simple, easy to use, easily understood indicators are needed. But what are their purposes and why are you collecting them like that? I'll wrap up with that.

Paul Stacey: Well, thank you very much.

And now we finally turn to the final part of our agenda. We've got ten to fifteen minutes still to this session so I'd like to invite all of you out here to now ask questions, express your own views on this and in order to capture the audio, we've got another microphone. We'll give you the microphone if and when you've got a question or comment you'd like to make.

Jen Budney (Kamloops Art Gallery): I have two points, two questions. First off, Andrew, thank you very much for walking through the city council meeting. When I hear those scenarios it scares me, though, because of course at least where we live, obviously the government is still our biggest funder. And so our biggest funder has the least amount of time to listen to a lot of those issues. So then that brings me to Doug and your paper on sustainability and especially your critical assessment framework. And just to ask, How far−because you've probably been at it longer than most−how far have you been able to integrate this into use within the museum system in Canada?

Doug Worts: I think the short answer is not very far. Part of the attractiveness of getting involved in the CURA was the hope that there would be opportunities to work with groups within this project to actually take the Critical Assessment Framework and to use it and push it and change it, as it was useful in different settings. Because as a group of nine people from across the country, we sort of cobbled together our work to mount these workshops once or twice a year from museum communities, but we still don't have the time to really apply it in a very focused way. We hope that's still to come out of this CURA process.

Paul Stacey: Other questions or comments?

Carol Greyeyes: Hello. My name is Carol Greyeyes and I'm originally from the Muskeg Lake Cree Nation, which is Northern Plains Cree.

I'm an artist and I work for the Saskatchewan Arts Board as the Indigenous Arts Advisor. It's my job to always speak for the original habitants of this land that we are enjoying. I've just been listening to everybody this morning and doing this presentation and a number of things are coming up. There's a big discussion about quality of life and people always say, "Well, why aren't Native people participating in our programming or in our activities, or etc.?" I haven't heard anything other than Marilyn's poems, which were really interesting and I thank the organizing committee for inviting her as a keynote, but I haven't heard any voices from that sector of the community. I want to acknowledge the original caretakers of this land and thank them for allowing us to be here. I'd thank them in person, but I haven't seen anybody yet.

Quality of life−you know you said that in Canada (and I'm looking at Doug) that we have a great quality of life, but the reality for the majority of aboriginal people is there is no clean water. Our reserve in Saskatchewan, it's a high-class reserve. We don't have any paved roads. We don't have water. We don't have clean water. We have electricity. There are so many people living without what we consider the basics of life. So there's that, but there's also−I would suggest to

Gilles and Alex – if you really want to measure the value of culture that you go to First Nations communities. Alex in his presentation said that if you want to kill culture, cut it off at around the age of twelve and that just sent a chill through me because I thought of residential schools and how that happened. It didn't kill us. And then I was flipping through a book on residential schools and this survivor had said that he was working with a psychologist and the psychologist said, "You would not have survived if it wasn't for these visits with your grandparents, where you got to do ceremonies and speak your language. You would not have survived the abuse." So if you want an example of how important culture is, in this case it was a matter of life and death.

It is about people's reaction to their environment and how they maneuver through it. If you want to measure the significance of culture, I would suggest you look at First Nations communities. Somebody this morning was saying, "Well you know at the art gallery we don't get a lot of response from the First Nation community here." And I thought, well you know if you don't have a viable food source, what's important? And is it in my best interest to participate in the other system? In the system that has, or in the worldview that hasn't sustained me throughout my life. So those kinds of things might be something that you would consider when you are looking at your analysis.

I'll just stop there, but thank you all. It's been very interesting.

Paul Stacey: Alex. Do you want to comment?

Alex Michalos: I agree with everything that you said. I have tried hard. The aboriginal communities are not homogeneous. We have several First Nations communities nearby. We are on Carrier Sekani land in Prince George and you can study eighteen different aboriginal languages there. I have tried and I have several aboriginal friends because we've been there for a while, have tried to get in to make friends with the band council and do quality of life studies and it's a slow thing to do. At least in my case, it's not for lack of trying. I belong to a group that's working on something called the Canadian Index of Well-Being and we had one meeting with the (what's the federated group with offices in Ottawa? – George Erasmus used to be the chair of it?). Answer: Assembly of Nations. We tried to get the Assembly to join with us because we wanted to have an aboriginal voice in this, in our index. And they never said no. In Prince George they've never said no to me. It's just that you start the negotiation and I haven't been able to succeed. And with the other larger group, they haven't been able to succeed either. So it's not an easy thing to do with the best of intentions, but you are right, it's something worth doing. I hope we can find better ways.

Douglas Worts: I want to say that I agree completely that the whole question of quality of life is usually seen through a system of number crunching and aggregation and that's why within our working group we developed one of the levels to really look at individual experiences, because it is essential to somehow understand what cultural experience looks like in the real experiences of individuals. I don't know how you aggregate it, integrate it into a stratified framework, but I think we have a sense that doing so is the task that needs to be undertaken.

Nancy Duxbury: There is an organization in Vancouver, the Centre for Native Policy and Research, that published a report in 2005[2] that looked at quality of life indicators for urban aboriginals in the Vancouver region, using a medicine wheel approach to organizing their whole process. One of the quadrants was culture and community or culture and family. I believe it had four indicators, which were tied to traditional languages, traditional practices and things like that. It might be a matter of finding a group like that to help make the bridges.

Alex Michalos: I could talk to Nathan because we had a nice chat but we never actually developed anything together. He sort of went his way. So we had the initial discussions. We have a special agreement between the University of Northern British Columbia and the Nisga'a Nation and they have their house of wisdom. They really want an independent university of their own, so we are trying to help them find their way to that. But even with great relations – and my wife was adopted into the Killer Whale, she's got relatives – but for some reason we still haven't been able to get a survey in any of the aboriginal communities, even where we have good friends.

Paul Stacey: Okay we'll take one last question, but then we are running a bit late so we should wrap up.

Jen Budney: Carol, I want to thank you for your comments. I just want to clarify something about the Kamloops Art Gallery. We do actually have quite a high level of participation by members of our First Nation's communities. We don't have a lot of members, perhaps, and that's what I was looking at for the next membership. We also don't have a lot of members from the Aberdeen area, which is way up on the hill in the suburbs. That said, I think it is important to recognize and it's tied into what Doug's presentation started off as today: that the very foundation of museums comes from a colonial enterprise and really has developed out of the kind of global capitalism that has seen so many communities and traditional cultures absolutely destroyed. So if we weren't in the process of destroying these cultures, we wouldn't have as many museums in the first place.

There is a bit of an irony attached to all of us sitting around from the museum community trying to figure out how we can make ourselves part of something really globally sustainable. Since you were talking, Doug, about ecological sustainability and in fact human survival, I'm wondering if there was a note of despair because I don't see those kinds of indicators here on the list that you generated and I'm not sure how we can even go about doing that. I think about that sometimes in the gallery when we are building up new walls for a show and then tearing them down six weeks later and transporting works across all of North America for six-week periods.

Douglas Worts: It's true. It's difficult to know how to address that. We have buried the global ecological impact of our lifestyles deep within our unconscious. As the foundation of human life on the planet shifts, what mechanisms do we have to identify and then address our most pressing contemporary issues?

I also just wanted to touch on that notion of museum because it's such a problematic word. If you go back to museum as the place of the muses, it's a place of deep creativity and reflection. Somebody, maybe it was a joke, I don't know, took that idea of "the muse" and attached it to a notion of bricks and mortar places that have limited collections and is obsessed with its own authority. Those are the challenges of the museum world: To give that up and to see culture and creativity as something that is always happening in the here and now of the general public.

Paul Stacey: Well this has been a fascinating discussion. Maybe you could join me in thanking the panel for their insights. [Applause.] Thanks to all of your for joining us for today's session. And the web address is www.smallcities.ca. It's all going to be available from the Small Cities website, so thanks everybody and on to the next session.

Commentary

After the live discussion, and as part of the preparation of the printed text, Mark Seasons (University of Wateroo) provided the following commentary on issues raised by the Roundtable.

This session produced some really interesting discussion and exchanges of opinion on complex issues: quality of life, cultural indicators, and planning and managing small and mid-size cities. Each participant brought different perspectives to the discussion. Yet, there was considerable convergence in terms of these issues and their resolution.

Some context is in order. There are roughly one hundred small and mid-size cities in Canada—urban places with populations in the 25,000-300,000 range. Some of these communities are located within the geographical and economic reach of Canada's major urban centres, and others are isolated and self-contained, located at a distance from large cities. In most cases, these places share many of the same complex economic, social, environmental and cultural challenges as their large city counterparts (e.g., homelessness, economic change, aging society, etc.). In other cases, there are significant differences between large cities and small-to-midsize cities in the scale and intensity of these challenges, which call for community-driven analysis and solutions. As a result, Viaud suggests that the small city policy agenda (and resultant indicators) should be acknowledged and that interventions should focus on economic development challenges, investment in social and cultural infrastructure, and capacity-building generally. This is a sensible starting point.

Sometimes these challenges are exacerbated by size and the limited capacity of small-to-midsize cities to plan for and manage change (e.g., the local impacts of structural economic transformation, demographic change), as both Tucker and McColl attest. In all cases, quality of life is both a goal and a community concern. There are many interpretations of what constitutes quality of life and these are evolving from traditional definitions to a more experiential and personal view—what a place feels like, how it is experienced (Worts, Michalos, Duxbury). Quality of life is recognized as a key determinant of community viability; people move to places where they want to live, rather than for employment opportunities alone (Tucker).

Quality of life is something that defines a community, makes a community distinctive and reflects the uniqueness of the community. At the same time, there is great interest in benchmarking the comparative quality of life among similar-sized communities (Viaud). As

Michalos notes, quality of life is something that must be defined by the community itself, and it has to be operationalized by the community too.

Culture, defined broadly, is a major contributor to quality of life in these communities. Certainly, culture includes the traditional interpretation: arts and culture – a thriving artistic community, theatre, dance, etc. It also includes community values, their expression and the self-image of the community and of us as individuals in that community (Worts). These are dynamic concepts, always in flux. In conceptual terms, culture is one of four foundational and integrative elements of sustainable development (the others being economic, social and environmental). Indeed, as Worts notes, culture must not be considered independent of the other elements of true sustainability. Further, we must not strive for a quality of life that compromises the sustainability of our communities and the planet (Worts). The key here would seem to be to interpret quality of life less in material terms, more in experiential terms.

Clearly, the goal of attaining and maintaining a good quality of life is, on the one hand, admirable and appropriate, and on the other hand, a frustrating and demanding task. We want to know how we might achieve a desirable quality of life. This leads us to the subject of indicators. Indicators are sets of data or information that tell us something about a community, or a policy, program or project. Indicators point to progress (or otherwise) in efforts to achieve stated objectives. They can indicate the extent of change that has been experienced. To be effective, indicators need to support and be fully aligned with a clearly defined goal or objective that has well developed outcomes and impacts; this is the conventional interpretation favoured by policy analysts. As Duxbury and Worts point out, this interpretation is at odds with a more subjective, values-based conception of worth. Mc-Coll suggests that both quantitative and qualitative measures of quality of life are important as we strive to understand and achieve this goal in our communities. We need to "think through a cultural lens," as Worts suggests.

There is no shortage of indicators and indicators models. There are quality of life indicators models (Federation of Canadian Municipalities) and integrative models that try to reflect the experience of living somewhere – for example, genuine progress indicators (Pembina Institute). There are also sustainability indicators that are used at urban (e.g., City of Hamilton, ON) and regional scales (e.g., Fraser Basin Council). The real challenge is to develop indicators that produce the kind of information that we need to make well-grounded decisions in the small-to-midsize city context, and to help create a small city policy agenda (Viaud). These indicators must also tell us about the experience of living in a place. The challenge is to create meaningful, relevant and useful indicators that convey objective and subjective impressions about the community.

To be effective and to have any impact, the indicators need to be in a format that can be easily managed by local governments—for example, by city planners and by local councils that are pressed for time and lack the resources needed for proper planning and analysis (Tucker, Viaud). The indicators must also be easily understood by community residents. This requires, in turn, that we know what we need to know, which can be a difficult proposition! Perhaps we should simply embrace the many unknowns, as Worts proposes? As Duxbury notes, indicators need to be relevant to the community, they need to generate knowledge, mutual learning and understanding (Tucker), and enhance connections (Worts). The definition of quality of life is a task and process that should involve all members of the community. The creation of indicators, and the monitoring of indicators, should also be a responsibility shared by the community.

In summary, we are in the early stages of a much-needed conversation about quality of life and its relationship to culture in our communities. The discussion generated by this workshop represents an important step forward in this journey of exploration. It is apparent that we need a new generation of indicators that helps us understand the nature of our small-to-midsize communities, enhances communication and learning, and leads to improvements in community health, sustainability and quality of life. Most important, we need a community-generated understanding of quality of life and of the roles and contributions of culture in its many dimensions in our communities.

Notes

1. Editors' notes: The roundtable presentations were first transcribed and edited for publication, and each speaker was given the opportunity to revise the text, to elaborate or rephrase for clarity. Throughout, as editors, we've tried to maintain the oral feel of the original event.
2. Cardinal, Nathan, & Adin, Emilie. (2005, November). *An urban Aboriginal life: The 2005 indicators report on the quality of life of Aboriginal people in the Greater Vancouver region.* Vancouver: Centre for Native Policy and Research.

Part III   Picturing West

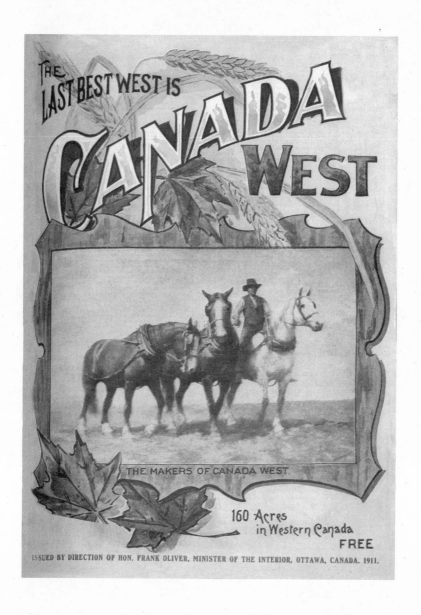

THE LAST BEST WEST IS CANADA WEST

THE MAKERS OF CANADA WEST.

160 Acres in Western Canada FREE

ISSUED BY DIRECTION OF HON. FRANK OLIVER, MINISTER OF THE INTERIOR, OTTAWA, CANADA. 1911.

Kalli Paakspuu

Photojournal Rhetorics
of the West

In an essay entitled "On Photography," Susan Sontag wrote that photographs "give people an imaginary possession of a past that is unreal" and "help people to take possession of a space in which they are insecure" (9). Leslie Devereaux argues that the signifying practices of photographs are culturally specified as a moral and ethical space between persons (71). Invented more than a century and a half ago, photography brought to the world visual realities that transformed communication and the transmission of information and knowledge. In the late nineteenth century, modernism produced a new world and the photo-eye provided a validating "being there." Comparable to the revolutionary technology of the printing press and its effect on language, early photographic representation created a language of speaking through the body practised by both the photographer and his subject in the photographic production.

The portrayal of Indians in these initial years of photography was shaped by various attitudes in the imagination of white society. Early photographers like Frederick Steele of Steele & Co. followed the well travelled paths of the railways and their branch lines or used stage coaches or riverboats. Generally the Indigenous community did not go to the photographers' studios for portraits: photographers were tourists that came after them in their territory and environments. Marcia Crosby has written about the "Imaginary Indian" and argued that this fiction "functioned as a peripheral but necessary component of European history in North America – the negative space of the 'positive' force of the colonialist hegemony" (269). In colonialism the camera became a tool for literalizing stereotypes and for symbolic control over the bodies of others through photographic surrogates (Pultz 20; see also Tagg). Because of these concerns, in contemporary society today, many Indigenous cultural organizations keep their collections in the home community to control their uses.

A photographic image produced within the conventions of nineteenth century colonial rhetoric may address and speak very differently to a contemporary Indigenous reader than it did to an original viewer. A portrait of a community member, for instance, engages its viewers in local knowledge and memories. The "orientational" features of visual conventions are relative to the time and place and are reenacted in photographic exhibitions. As cultural brokers, curators use the museum or gallery as a performance stage for discourse relating to public history, where local and global politics are contested (Cronin 3; see also Karp and Lavine). A photograph as a text thus may have very different social uses for the photographer and the human subject. Meanings are both temporal and embodied within practices that organize consciousness culturally and socially; photographer and subject are positioned differently in these relations. A responsive camera observes and interprets without provoking. An interactive camera records its interchanges, and a constructive camera interprets its subject by breaking it down and reassembling it according to an external logic (MacDougall 4).

The making of a photograph embeds, in its document time, the social organization of its production, which cannot be fully known by the viewer. The subject represented in the photograph always has a physical relationship to the camera that is one reality, part of the camera's reality, part of the reality being filmed, and part of the reality in the photograph. Appearance is a type of visual knowledge and a physical showing is a way of saying the unsayable. The photograph is an expression of real relationships between camera and human interactions which reveal aspects of both. In the later nineteenth century, new meanings and technological advances in photography, like the invention of the Kodak camera and roll film, expanded its uses in both personal and industrial settings. The early photograph required the subject to be unmoving while the image recorded an embodied physical dialogue that became a material imprint and visual artifact. Within this context, the photography of westerner Harry Pollard makes a significant contribution to regional narrative as a significant locus for Western knowledge, cultural exchange and Indigenous alterity. Pollard's work is ethnographic and photojournalistic. Scopic views consistently treat the domestic and ceremonial with an eye trained for telling cultural narratives through a realist mode.

Harry Pollard used the photojournalist form to locate his subjects in a living culture and the natural rhythms of their environment. Late 19th century photographic uses did not generally include the photojournalist in Canada – though Andrew Rodger describes John A. Macdonald's funeral cortege in 1891 as photojournalism (9). The notes Pollard kept on his subjects were detailed and respectful and included the subject's personal name when known. Pollard's photography consequently offers an alternative to what Georges E. Sioui has termed "Amerindian autohistory," where a convergence with non-Native documents and the "scientific" validity of Native historical sources make "colonial documentary sources...the ultimate fortress of Euro-American discourse on Amerindians" (59). Pollard's identification with the Blackfoot peoples may have paralleled his own efforts to create a viable livelihood in the region. Like bell hooks' Black American photographic wall (1995), Pollard records the quotidian and ceremonial in a body of work that is an Indigenous history alternative to the popular culture forms circulating outside the reserves. Like hooks' wall, Pollard's photographs survey assimilation and resistance.

Harry Pollard's photojournalistic aesthetic grew from a family practice where Pollard as a young boy learned the production of daguerreotypes and wet plate photography. His father, the principal photographer of Tillsonburg, Ontario, raised him in the entrepreneurial world of portrait photography, where he developed great technical skill and mastery. From an unpublished essay, his granddaughter Joy Firmstone recorded Pollard's words: "That was in the days when the flash went off with a big belch of smoke. My first job was coating the old tin types that father made" (Firmstone 1). With the completion of the Canadian Pacific Railway in 1885, a new policy by Sir William van Horne gave photographers and painters free passage on the premise that their images of the west would encourage settlers and tourism. Spectacular views of mountains and primeval forests produced through the CPR inspired Harry Pollard to board the CPR to Calgary and open a studio on Stephen (8th) Avenue, five years after the city incorporated with a population under four thousand. Active within the professional photographic fraternity of Alberta, Pollard soon gained national prominence with his promotional pictures of the Rockies, Calgary, and foreign countries. In 1924 he became the press photographer for the Associated Screen News and Canadian Pacific Railway. But when he shifted to work as a press photographer overseas in later life, his early photography fell into obscurity, only later to become available in the public archives.

Before photographic film, photographers used glass plates, making films by putting emulsion directly on the glass surface. A large black sheet draped over the camera and the photographer's head was necessary for the photographer to focus upon the image on the ground glass. Until the First World War this wet plate system was favoured by many photographers because they could control the development and artistic effects of printing. Despite the introduction of roll film and the Kodak camera in 1888 and the consequent revolutionary competition of amateur photography, Harry Pollard continued to use the 8 by 10 portrait box camera with a Bosche and Lombart lens, the first of its kind in the Canadian West. This lens made it possible to take both a close-up picture or a wide-angle group shot. Pollard also had the first 360 degree circuit camera, which produced panoramic pictures in a complete circle.

Given the competition of two established photographic studios in Calgary, Pollard diversified with excursions to ranches, farms, cattle round-ups and Indian reserves. As an artist entrepreneur, Pollard stated, "I took pictures of anything and anybody–anywhere I could earn an honest dollar" (Firmstone 4). An easterner in a 1906 issue of the *Calgary Eye-Opener* described Pollard's studio as "one of the most elaborate, complete and thoroughly adapted Ateliers in Canada, if not in America" (Firmstone 3) . On a visit to the Blackfoot camps, Pollard met the American western artist and wrangler, Charles Russell, whose paintings portrayed the people in domestic and warlike activities, often as traders and self-sufficient individuals (Aldrich 3). By its partial "insider" perspective from a six-month experience with the Blood Indians, Russell's imagery challenged Eurocentric representations of the West. While sketching, Russell said to Pollard, "Why don't you do what I'm doing–make records of this great west?" (Firmstone 4 - 5).

Following the example of photographer Father Lacombe, Pollard established friendly relations and trust before visiting the Indian camps with his camera. His scrapbook contains this undated article from *A. T.A. Magazine*:

> Accompanied by a driver from the local livery stable,
> Harry Pollard would load up a democrat with provisions
> of tea, sugar, flour and tobacco and drive out for a pow
> wow on one of the reserves in the southern part of the
> province. There, given permission to set up his tent, he
> would patiently set about making the Indians understand
> his genuine interest in them and their tribal customs.
> (Firmstone 5-6).

Firmstone reports that Pollard traveled to the various Indian reserves at Gleichen, Cluny, Morley, and Sarcee to photograph individual chiefs and braves: "On a good day the chief of the tribe would have a teepee set up next to the chieftain's and then order his minor chiefs and braves to pose" (5-6). But Pollard constantly had to re-emphasize trust and collaboration for his enterprise, as noted in an excerpt from *Herald Magazine*:

> The big 8 by 10 camera would be set up on its tripod, the photographer would disappear under the thick black cloth, and the picture would be taken – often the Indian would be unwilling and all were somewhat supersti-tious of the hidden eye.... Often a brave simply refused to have any thing to do with "the white man's mystery box." But generally the photographer was successful because the chief generally was near at hand to see his orders were obeyed. (Silversides 7)

Pollard often used the guest teepee of the camp and not his own portable tent. The chief commonly set up Pollard's teepee next to his, integrating Pollard's teepee into the community. From this central position Pollard had unparalleled access to both ubiquitous and ceremonial spaces, which he photographed. But the chief's directing Pollard's photography effectively created two separate referential worlds, thereby doubling the cultural referents and producing a truly transcultural photographic form. Further, Pollard's photography captured events shared in collective memories over many years with returns to the same locations, persons and subjects. In photojournalistic form, Pollard's work thus became self-referential as it surveyed time passing, children growing, and people ageing.

The majority of photographs taken in Canada and the United States in the nineteenth century were portraits made for sitters for private purposes. This photographic portraiture became a visible sign of prosperity or celebrity and was not affordable to everyone. The nine-teenth century, therefore, soon featured two kinds of photographs: private images made and paid for by the sitter or individual, and pub-lic images made speculatively and designed to be marketed and sold to consumers as stereographs, cabinet cards, exhibition prints, and postcards. A sitter's payment may have been money, food or material supplies, or perhaps a copy of the photograph, since commercial sales offered secondary uses and profits for the photographer. Generally these commercial images, whatever their source, were marked with words scrawled across the image, with titles printed along the mounts, brief narratives printed on the backs or with captions, or texts in a descriptive pamphlet. These words typically reinforced one particular reading of the photograph at the expense of others, erasing ambiguity and promoting a preferential reading.

Mediated by a mechanical and photochemical technology, a photograph of a person or of people is a meaningful interchange in which the person imaged is always a presence. The possession of a portrait enables the owner to maintain control over the uses and interpretation of that image. In the public realm this control disappears as photographers, publishers and viewers affix their own explanation to the picture. Private moments are transformed into public spectacles, personal pictures into commodities, and records of events into free-floating metaphors. And because of their commercial value at the time, such as in postcards or illustrated stories, in the Canadian and American archive many of the photographs of Native Americans were copyrighted by their photographers. And in the United States, a custom initiated in the James E. McClees Studio in 1857 was delegation photography, in which photographs became used as a proof of presence in legal situations, such as treaty negotiations.

Harry Pollard's early career as a photographer overlapped with that of E. S. Curtis, who photographed some of the same people and communities. Both began as independent artists and developed respected reputations with Native Americans. Pollard documented the accoutrements of trading practices like Hudson Bay blankets and western style hats and the display of the Queen's medals. Pollard's straight photography also documented the Blackfoot iteration of culture. His inclusion of transcultural effects created a legacy different from that of Curtis, who used pictorialism and photo darkroom methods to remove evidence of White civilization, thereby idealizing and exoticizing Indigenous cultures.

The Harry Pollard Collection totals 12,000 negatives in the Provincial Archives of Alberta. The collection includes at least 200 portraits of Indigenous peoples photographed between 1900 and 1910. Sixty of these are life-sized portraits of Blackfoot, Blood, Cree, Sarcee, and Stoney Tribes, with some 8 by 10 glass negatives enlarged to 16 by 20 inch portraits and tinted with oils. A standard practice in the early days of photography was for photographers to acquire and store under their own copyright works by other photographers, works like the portraits of important individuals. Collected photographers like William Hanson Boorne and others in the Pollard collection are thus accredited to Pollard. Pollard's collection, therefore, contains the portrait of Chief Crowfoot (See Fig. 1), for example, with a C.P.R. perpetual pass for his role in the Blackfoot uprising.

Pollard's photography anticipated new technological uses through

Fig. 1. Chief Crowfoot, 1885. (Harry Pollard Collection, p. 129)

framing, composition, montage, and his collecting practices. Though the Native American subjects may not have understood the photographer's artistic purposes, by their very collaboration they actively interpellated the original photographic forms with traditional knowledge and values that addressed their people. The dramaturgical model of Erving Goffman (1959), a symbolic interactionist, suggests that a performance relationship exists between the photographer and the subject shaped by bodily expression and interaction. For a positive

Fig. 2. Inside the Medicine Lodge, 1910. (Harry Pollard Collection, p. 52)

result, a portrait sitter needs to match the competence of the photographer's performance. The sitter's expression reflects the level of success in this collaboration. "Inside the Medicine Lodge" (See Fig. 2), for example, features two men and two women in cotton clothing and blankets among handmade, highly portable personal furnishings. The centre frame displays two large cushions. Taken from the inside of the teepee, the photograph reveals the interior teepee architecture and a relaxed comfort level in the photograph's participants—despite the use of a blinding flash. For the initiate, medicine bundles and sacred ceremonial objects are easy to recognize. The top knot on the head of the man in the centre left signifies spiritual healer, and is likely someone like the cultural historian Kyaiyi-stamik (Bear Bull) (see Fig. 8).

Pollard's photograph of the Blackfoot Council (Fig. 3) witnesses a formal event, which Pollard composed with the most elaborately clothed and top knotted elder in the centre, flanked by two men on each side. Two life-sized painted horses are clearly visible on the background teepee. The Council's formal arrangement in front of the teepee may have been mutually decided by the photograph's participants. Of interest in Pollard's record is the listing of only three

Fig. 3. Blackfoot Council. Left to Right: Calf Child, Weasel Child, Many Turning Robes. (Harry Pollard Collection, p. 25)

persons when five were actually present. Perhaps he was planning to add other names later. That four men stand and one sits on his haunches makes the picture an unusual group portrait. Marked by an uncommon warmth and informality, Pollard's image expresses a balance of power between the photographer and the subject. The facial expressions are relaxed and express harmony despite the formality of the situation. A subject's direct look at the camera is an expression of the impulse to "pose" and control one's photographic representation (Nichols 91). Deeper structures of knowledge are linked to the surface reality of a photograph, and a community's use of these photographs functions within family and local historical knowledge (Poignant 7) to activate deep memories (Edwards 148) and to retrieve missing names and stories.

In another photograph, Big Belly (Fig. 4) proudly displays the treaty medals and the clothing from Article 6, Treaty Number 7. The clothing was a negotiated treaty benefit that provided every chief a set of European style (or white man) clothes. The full outfit was a brass-buttoned coat, side-striped trousers and plug-hat. A portrait of a chief wearing the Queen's Medal is a display of strong faith in the great "White Mother." As an item that the Sarcee listed in a treaty negotiation with the Queen, the clothing represents an assimilationist policy, which was a desirable outcome for the Canadian government. The act of wearing it, however, did not make Big Belly, with his waist-long braids, pass for a white man. In fact, the complete presentation of the self is not only for Pollard, the photographer, but also for the little girl at the left side of the frame, for whom this performance is a decided disindentification. The clothes and medal, as symbols of assimilation, become an appropriation from the colonizer that take on a new political meaning in a reservation camp. These are not simply the Queen's clothes. With his profile clearly presented to the camera, Big Belly's gaze to the side places him in a spatial relationship to the land as one who surveys and commands the space in a symbolic representation. His relaxed facial expression and body position show comfort and active participation in the portrait-making process. Pollard's gaze thus follows everyday life and the Sarcee resolve to live within their core values – a defining difference from the visual records of "vanishing race." The wearing of the full outfit at a ceremonial camp, thus, is a disidentification with the colonizer's apparel, if not even more clearly a contradiction of assimilation.

Photographs of everyday activities, like "Woman Smoking Meat"(Fig. 5) at the Blackfoot camp, offer a longer narrative through the dramaturgical language of photography. The teepee in the background painted with buffalo heads evokes the tribal history and the centrality of the traditional buffalo hunt. A narrative of resistance emerges through this buffalo imagery, which also figures prominently in other photographs of the Sundance Lodge and by the woman's transcultural attire. A metallic hook dangles from the meat curing pole. The photograph is descriptive of food preparation practices for later generations. Pollard selects a moment when the woman looks away from the camera to compose an iconology that reveals life's physical demands written in her body. Unlike in the Blackfoot Coun-

Fig. 4. Big Belly, Sarcee Chief (1910). (Harry Pollard Collection, p. 58)

cil photograph, here Pollard here makes no effort to include the subject's name in the title of the photograph, a fact that suggests a lack of familiarity in the relationship.

In "Making of a Brave," photographs taken from 1904 to 1916, Pollard's collection documents the Blackfoot Sundance Ritual, a ceremony long suppressed by American and Canadian governments. Since Pollard also collected photography on this subject from Alex J. Ross and William Hanson Boorne, Pollard's is possibly the most complete record of this native spiritual and resistance movement to exist.

Fig. 5. Woman Smoking Meat (ca. 1910). (Harry Pollard Collection, p. 40)

His documentation of the Sundance represents a creative challenge of photographing a live, unstoppable event with a technology best suited for posed images. Through repeat performance, the photographs' subjects took the photographer into the moment as someone who witnessed and lived it with them. By invitation, Pollard attended the 1904 Blackfoot ceremonies on the Bow Flats south of Cluny. His knowledge and experience of the Sundance guided him to a photojournalistic documentation of sequences of the ceremony. At least a hundred teepees were set up in preparation for the Sundance, which

Fig. 6. Ceremony of Erection Sundance Lodge. (Harry Pollard Collection, p. 50)

included ceremonial dances that took two or three days to perform. In several of the Sundance series shot in 1910 and 1912 he photographed the ceremony of the erection of the Sundance Lodge (Fig. 6), a full view shot of a huge community construction effort where women, children and men participated. Photographing the ritual as practiced by the medicine man, Pollard was also present to photograph the "calling," a Sundance performed by virgins.

Within the National Museum of the American Indian in the United States thousands of images communicate an American history through a saga of conversion and transition palpable even today. As documents of lived encounters, early photography joins narratives of public memory to a non-indifference to its transitive aspects (Simon 186). The moment of taking the picture is selected from a phenomenological streaming where the photographer marks a time, place and a presence that congeals social relations within historical relations. Both the photographer and the subject use the encounter to actively construct a myth that is a natural history (Barthes 1981) and which normalizes a world through signs based in the physical world, gestures, facial expressions, clothing and other embodiments. These are memorial spaces of temporal and ontological boundaries where a Derridean "learning to live with ghosts," as elaborated in *Specters*

Fig. 7. Calf Child – Blackfoot. (E. S. Curtis *The North American Indian*, v.18)

of Marx (1994), extends community embodiment and reconfigures a "politics of relationality" in public life (Simon 187).

In her study of family photographs, Marianne Hirsch introduces the concept of postmemory, a generational difference from history by deep personal connection (22). As visual evidence from past generations, personal connections are made on many levels that include knowledge of persons, geography, place or culture. The photographic aesthetics of postmemory is "a capacity to signal absence and loss and, at the same time to make present, rebuild, reconnect and bring back to life" (Hirsch 243). A politics of relationality not only implicates us in a past we did not live, but impacts us with the possibilities of life in relation to the living, the dead and the unborn. For Canadians, the history of the western frontier is particularly significant, because a majority of the settlers in western provinces do not have a fifty-year history within their region.

Calf Child, who appears in top hat and elaborately dressed in Pollard's Blackfoot Council photograph, also made a portrait with E. S. Curtis (Fig. 7). In Curtis's *The North American Indian*, Calf Child appears in an everyday western shirt with his hair braided in the same style as in Pollard's group portrait. His relaxed face expresses a half smile and the portrait, without exoticisation, is deeply nuanced. Calf Child uses the social occasion to express individuality and a performance of culture. Curtis's institutional context in *The North American Indian*, however, accords Calf Child a presence in the vanishing race narrative – which with its expiration date becomes another form of exoticisation, if not exclusion.

An act of self-definition always has another reference point in the narratives of both participants in the photographic encounter. In Curtis's portrait of Kyaiyi-stamik, ethnological detail is emphasized through the braided hair, the elaborate top knot and the ornamental shells and beads (Fig 8). The striking profile of the nose with the noticeably relaxed open mouth makes a particular statement in the portrait's use in *The North American Indian*, where a pictorialist aesthetic defines a nostalgia for "Glory Days." Jeff Thomas, an Iroqouian photographer and curator, brings an Indigenous perspective to the reading of Curtis's portrait, which is often seen without Curtis's descriptive caption or text:

> The Curtis portrait of Bear Bull was designed, through the use of profile and open space, to illustrate the top knot over his forehead. Curtis' brief caption provided the following information: "Illustrates an ancient Blackfoot method of arranging the hair." In Bear Bull's community the top knot was a signifier of his role as a spiritual healer, its origin reaching back into Aboriginal history. Bear Bull was also a cultural historian who Curtis used to describe the warrior society structure. Looking at his profile, the deep lines in his skin reveal a roadmap to that ancient society, a place of pride, dignity and au-

tonomy. Bear Bull's portrait should also be read along
with the social realities facing his community at the time.
Bear Bull was born in 1859 between the Battle River
and Saskatchewan River and this portrait was taken ca.
1900 when he was living on the Piegan Reserve, in the
soon-to-be established province of Alberta. His world
was disrupted, first by smallpox and fur and whisky traders; followed by government and railway survey teams;
then the loss of the buffalo herds, government treaty
delegations, the reserve system, settlers, farms and cities.
As a result, his family and community were torn apart
by government policies of assimilation and his children
forced to pass through the dark corridor of the residential school system. Museum field teams descended upon
Bear Bull's community to collect and preserve, in white
museums, the words and artifacts that were representative of his vanished world. (Hudson and Thomas)

Curtis's captioning of First Nations images in this early period
rarely commented on the political context or power dynamics in
which the photograph was created. Curtis's views followed an aesthetic of "the best of modern methods" and "transcriptions for future
generations" that avoided signs of civilization. Curtis describes his
project as follows:

While primarily a photographer, I do not see or think
photographically; hence the story of Indian life will not
be told in microscopic detail, but rather will be presented
as a broad and luminous picture. And I hope that while
our extended observations among these brown people
have given no shallow insight into their life and thought,
neither the pictures nor the descriptive matter will be
found lacking in popular interest. (Curtis 1907: XV)

Though a power dynamic may not be overtly evident here, Curtis
sets up the fourth imaginary wall (as in theatre) by positioning the
camera at an ethically safe distance. Congruent with this lack of sensitivity to the nuances of cultural force, Curtis's work as a tribal history also never acknowledges the divide along the 49th parallel, for
example, or the existence of Indigenous nations, which he refers to as
tribes. Not once does he acknowledge the trauma of the residential
school, nor the hostile relations through the relocation of the peo-

Fig. 8. Kyaiyi-stamik (Bear Bull), a member of the Blackfoot Nation, Alberta, 1926. (Photographer: Edward S. Curtis. Photogravure. National Archives of Canada. C-019753)

ples to reservations, nor their starvation. The social relations of his production process are invisible, as are the apartheid relations which continued to exist between the Indigenous and the settler. Curtis does grant this concession: "As a body politic recognizing no individual ownership of lands, each Indian tribe naturally resented encroachment by another race, and found it impossible to relinquish without a struggle that which belonged to their people from time immemorial"

(Curtis 1907: XV). The removal of entire communities from their homelands to reservations, however, paradoxically created the later need for sites of cultural reproduction and reorganization where local language and customs could be practiced as inheritances.

In landscape photography both Pollard and Curtis, of course, presented local customs ubiquitously. Their views of the Blackfoot camp, for instance, reveal teepee placement. In subsequent years these teepee placements would be repeated by families. As expressions of the community's complex social structures and governing principles, these spatial structurings included implications of sovereignty.[1] Picture making with photographers like Curtis and Pollard thus provides continuous examples of co-operative and constructive engagement sustained through (and, perhaps, in spite of) early federal governments' efforts to contain Indigenous peoples in reservations.

However, as many of the Indigenous subjects were not the commissioning patrons of the photographer, the photographs' subsequent public use in a transforming world was certainly beyond the subjects' understanding. Curtis's subjects could not understand the uses of the subscription project, for instance, nor the accessibility of a complete digital collection on a Library of Congress website a hundred years later. Though both photographers bring into circulation different visions of nation, their photographs continue to reproduce the existing power relations of their original contexts of production, which are reiterated in later exhibitions.

As noted above, older visual records were class-based because a painter, photographer or scholar needed material resources and patronage to undertake a documentation project. These opportunities were not options for everyone and required entrepreneurial skills and financing, which, in turn, influenced the kinds of subjects documented and their aesthetic form or genre. Materials and equipment used by photographers and painters were particularly expensive if there were no buyers. Ironically, because of constraints that Curtis accepted, much of his photographic project erased the day-to-day and location-to-location differences that he wanted to record, so, as a genre, his work became something of a conventional framing and representation of an outsider looking in.

Curtis's pictorialism is an expression of the photo secession movement that included photographers Alfred Steiglitz, Edward Steichen and Gertrude Kasebier, who followed an aesthetics of impressionist painting. Pictorialism arose at the end of the nineteenth century as the first fully international group of advocates and practitioners of photographic art (Nordstrom and Wooters 33) in resistance to the amateur use of the Kodak camera. For Curtis, pictorialism fitted easily into a commercial context. In 1906 railroad magnate J.P. Morgan lent Curtis $15,000 per year interest free for five years to do the fieldwork to produce the twenty-volume *The North American Indian*. When in 1910 Curtis needed to renew the agreement for a $60,000 advance, his company restructured as The North American Indian, Incorporated, and was retained by the Morgan Company. The subscription system used to finance his The North American Indian fitted with a genre and a colonial rhetoric that positioned Curtis's subjects into a physically irretrievable past. But corporate endorsements in his day elevated Curtis's work in the public American memory, so his photography was exhibited widely in his lifetime.

In contrast to Curtis, Pollard never commercialised to any comparable scale the Blood and Blackfoot photographs of his early period. In later years, Harry Pollard diversified from portrait photography and travelled the country, recording all aspects of the development of Alberta from agriculture and mining to construction and scenery. He frequently used a photo essay approach to tell an entire realist story of agriculture, ranching and the people, with the intention of writing an illustrated history of southern Alberta.

The authority of any photograph asks us to consider its genesis, whether, for instance, it is a view by an anthropologist, tourist, artist, government official or amateur. Within the context of this discussion, photographs therefore invite the viewer to consider other aspects of interpretation relating to colonizing ideologies. Despite the limits and boundaries of any framing apparatus, another hierarchy of meaning co-exists with a separate agency: the other side of a double narrative which is the subject's presentation of self. By its resistance to colonial ideological forms, this narrative can be seen as an anarchic reorganization, similar to a rhizomatic hypertext. Framing a picture has two other intertwined impulses – to frame, but also to show what is beyond the framing convention in a shorthand. The body idioms of the photographer and his subject circulate oral story forms in the photographic encounter, which, like a hypertext, change meaning through different readings and their contexts. In Western visual art the human body has been a principal subject since the Renaissance and a central locus and metaphor for understanding and exploring political change. In representational practices, the body does not appear as itself, but as a mnemonic sign. Through the use of context, framing and style, an artist limits these metaphorical meanings of the body.

In retrieving traces of the past fixed in the document time of the photograph, a power is displayed in repetitions and resistances in the present. The photographic encounter has both a synchronic and diachronic narrative within a material history that references other interactions, and an intertextuality with other representational forms. A photographic portrait inherits the conventions of painterly study of character but still reinvents the form within a different set of conventions. A photograph's meaning is intrinsically tentative, oscillating in a hypertext between the intentions of the photographer and the subject, and then, finally its reader. In the frame, the social and actual lived relation between the photographer and the subject is taken for granted.

Nevertheless, the body becomes a performative site of personal and public memory. When we examine the bodily traces in the photograph, we may ask what these representations and resistances mean. In a time when Indigenous people were denied their religious and cultural practices and were forcefully located on reservations by federal governments, this "writing the body," with its boundary and surface, was a public performance defining an alterity of political and cultural significance. Today, the photograph as writerly text invites the reader to rewrite and reconstruct its meaning in an open system.

In archived photographs that are historically discontinuous, narrative making becomes a creative effort to reconcile breaks, contradictions and ruptures. When photographs are used as a "window," the breaks in the narrative become both instruments and objects of research. Curator Jeff Thomas notes that he uses presentation techniques as a symbolic challenge to traditional framing techniques and institutional authority, to create an openness to new "objects" for viewing and stories (Hudson and Thomas). In its developments in a Western milieu, photography's vision is historical and significant for understanding situations where cultural encounters have been unequal, as in gender and race relations, and in the conquest and oppression in an expansionist West. Native American leaders Red Cloud, Sitting Bull and Geronimo appropriated the photographic stage for their own purposes, using it to carry messages of peace. And in the lucrative commerce of early practitioners, Romantic Indian views stabilized and anesthetized public perceptions of relations that only a few years earlier had been hostile. In a time when Indigenous people were denied their religious and cultural practices, a "writing the body," with its boundary and surface, was a public performance that resisted certain readings of history and narrated more complex histories. A method of reading the image is to consider the tensions of the moment recorded and the long histories that bring the participants into the encounter in a local or global frame.

Pollard and Curtis both sensed a history and presence in a geography that was an inhabited place. But as a redefinition of a landscape genre, Pollard's photography especially offers a deconstructive power in a close reading of certain images where we experience an empathy between sitter and subject within a narrative of Pollard's life experiences. A decolonizing aesthetic also exists in Pollard's notes, with specific references to people by name, place and date, recognizable skylines, campsites and their spatial formations. The long exposures made demands on the subject, which also offered opportunities to express fears and desires in a physical performance of culture. Alterity figures into a form of public address where certain kinds of interactions tell people who they are and who they most certainly are not. And local community readings focus on recontextualizing the photographs in ways that teach historical and cultural knowledge. As a visual history of Alberta, Pollard's photography shows how First Nations lived in the nineteenth century, shortly after European contact, so they are valuable in educating younger generations about a past of disruptions, with their social consequences.

Note

1. In Canada, First Nations have sovereignty by virtue of original occupancy, which has never been relinquished by treaty agreements negotiated by international law. Osgoode Hall Law professor Kent McNeil outlines that Canadian law has two sources that impact on First Nations rights to self government: legislation like the Indian Act, and case-by-case court decisions: "in 1982 section 35 of the new Constitution Act recognized and affirmed the existing Aboriginal and treaty rights of the Aboriginal peoples of Canada. These rights are undefined in section 35, and so Canadian courts have taken on the task of defining them" (1).

Works Cited

Aldrich, Lanning, ed. *The Western Art of Charles M. Russell*. New York: Ballantine, 1975.

Barthes, Roland. *Mythologies*. Trans. Annette Lavers. New York: Hill and Wang, 1972.

Cronin, J. Keri. "Changing Perspectives: Photography and First Nations Identity." M.A. Thesis, Queen's University, Kingston, 2000.

Crosby, Marcia. "Construction of the Imaginary Indian." *Vancouver Anthology: The Institutional Politics of Art*. Ed. Stan Douglas. Vancouver: Or Gallery, 1991.

Curtis, E.S. *The North American Indian*. 20 vols. Cambridge Mass.: Cambridge UP, 1907. Also available online at <curtis.library. northwestern.edu>.

Derrida, Jacques. *Specters of Marx: The State of the Debt, the Work of Mourning, and the New International*. Trans. Peggy Kamuf. New York: Routledge, 1994.

Devereaux, Leslie. "Experience, Re-Presentation and Film. *Fields of Vision*. Ed. Leslie Devereaux and Roger Hillman. Berkeley: U of California P, 1995. 56-76.

Edwards, E. *Raw Histories: Photographs, Anthropology and Museums*. Oxford: Berg, 2001.

Fabian, Johannes. *Time and the Other: How Anthropology Makes Its Object*. New York: Columbia UP, 1983.

Firmstone, Joy. "Harry Pollard: Chief Little Picture Man." History 432 [University of Alberta]. Provincial Archives of Alberta, April 14, 1975.

Goffman, Erving. *The Presentation of Self in Everyday Life*. New York: Doubleday, 1959.

Harlan, Theresa. "Message Carriers: Native Photographic Messages." *Views: The Journal of Photography in New England* 13-14 (Winter 1993): 3-7.

Hirsch, Marianne. *Family Frames: Photography, Narrative and Postmemory*. Cambridge: Harvard UP, 1997.

hooks, bell. *Art on My Mind: Visual Politics*. New York: The New York Press, 1995.

Hudson, Anna and Jeff Thomas. "Edmund Morris: Speaking of First Nations." *On Aboriginal Representation in the Gallery*. Eds. Lynda Jessup and Shannon Bagg. Hull, Quebec: Canadian Museum of Civilization, 2001. 127-148.

Johnson, Tim. "Introduction: Gazes Forward from the Past." *Spirit Capture: Photographs From the National Museum Of the American Indian*. Ed. Tim Johnson. Washington: Smithsonian Institute Press, 1998.

Karp, Ivan and Steven D. Lavine, eds. *Exhibiting Cultures: The Poetics and Politics of Museum Display*. Washington: Smithsonian Institute Press, 1991.

Loft, Steven. *Transference, Tradition, Technology: Native New Media Exploring Visual & Digital Culture*. Walter Phillips Gallery Edition, Banff, 2005. 88-103.

McNeil, Kent. "What is the Inherent Right to Self-Government?" 3 October, 2006. Hul'qumi'num Treaty Group and National Centre for Governance, Governance Development Forum, Parksville, B.C. 9 July, 2008 <http://fngovernance.org/pdf/Hulquminum-SpeakingNotes.pdf>.

MacDougall, David. *Film, Ethnography, and the Senses: The Corporal Image*. Princeton: Princeton UP, 2006.

Nichols, Bill. *Blurred Boundaries: Questions of Meaning in Contemporary Culture*. Bloomington: Indiana UP, 1994.

Nordstrom, Alison and David Wooters. "Crafting the Art of the Photograph." *Truth Beauty: Pictorialism and the Photograph as Art, 1845 - 1945*. Ed. Thomas Padon. Vancouver: Douglas and McIntyre, 2008.

Poignant, R., with A. Poignant. *Encounter at Nagalarramba*. Canberra: National Library of Australia, 1996.

Pultz, John. *The Body and the Lens: Photography 1839 to the Present*. New York: Harry N. Abrams, 1995.

Rodger, Andrew. "Portrait Gallery: Sir John A. Macdonald." *The Archivist*. National Archives of Canada, 20.3 (1999): 109-110.

Silversides, Brock V. *The Face Pullers: Photographing Native Canadians 1871-1939*. Saskatoon: Fifth House, 1994.

Simon, Roger. "The Pedagogical Insistence of Public Memory." *Theorizing Historical Consciousness*. Ed. P. Seixas. Toronto: U of Toronto P, 2004. 183-201.

Sioui, Georges E. *For an Amerindian Autohistory*. Trans. Sheila Fischman. Montreal: McGill-Queen's UP, 1992.

Tagg, John. *The Burden of Representation: Essay on Photographies and Histories*. Amherst: U of Massachusetts P, 1988.

Ginny Ratsoy

Re-viewing the West: A Study of Newspaper Critics' Perceptions of Historical Drama in a Western Canadian Small City

History is our lost referential, that is to say our myth.

Jean Baudrillard (43)

In her essay "The Alarming/Boring Binary Logic of Reviewing English-Canadian Drama in Britain," Jen Harvie laments a tendency of British reviewers to read Canadian plays as realist. For example, Harvie notes that the British critics see the works of Judith Thompson "as direct representations of an unpalatable Canada" to the extent that one critic, on the strength of his reading of her famous work *Lion in the Streets*, advised readers against moving to Canada (132-133). This reading is particularly striking given that Thompson's work is widely perceived in academic circles as being, as Harvie states, "an argument for understanding reality not as objectively accessible, but as only ever subjectively produced" (132).

I cite Harvie's complaint for three reasons. First, it illustrates an extreme but not rare perspective on reading dramatic performance: as a somehow unmediated re-creation of an event, a person, or, in the case of Harvie's example, a place. In addition, it illustrates the sometimes considerable gap between journalistic reception and academic reception. Finally, it concerns itself with something that scholarly writing on Canadian drama rarely considers: newspaper reviews. For instance, in a collection of eighteen articles in a book entitled *Performing National Identities* and, significantly, subtitled *International Perspectives on Contemporary Canadian Theatre*, Harvie's essay is the only one solely devoted to a study of newspaper reviews of Canadian plays.

Like Harvie's work, the few other articles that have examined journalistic reception of Canadian plays have tended toward the evaluative. James Noonan's "The Critics Criticized: An Analysis of Reviews of James Reaney's *The Donnellys* on National Tour," dating back to 1977, for example, is highly prescriptive. The single issue of *Canadian Theatre Review*, published in the winter of 1988, to its credit, includes articles from a variety of perspectives written by academics and newspaper journalists; it also, however, leans to the evaluative – and to the perspectives of Ontario-based reviewers.

The seminal academic text devoted to an examination of journalistic criticism of theatre in Canada wasn't published until 1999. *Establishing Our Boundaries: English-Canadian Theatre Critics* is a series of essays edited by Anton Wagner, most of which, as Michael McKinnie notes in a review essay, tend to privilege notions of the "singularities of the historical subject and historical action" (218). Almost every article's title includes the name of the critic on whom the article centres: for instance, Robert Nunn's "Theatre – Transgressions or Tribal Celebration? Ray Conlogue at the *Globe and Mail, 1978-1998.*" Necessarily with this approach, a fair bit of biography is included: the critic's upbringing, education, previous employment experience, and sometimes surveys of political and philosophical views. This approach generalizes about the individual critic's development: "Becoming Actively Creative" or "The Critic as Cultural Nationalist," for example. As McKinnie notes, the essays largely adhere to a "more traditional model of historiography – the descriptive survey – and to a traditional understanding of artistic practice: an Arnoldian evaluation of the 'touchstones' of aesthetic development" (218). While it is a thought-provoking, astute piece, McKinnie's review does not address something that is significant to my purposes: *Establishing Our Boundaries: English-Canadian Theatre Critics* is structured around larger centres and the mainstream of criticism.[1] In fact, almost every article has a large city and a major newspaper in its title.

I suggest a paradigm shift is in order in a discussion of newspaper theatre criticism in the small city, particularly because my paper participates in the CURA small cities project, specifically on the role of professional theatre in a community.[2] Kamloops is a city of approximately 85,000 people in the British Columbia Interior. A four-hour drive from the nearest major centre, Vancouver, it is home to only one professional company, Western Canada Theatre, which had its genesis in a high school drama class of the late 1960s and is part of the regional theatre movement that began in Canada in the late 1950s. Rather than description to the end of critique, and rather than examination of an individual critic's response over a sustained period of time, this chapter, while not effacing the reviewer, focuses on an *analytical* examination of selected pieces of newspaper criticism of a series of plays.

Moving the focus of scholarly examination beyond critique and description/biography not only better suits my purposes, but also is more reflective of the conditions of small-city newspapers and communities. Small-city newspaper reviewers almost without exception have more than one beat; typically they are also critics, reporters on and reviewers of almost all artistic endeavours, and sometimes more. In a recent interview, veteran *Kamloops News* arts reporter Mike Youds, comparing the role of reviewing in small cities and larger centres, indicated further considerations are at play:

> We tend to adopt a critical perspective that considers not
> only our readership but the context of the production
> within the community. In other words, even in the case
> of a professional company such as WCT, there is a great
> deal of community effort and a lot of tax dollars invested
> in the institution .... There is a much greater familiarity
> between audience and company that any critical exami-
> nation of work might take into account. Also, the field
> is much smaller. The scope of arts and entertainment is
> much more limited, so there naturally tends to be greater
> attention paid to, and public appreciation for, what is
> available.

I would argue, therefore, that the specific qualities of small-city reviewing call for a collective, rather than a personality-driven, investigation.

I will concentrate specifically on two questions: whether the reviewers evince an understanding of and appreciation for theatre as something beyond direct representation, and what connections the reviewers make between performative Kamloops and the contemporary newspaper reader/theatregoer. That is, do the reviewers consider artistic purposes as paramount to attempts at recreation of reality, and how do the reviewers perceive the relationship between the theatre-going community and the work of performing art?

In addition, I will give some consideration to the question of whether there is an academic-journalistic divide. The scholarly work published on plays with a Kamloops origin is small at this point,[3] so I will use a somewhat broader base of comparison: articles written about theatre in British Columbia. In my introduction to *Theatre in British Columbia*, a collection of eighteen essays published in 2006, I observe that the writers of those articles construct British Columbia drama as "self-consciously outside of the norm" and "embrace, indeed revel in" that difference (xxii). Does a similar construction reveal itself in local newspaper reviews?

My purpose is emphatically not to judge: my concern is not with what a critic should be, with inventing an impossible standard to which the small-city critic (who, like her large-city counterpart, is publicist/reporter/reviewer/critic/educator—and more, all under deadline) should conform. The question of what a theatre reviewer *should* do is beyond the parameters of this paper, although I will pay some attention to what these particular critics *do* in fact do, in regard to those roles. An examination of the response to five plays produced by Western Canada Theatre over a period of more than two decades is an approach that allows for an analysis of the critical reviews of several reporters, primarily at two newspapers, and of plays under the artistic helms of two artistic producers. I have selected the plays which would seem to be the most likely to engage CURA research purposes; that is, because they have apparently direct connections to the small city of Kamloops, BC (by originating from the city and/or by having strong local content) rather than having first been created and produced and being *about* elsewhere, they would seem to be most likely to engage questions of community. Each play was created with the input of members of the general Kamloops community or WCT personnel or commissioned by the company.

Timestep, conceived and directed in 1983 by Vancouver playwright Campbell Smith when WCT was under the directorship of Michael Dobbin, is based on extensive interviews with senior citizens and children in Vancouver and Kamloops, whose narratives were scripted and staged in the manner of story theatre, which has actors enacting the reminiscences of their characters. The dialogue presents a selective social history of Canada in the early twentieth century. Expressionistic, the play relies on an accumulation of impressions rather than a conventional plot.

Boris Karloff Slept Here, a 1985 collective creation spearheaded by David Ross, who assumed the directorship the previous season, is a musical based on Kamloops history from 1840-1915. The eleven writers and performers, including Ross and such well-known Vancouver performers as Margo Kane and Meredith Bain Woodward, relied for their material on conventional local history books as well as extensive interviews with local Aboriginal elders, storytellers, and educators. The play begins with an important story in Shuswap culture and in large measure functions as a humorous but incisive critique of colonization, foregrounding the unequal power balance between the European colonizers and both the Shuswap people and non-white settlers. It employs episodic vignettes characteristic of revues.

The biographical comedy *Flyin'Phil*, a two-actor play about Phil Gaglardi, the colourful, controversial and eccentric Social Credit MLA and BC Minister of Highways, preacher and Kamloops mayor was produced in 1992. Written by Ian Weir and former WCT publicist Judi Bryson, *Flyin' Phil* is directed by Ross – who also plays Gaglardi –and includes many of Gaglardi's own words, as well as a foil character who takes on numerous roles.

Western Canada Theatre commissioned the Weir-Bryson team to write *The McLean Boys*, which takes as its subjects four young mixed-race (Shuswap and European) men, Alex Hare and the three brothers Allan, Charlie and Archie McLean, and the events surrounding their 1879 killing of the town constable Johnny Ussher and a shepherd, James Kelly. Produced in 1996, the play also features a cast of shadowy, expressionistic non-Aboriginal characters, eschews chronology, and, while it does not valorize the quartet, can be read as undermining the conventional genre of the Western in both its content and structure.

WCT also commissioned renowned Cree playwright Tomson Highway to write the tragi-comic *Ernestine Shuswap Gets Her Trout*, which takes as its point of departure the Laurier Memorial, a 1910 petition from local Aboriginal chiefs to Prime Minister Wilfrid Laurier. Produced in 2004, the play features four fictional Aboriginal female characters, who, while preparing a feast for Laurier's arrival, enact the grievances outlined in the document, as well as reading aloud and critiquing various parts of it. In a graphic reminder that the grievances extend to the present, the actors present audience members with part of the written document as they leave the theatre.

Each play is in one way or another historical. What I found in an earlier study of novels and short stories set in the Kamloops area seems to hold true for playwrights as well: "Writers about Kamloops have a preoccupation with creating a past" (207). Even *Flyin' Phil*, written about a man who was alive at the time of writing, because it is biographical, necessarily delves into his personal and BC's history. These plays, in significantly varying ways, are also examples of documentary theatre: based on "real" events and people, they variously incorporate fragments of written (and, in at least two cases, oral) chronicles of the period in which they are set. Drawing on the practices of Piscator, Attillio Favorini furnishes an applicable definition of documentary drama: "Plays characterized by a central or exclusive event, on dialogue, song and/or visual materials (photographs, films pictorial documents) 'found' in the historical record or gathered by the playwright/researcher, and by a disposition to set individual behavior in an articulated political and/or social context" (xx). I shall return to Favorini's definition.

It is salient to my discussion to note further that the five plays, again in varying degrees, share with Canadian historical drama as a whole certain defining characteristics. The material conditions of Canadian theatre have generated an oppositional, non-representational approach to the treatment of history. As Ric Knowles states,

> Canadian drama has been shaped by the fact that it
> has tended to occupy alternative spaces and to play an
> alternative role culturally: for reasons of size and budget,
> its treatment of historical subjects has required nonil-
> lusionistic devices...moreover, its tendency under the
> circumstances has naturally been toward both politically
> alternative deconstructions of dominant national myths
> and meta-theatrical questionings of dominant dramatic
> forms that it views as oppressive or colonialist in impact.
> (123-4)

Furthermore, the five plays are relevant in their reflection, not only of an imagined small city community, but also of an imagined Western Canada. Specifically, they, and their historical context is most relevant here, are read as interrogating conventional notions of West, through their plots, depiction of characters, and, at least as significantly, through their structure.[4] Although five may seem to be a small sampling, I suggest a study of the reviews of the plays which I see as central in the development of the theatre company's history and sense of identity—largely *because* of their local inflection—is legitimate and can provide a foundation for an examination of questions of community. Of the eleven local reviews composed by professional reviewers, I would classify five as exclusively favourable to the play under discussion, five as largely positive (but expressing some reservations), and one as slightly more positive than negative. The fact that local reviewers tend toward the favourable is hardly surprising. Anton Wagner, cited earlier, has noted such a predilection country wide: "Writers on the theatre in Canada since the beginning of the eighteen hundreds have faced the necessity of fighting for the very survival of live theatre. This has often meant encouraging audiences to attend performances the theatre writers themselves knew to be of less than outstanding artistic merit" (18). Moreover, one of the eight objectives of the Canadian Theatre Critics Association (whose members include newspaper reviewers as well as academics and others) is "To encourage the awareness and development of Canadian theatre nationally and internationally through theatre criticism in the media." Along with the critic as reporter and the critic as educator, the critic as booster has a long history in Canada. Particular additional circumstances may influence the small-city reviewer: likely to have more than passing familiarity with personnel of the only professional company in town, and, by the time of experiencing the performance, likely to have written one or more pieces in anticipation of the play (features on specific actors and the like) she or he, consciously or unconsciously, may be predisposed to viewing the play through a sympathetic lens, particularly when that play is perceived as having substantial local connections. While maintaining that "the first obligation should be to the reader/subscriber," Youds indicates that local elements such as setting, creation, involvement, direction, and cast might have a particular influence on the small-city reviewer. He adds, "The cultural integrity and authenticity of the small city depend on the degree to which residents interact with the local, obviously, and this interaction cannot be taken for granted. It's an uphill battle against mass-media saturation and competing interests." Preserving the identity of a small city, then, is also a consideration of the critic.

However, the evaluative aspect is of interest to me only insofar as it relates to the analytical one. Rather, my interest lies in the fact that over one half of these favourable reviews perceive the play under examination as outside of the norm. Mick Maloney's review of *Timestep* in the *Kamloops Daily Sentinel* finds the piece as "well, an unusual play" and commends Dobbin for having "the courage to take a chance on a production which would be out of the norm." Maloney's sentiments are echoed by Sandra Albers' *Kamloops Daily News* reading of the work as "a play without a plot... rather daring theatre." Similarly, in his *Kamloops Sentinel* article "*Boris Karloff Slept Here* Will Surprise and Offend," John Morran observes that the play "tells little about the chronological history of Kamloops but a lot about the relationship between different cultures that met and frequently collided here." Sandra Albers reads that collective creation as a "moving mixture of factual truth and historical symbolism." In her review of *The McLean Boys* in *Kamloops This Week*, Jeanne Soodeen exhibits an understanding of and appreciation for the expressionistic devices of *The McLean Boys* through such descriptors as "extraordinary theatrical portrayal" and "fantastic story telling technique." Soodeen commends the play's use of a series of actors who take on various roles of establishment figures for "filling in the background and history, a useful technique in dispersing information, challenging the motivations of the McLeans and answering questions presented in the [main]intriguing plot." Alan Wishart's *Kamloops This Week* review of *Ernestine Shuswap Gets Her Trout*, entitled "The Birth of a Myth," declares,

> Usually, when you say someone doesn't let the facts get in the way of a good story, it's not a compliment. In this case, though, Tomson Highway has done an excellent job of taking an important moment in the history of the region and spinning from it a tale of mythic proportions .... Do not go to this play expecting to see an exercise in reality.

The widespread acknowledgement of the works as less than faithful in their adherence to the historical "facts" is revealing. The reviewers implicitly or explicitly recognize, even laud, the difficulty, impossibility, and even inadvisability of attempts to "re-enact" or "faithfully re-create" and, perhaps this is made most explicit in Morran's and Wishart's reviews, perceive a greater artistic *and community* purpose than attempts at re-enactment. Equally enlightening are their responses to the plays' dramatic structures. Although they do not define a norm from which these plays differ, the reviewers demonstrate an implicit understanding of the norm as what Ric Knowles describes as the "Aristotelian/oedipal/biblical narrative [that] has become the standard structural unconscious of dramatic naturalism in Canada as elsewhere" that inscribes "meanings and ideologies" that are fundamentally conservative and patriarchal"(31). In other words, the norm of dramatic structure is a narrative pattern that employs linear chronology, performs single, male experience, and reaffirms the status quo. In general, therefore, the reviewers construe the deviations from normative content and form as adding to rather than taking away from the enjoyment of the production. They are often, in fact, perceived as inherent to the play's appeal (rather than minor weaknesses the audience can overlook in an otherwise positive production) and tied to larger perceptions about community. Morran's "the relationship between different cultures that met and frequently collided here" and Wishart's "taking an important moment in the history of the region and spinning from it a tale of mythic proportions" are merely the most striking illustrations of this perception.

Only rarely does a reviewer perceive differences as negative. In an otherwise largely positive overview, Sandy Wiseman's reflections, therefore, stand out when she writes of *The McLean Boys*:

> Those familiar with the McLean story—might find WCTC's production doesn't flow exactly like you might anticipate. Throughout the first act I waited for the "murder scene" when the boys kill the police officer Johnny Ussher. It never came. As the second act started and still no dastardly deed, I started to lose interest. The pace picked up very nicely once the climax of the killing scene was reached about halfway through the second act.

If Wiseman believes the killing was the catalyst for subsequent events, she is perhaps confusing climax with point of attack. Either way, her objection raises the very good question of where the story does actually begin and end—a question, I suggest, that the play's non-linear form *deliberately* foregrounds

There is another notable exception to my generalization that the reviewers eschew an implicit or explicit adherence to the mimetic—their responses to *Flyin' Phil*. Again, the reviews are, on the whole, positive, as indicated by the titles of two of the three: "Flyin' Phil Soars at Sagebrush" and "WCTC's Flyin' Phil Soars." The third, in *Kamloops North Shore Today*, is less glowing, ending with this sentence: "Given a longer run to sort out a few glitches, it could soar." Much of their praise goes to Ross's acting; specifically, each reviewer devotes considerable space to assessing Ross's success at depicting Gaglardi realistically, mimetically, that is. Michele Young in the *Daily News* notes Ross's "voice, speech patterns and physical actions remarkably imitated those of the preacher/politician"; David Lennam in *Kamloops This Week* observes, "Ross has Phil down pat—the cadence of his voice, the stiff arms, the powerful gait and most importantly, the little hand gestures." It appears that when a historical figure of local prominence is still literally visible, details of "authenticity" assume a greater relevance than when the historical material is more dated. Further, as the reviewers themselves note, this is as much (or more) performative biography as performative history—and is thus, arguably, a somewhat different genre than the other plays under discussion. Perhaps an additional factor is at play here: *Flyin' Phil* is the closest of the works to "the Aristotelian/ oedipal /biblical narrative" as Knowles defines it.[5] Although *Flyin'Phil* deviates from the model to some extent, the play's form, it could be argued, encourages a more mimetic reading.

Even so, the reviews embrace the "non-reality" based aspects of

Flyin'Phil, which has a foil to Ross's Phil in the form of a single actor, Dolores Drake, who takes on twenty roles of various political and personal figures in Gaglardi's life. Michele Young's response to the non-representational aspect of the play is typical of the three local newspaper reviews. She suggests it is a dramatic device which her readers may find off-putting on paper but applauds the device and Drake's performance, evincing an understanding of the dramatic rationale for the rather over-the-top aspects of the play: "Subtle, the production is not. But then again, neither was Flyin' Phil." All three reviews recognize and applaud the play as a work with an emphasis on character and as a work of art rather than an attempt at historical re-enactment.

As modernist multiethnic scholar Benedict Anderson has famously noted, "All communities larger than primordial villages of face-to-face contact (and perhaps even these) are imagined. Communities are to be distinguished, not by their falsity/genuineness, but by the style in which they are imagined" (6). As they write to and of a Kamloops community, what community do the reviewers imagine? What discursive stance do the reviews adopt; that is, do they maintain the distanced, "objective" voice associated with newspaper reporting, or do they more actively engage with their audience? If the reviewers understand and appreciate the differences between attempts at historical veracity and artistic creation, what relevance do they see in these creations to the contemporary newspaper reader and theatre goer – to the part of the community they are addressing? Do they read the performances as entertaining, somewhat educational insights into a discrete, complete past, or as having relevance to the present, particularly to the small city community? In short, through their readings of the plays and their engagement with their readership, how do the critics imagine their community?

Reviews of *Timestep, Flyin' Phil,* and *The McLean Boys* take what I will refer to as a medial perspective. They make direct reference to audience, often in the form of advising readers in general of specific segments of readership to attend the performances, and sometimes address the audience directly. For the most part, however, they employ first and third-person reportage and focus on their perceptions of the play under consideration. There is a certain level of detachment, a "middle distance" if you will, between the "objective" reporting of, for example, a news article and a style that engages in a fuller discourse with readership. In addition, while reviewers of these three plays appreciate the works as unusual, well-made historical works that deliver interesting, relevant messages, they tend to frame those messages in the background of the past: what Kamloops and area once was.

Perhaps it is not surprising that the sense of audience is most present, most overt, in the reviews of *Boris Karloff Slept Here* and *Ernestine Shuswap Gets Her Trout*; these are, after all, the plays in which the "character" of the Kamloops area is most developed. In varying degrees, the other three plays are read as "character" works in more conventional ways: the histories of "ordinary people" in the first case, the history of a successful individual in the second case, and the history of a marginalized (in terms of ethnicity, age, and social class) quartet in the third case.

In terms of both closely discoursing with audience and seeing a present relevance in the plays, a closer stance is evident in the two plays that are more collective in focus. Both Morran and Albers use the first person plural in their discussions of *Boris Karloff Slept Here*. Morran states that the play "shows us history is made by imperfect people in an imperfect world" and Albers very directly engages her reader on at least two levels when she writes, "It makes us re-examine our own attitudes a century or so in time beyond the play's setting." Albers's observation, with the use of the collective "we," can be read as a recognition that the contemporary audience is receiving a lesson about the community's past that extends beyond the past – that the play's reading of the racism rampant in the colonial past of Kamloops is not absent in the "real life" of the contemporary reader/audience.

The reviews of *Ernestine Shuswap Gets Her Trout* evince the most fully formed sense that they are written to a specific group and the clearest indication that the play's relevance goes beyond its chronological time setting. As I also mentioned, Wishart emphasizes the communal significance of *Ernestine Shuswap Gets Her Trout*: the word "myth" or a variant is employed four times; in fact, even the new lobby in the Sagebrush theatre "is almost of mythological proportions." Further, he not only uses the word "audience"; he also, through a comparison of the effect of an early Greek myth on its audience with the effect of the play on its 2004 Kamloops counterpart, uses the first person plural: "Hey, we're in on the ground floor of a myth here."

Wishart's reading of the play as having monumental significance for a local audience is relevant for a number of additional reasons. I remind the reader that Tomson Highway's *Ernestine Shuswap Gets Her Trout* can be read as a highly complex deconstruction of Western notions of history and, to an even greater degree than *Boris Karloff Slept Here*, an indictment of past *and present* racism against First Nations people. In that sense, if it is an explanation of origins that is of great significance to the identity of a community (a common definition of mythology), it is a decidedly postcolonial conception of origins.[6] As Wishart acknowledges with his words, "Do not go to this play expecting to see an exercise in reality.... Each character, in her own way, embodies part of the spirit of the First Nations people of the region and each brings that spirit out," the play is in opposition to the "standard structural unconscious of dramatic naturalism in Canada" of which Knowles writes. It is also a play that, arguably, is hard to read as anything but an indictment of the project of colonization (31). However, by way of underscoring his "warning" to his readers that the play is not kitchen-sink realism, Wishart writes, "These four women are not your neighbours." This assertion could be read as undermining any sense that the myth has a life in the present in the way that, for example, Sandra Albers's reflection on *Boris Karloff Slept Here* does. While Wishart perceives an undeniable importance in the play to the local audience, he does not fully acknowledge that importance as having a life *in* the present; rather its significance is in origins, not in development.

Mike Youds's review, on the other hand, suggests that the four female characters are, in fact, the readers' neighbours. Whether or not the readers are cognizant of the fact is another matter. It is perhaps the most reflective, subtle, and focused on audience of all the reviews I examined. Youds begins with an epigram from the Laurier Memorial: "We condemn the whole policy of the BC government towards the Indian tribes of this country as utterly unjust, shameful, and blundering in every way." The review proper begins with the words "Kamloops audiences" and includes a significant reflection on the deep and ongoing connections of the historical play to the present community and a speculation about the present community's response to the play. Youds devotes considerable space to a discussion of how the play is both unfamiliar and familiar: the geography is familiar, but, Youds posits, the play is unlikely to be familiar to most audience members beyond that. Highway, he writes, "takes audiences on a remarkable journey through time to a place, a people, a language and an existence that seems foreign, only it is not. In fact it could not be closer to home." He concludes by quoting the company's brochure slogan for 2003-4: "More than any other WCT play this season, this one delivers on the promise to 'see the world from the edge of your seat'" and adds a proviso: "In this case, though, the world you see is another dimension of the place you inhabit." I suggest Youds is indicating cultural differences, even a substantially unbridged cultural gap, between most readers and audience members and the First Nation characters, content, and form of the play. He is evincing an acute, if understated, recognition of the vast complexities of the shared space: the geography is shared, but the potential audience is worlds apart metaphorically from the culture. He suggests the majority of the audience is unlikely to connect itself, or at least its present, to the play about the community. According to communitarian theorist Derek Phillips, sociologists define "community" as having two major aspects: "One, the territorial, conceives of community in terms of locale, physical territory, geographical continuity, and the like. The other, the relational, conceives of community in terms of the quality of human relationships and associations" (12). Youds conjectures that much of his audience will grasp only the former.

In addition, implicit in Youds's words is the recognition that the play presents an Aboriginal notion of time that is more complex than linear, Western concepts of time. He indicates that the play's relevance is more than historical: the existence seems foreign but it could not be closer to home – in place *and* time. Note his use of the present tense: "the world you see is another dimension of the place you inhabit." To an even deeper extent than those I have looked at previously, Youds's review of *Ernestine Shuswap Gets Her Trout* demonstrates a recognition of Knowles's contention that "dramaturgical form... and structure" are "forums for the social negotiation of cultural values" for "the production of meaning" (15). Youds, in fact, adapts an aspect of the play's dramaturgical form to his reading of it.

Reflecting upon his review several years after the fact, in a recent conversation Youds indicated his sensitivity to both the play itself and its context within the community from which it emanated: "One of my gut responses to *Ernestine* was that it could be misinterpreted as historical fact, especially with the direct references to the Laurier Memorial, Kamloops, and an actual historical event. It is important for the audience to understand that this is storytelling in the mythical tradition, relating to but not dwelling on historical facts."

I have interspersed throughout this paper several possible explanations for what I read as a closer engagement of the reviewers with *Boris Karloff Slept Here* and *Ernestine Shuswap Gets Her Trout.* I would like to return to Favorini to formalize and synthesize that discussion. Drawing again on Piscator, Favorini has developed "a continuum of reality-driven representations" that is useful to that purpose:

Historical Drama	*Documentary Drama*
integration propaganda	dialectical propaganda
(re-shaping behaviour for stable	(demystifying a
social setting)	complex situation)
author/ity	authentic/ity
individual	collective
metaphorical	metonymic
character	event
theatricalized history	historicized theater (xx)

We might productively conjoin Knowles and Favorini here: the "Aristotelian model" as Knowles perceives it would seem to have much in common with the characteristics Favorini assigns to historical drama. As indicated earlier, each of the five plays resists the Aristotelian/historical drama model *in varying degrees.* On a continuum, *Flyin' Phil* does so least, *The McLean Boys* somewhat more so, and *Timestep* to a somewhat greater degree again. Closest to full documentary theatre are *Boris Karloff Slept Here* and *Ernestine Shuswap Gets Her Trout.* To more fully incorporate Knowles's concepts, the latter two plays are also closest to his vision of "transformational theatre" – works which "by virtue of their rejection of the inherited Aristotelian, modernist, and above all oedipal models" facilitate basic social change (80-81). While a quantitative measure of the social change affected by these plays is beyond the scope of this paper, my own analysis in the body of the paper would suggest that the reviewers themselves were most affected by the plays that come closest to unadulterated documentary drama, and most engaged with their readership when discussing them. With its opposition to notions of hierarchy and other conventions and focus on collectivity and event, historicized theatre most successfully evokes a sense of an imagined community. Somewhat paradoxically, that which least pretends to objectivity most elicits a sense of identification and community; that which calls attention to its invention sparks closer engagement.

In the case of his review of *Ernestine Shuswap Gets Her Trout,* Youds was conscious of feeling a particular connection to the play and a specific obligation to the reader. He reflects on that review:

> It was important to highlight the collaboration between
> native and non-native organizations [in the production
> of the play] especially considering that the play is based
> upon an historical injustice that many feel has never

been fairly or adequately addressed. Here, both the city
and the river serve as metaphors for possible reconcilia-
tion of Indigenous and non-Indigenous Canadians. This
can only come through communication. *Ernestine* speaks
to us on this level, but I'm not sure how many in the
audience understood its directness.

When reviewing plays with strong connections to their community of
readers, the small-city theatre reviewers/publicists/critics/reporters
are inclined to respond affirmatively, are cognizant of the shifting
parameters of history and biography, and, above all, are aware of the
constructed nature of theatre. Artistic and communitarian purposes
take precedence in their reading of locally set, historically focused
work. They place substantial emphasis on relevance to contemporary, local audience and construct their readership and the theatre's
audience as heterogeneous. They construct the local community
as geographically encompassing the larger area, sharing a physical
space, and holding a wide set of values and aesthetic preferences, at
the same time as they imagine that community as sharing enough in
common to derive from the plays aesthetic pleasure, historical edifica-
tion, and perhaps personal and political meanings resonant to their
contemporary situations. These reviewers perceive community not as
a monolithic, fixed entity with identical tastes and perceptions, but
as a heterogeneous collection with which they, in varying degrees,
converse.

Furthermore, the discrepancy Jen Harvie notes between academic
and British newspaper writers' readings of Judith Thompson's plays
is not paralleled in my studies of Kamloops reviewers of local plays
and academic critics of plays about British Columbia. What I wrote
in 2006 about the latter in my introduction to *Theatre in British Columbia*, whose articles examine BC theatre from the 1970s to the present,
applies to the former. Both the reviewers and the scholars read the
works as "resisting or acting in isolation from the mainstream." They
are "celebratory of off-centredness and complexity," they show "a
keen recognition of and appreciation for the incorporation of myriad
structures into dramatic work," and they acknowledge "the artificiali-
ty and slipperiness of boundaries ... among various theatrical conventions, styles, and movements"(xxii). It appears that in the extreme west
–British Columbia–at least, there is congruence between academic
and journalistic criticism: both realms appreciate, indeed, revel in,
perceptions of difference. Both groups construct home-grown drama
as creatively reflecting historically distinctive, even eccentric, notions
of West–and are at home with that depiction.

Notes

1. A notable exception is Chapter Ten, by Mayte Gómez, "Oscar Ryan at the *Canadian Tribune,* 1955-1988. Although as a Communist publication, the *Canadian Tribune* fell outside of the mainstream, its place of publication was Toronto.
2. The Small Cities CURA, Mapping Quality of Life and Culture CURA Research Program, funded by the Social Sciences and Humanities Research Council of Canada, maps quality of life and the culture of small cities in British Columbia. Twenty-six TRU researchers work with 37 community research partners and numerous community partners, as well as collaborating with several universities across Canada.
3. See Hoffman, James. "Political Theatre in a Small City: The Staging of the Laurier Memorial in Kamloops" and Ratsoy, Ginny. "The Creation of Shifting Local Identities: Historically-Based Theatre in a Canadian Small City."
4. In this respect, the five works share a commonality not only with Canadian historical drama as a whole, but also with non-performative Western Canadian literature which, as Arnold Davidson assesses it, "serves to subvert the standard Western dialectics of power, the established relationships between the pioneer and the prairie, the cowboy and the Indian, the masculine and the feminine" (13).
5. It should be noted that, in the program for *Flyin' Phil,* the playwrights insist that they "had no interest in writing hagiography" and were not under any illusions about the play as "the Definitive Truth about Phil Gaglardi."
6. Interestingly, Wishart's reading of the play places it nicely in accord with the reading of Western Canadian *novels* by scholars such as Arnold Davidson, who asserts that "Contemporary mythic fiction ...gives us mythic portrayals of the need for myth, and the myth most needed is a mythic picture of the past .... Furthermore, the search for the missing myth is regularly mocked and parodied in the very works that also portray that same search as essential" (17).

Works Cited

Albers, Sandra. "It's a History Lesson That's Fun." *Kamloops News* 11 Mar. 1985.

Albers, Sandra. "'Timestep' for the Time of Your Life." *Kamloops News* 28 Feb. 1983.

Anderson, Benedict. *Imagined Communities.* London: Verso, 2006.

Baudrillard, Jean. *Simulacra and Simulation.* Ann Arbor: The U of Michigan P, 1994.

Canadian Theatre Critics Association. <www.canadiantheatrecritics.ca>.

Davidson, Arnold. *Coyote Country: Fictions of the Canadian West.* Durham and London: Duke UP, 1994.

Dowden, Barry. "Flyin' Phil a Little Larger Than Life." *Kamloops North Shore Today* 29 Jan. 1992.

Favorini, Attilio, ed. *Voicings: Ten Plays from the Documentary Theater.* Hopewell, NJ: Ecco Press, 1995.

Harvie, Jen. "The Alarming/Boring Binary Logic of Reviewing English-Canadian Drama in Britain."*Performing National Identities: International Perspectives on Contemporary Canadian Theatre.* Eds. Sherrill Grace and Albert-Reiner Glaap. Vancouver: Talonbooks, 2003. 130-144.

Hoffman, James. "Political Theatre in a Small City: The Staging of the Laurier Memorial in Kamloops." *The Small Cities Book: On the Cultural Future of Small Cities.* Ed. W.F. Garrett-Petts. Vancouver: New Star Books, 2005. 285-302.

Knowles, Ric. *The Theatre of Form and the Production of Meaning.* Toronto: ECW Press, 1999.

Lennam, David. "WCTC's Flyin' Phil Soars." *Kamloops This Week* 26 Jan. 1992.

Maloney, Mick. "*Timestep* is Kind of, Well, an Unusual Play." *Kamloops Daily Sentinel.* (nd) 1983.

McKinnie, Michael. "The Contradictions of Canadian Theatre Criticism." *Essays on Canadian Writing 70* (Spring 2000): 218-225.

Morran, John. "*Boris Karloff Slept Here* Will Surprise and Offend." *Kamloops Sentinel* 10 Mar. 1985.

Noonan, James. "The Critics Criticized: An Analysis of Reviews of James Reaney's *The Donnellys* on National Tour." *Canadian Theatre Review* 3:2 (Fall 1977): 174-182.

Phillips, Derek. *Looking Backward: A Critical Appraisal of Communitarian Thought.* Princeton, NJ: Princeton UP, 1993.

Ratsoy, Ginny. "Away from Home, or Finding Yourself Back in Kamloops: Literary Representations of the Small City." *The Small Cities Book: On the Cultural Future of Small Cities.* Ed. W.F. Garrett-Petts. Vancouver: New Star Books, 2005. 205-220.

__. "The Creation of Shifting Local Identities: Historically-Based Theatre in a Canadian Small City." *Signatures of the Past: Cultural Memory in Contmporary Anglophone North American Drama.* Eds. Marc Maufort and Caroline DeWagter. Brussels: P.I.E. Peter Lang, 2008.

Ratsoy, Ginny, ed. *Theatre in British Columbia.* Toronto: Playwrights Canada Press, 2006.

Soodeen, Jeanne. "McLeans Sighted at Local Establishment." *Kamloops This Week* 28 Jan. 1996.

Wagner, Anton, ed. *Establishing our Boundaries: English-Canadian Theatre Criticism.* Toronto: U of Toronto P, 1999.

Weir, Ian and Judi Bryson. "Playwrights' Notes." Western Canada Theatre Company's *Program Magazine* 1996.

Wiseman, Sandy. "'Archie' Best Part of New Play." *Kamloops Daily News* 27 Jan. 1996.

Wishart, Alan. "The Birth of a Myth." *Kamloops This Week* 25 Jan. 2004.

Youds, Mike. "Highway's *Ernestine* Dishes Out Big Banquet of Food for Thought." *Kamloops Daily News* 24 Jan. 2004.

__. Personal Interview. July 15, 2008.

Young, Michelle. "Flyin' Phil Soars at Sagebrush." *Kamloops Daily News* 24 Jan. 1992.

James Hoffman

Community Engagement and Professional Theatre in the Small City in British Columbia

Promotional material is revealing. On the cover of the recent brochure announcing Western Canada Theatre's 2008/2009 season of plays, a dramatic image of a blackened sky envelops a city below—a city whose bright expanse casts dim flashes of light onto a low, roiling horizon. As the city glimmers like a beckoning oasis in the night, a person, whose back only can be seen, sits close by, Buddha-like, as though on a hilltop, watching both the distant city and, above it, a spectacular image of the moon whose rays burst through a patch of ghostly clouds. Near the top, set firmly against the blackest sky, the title of the season's plays is announced in large, white, lower-case letters, "right before your eyes ...," while, lower down, the theatre company's name and logo are spread radiantly across the moon, taking on its luminous glow. All in all, this is quite a striking scene: I can imagine that the person watching it is truly experiencing an overwhelming, transcendent moment.

The image neatly sums up the topic—and many of the questions—of this article. Professional theatre companies, I can assume, want very much just what this image portrays: a local audience member wholly occupied in watching a spectacular performance by the city's professional theatre company. The show is brilliant, embracing in its compass all of nature as well as the sparkling city at its centre. In this marvellous epiphany of universal and local conjunction, what could be more meaningful? But wait. Who is this audience member? I don't know because this person exists only in shadowy outline. And what city is this? Again, I don't know: there are no geographic or other markers. In fact, as I learn, it is nowhere in particular: the image of the city is taken from stock photos, as is the solitary figure and the wondrous night sky. So, I ask, with such an absence of local signifiers, what then do these images really convey? Clearly, while this picture is a powerful fantasy of professional theatre companies, at the same time it also represents several compelling issues that I believe these companies need to address.

In brief, despite the image and its longing for an ideal moment of performance, there is an uncertain relationship between the theatre company and its community. I can, for example, further question the anonymity of the brochure's cover. Not only are the audience member and the city given no local context, but also the season's title, and therefore its implied theme, "right before your eyes…," makes little particular commitment to anything beyond that of generalized entertainment and "making magic" (from a WCT letter to subscribers, April 18, 2008). The initial suggestion of a local inflection, a turning towards the city, instead turns into a tangible distancing; similarly, I notice, this undifferentiated approach is repeated in the list comprising the upcoming season of plays. Of the ten plays listed, five on the main stage at the large Sagebrush Theatre and five at the smaller, black box Pavilion theatre, just one could be classified as local in terms of subject matter: only the Saucy Fops production, newly written by a Kamloops playwright, will possibly have any direct resonance to life in the Kamloops community.

So, while it must be pointed out that Western Canada Theatre is doing many things extremely well—it is one of British Columbia's most successfully managed theatre companies, operating well in the black and permanently employing seven (in the summer) to twenty-five (in the winter) persons, not counting actors—it nonetheless faces specific challenges as it, like other professional companies in small cities in British Columbia, attempts to better understand its identity and mission in its community. This is especially important as the companies variously face not only financial, personnel, and venue issues, but also matters of direction. Working primarily as professional entertainment institutions has sustained but also limited them to this point in time; they must now begin to question their mandate and their role in rapidly changing communities, especially as for several, there is the prospect of working under new artistic directors. To begin this inquiry, let us look at what I am calling their secretive existence.

If there were an award for "best kept theatre secret" in British Columbia, it might well go to three very active professional companies that have contributed so much in their small cities: Western Canada Theatre in Kamloops, Theatre North West in Prince George, and TheatreOne in Nanaimo. These companies have been presenting annual seasons of generally well attended plays and musicals for a combined total of almost eighty years; a good number of the plays have been premieres and some have narrated local stories—such as the recent *Ernestine Shuswap Gets Her Trout* in Kamloops (2004) and

Being Frank in Nanaimo (2007). *Ernestine* tells the story of First Nations women engaged in preparations for a feast honouring the visit of Prime Minister Wilfrid Laurier to Kamloops in 1910, while *Being Frank* recounts episodes in the life of Nanaimo's colourful mayor, Frank Ney. In addition, the companies sponsor regular community events such as film festivals, children's theatre, wine tastings, auctions, touring shows, and the like. These activities, combined with ongoing resident personnel and control or ownership of performance venues, generate annual budgets sometimes reaching over a million dollars, as well as involvement with other cultural and civic organizations. By most indicators of community success, all of this appears very positive.

In addition, the companies function in seemingly ideal communities. Not only do they escape some of the possible negatives of the big city, such as high costs and competition from other professional theatre companies, but they work in what are perceived to be friendly, comprehensible locales, cities close to their rural and regional antecedents, with a strong sense of community. In discussing small cities, Lucy Lippard tells us they are "warm, manageable places where it is easier to become involved in civic and political dialogue" (60), while, closer to home, Lon Dubinsky notes the "vital cultural life" and "culture of participation" (66) characteristic of Kamloops.

There is also the distinct advantage of working in an environment where the professional theatre company can have a comparatively strong impact. David Ross, former artistic producer of Western Canada Theatre, now retired, is proud that his company can attract up to ten per cent of the population of Kamloops to one of his shows, a feat unthinkable for a professional company in Vancouver. Since all three companies function as the single professional theatre in their cities, they enjoy a certain empowerment by automatically setting the standards for stage performance in their cities and, for the most part, remaining critically untouchable. When, for example, arts critics review their shows the critics knowingly engage in a double act, that of providing both critical and supportive consideration of the company. What this means, with few exceptions, is that local theatre criticism consists of a summing up of plotlines and characters, along with a suggestion whether attendance is or is not recommended. Usually it is, because to recommend against can seem anti-community. If, for example, reviewers criticize too harshly they risk alienating their readership, many of whom will be regular or season subscribers and who, of course, have little other choice in what professional live theatre they attend; worse, if they seriously turn away audiences, they risk shutting down the city's only professional theatre. No critic would want that dubious accomplishment on his or her shoulders. Then again, critical boosterism is inherent in the small city as the critic normally measures a show under review only against other shows by the same company.

These professional cultural groups are increasingly seen as important players in the civic scene. Western Canada Theatre, long a member of the Kamloops Chamber of Commerce, recently initiated a discussion leading to the Chamber's advocacy for increased federal government arts funding for the Canada Council, funding that would ultimately benefit professional cultural groups in Kamloops; as reported in the Kamloops *Daily News*, it was a resolution made "to ensure our community has a good quality of life" (July 4, 2007, A5). As for the small cities themselves, they are increasingly taking leadership in cultural development: Kamloops' Cultural Strategic Plan, adopted in 2003, begins its preamble with the following:

> The Kamloops Cultural Strategic Plan lays out a blueprint for cultural development for Kamloops for the next decade. It is a comprehensive strategy which is based on the recognition of the diversity of the cultural sector in Kamloops, from small to large, amateur to professional and representing every conceivable genre from the visual arts, to heritage, the performing arts and the cultural industries. The strategy is rooted in the belief of the community-building capacity of the cultural sector and looks at how the sector can continue to contribute to the quality of life of Kamloops residents. (5)

Finally, the companies operate in a province that is comparatively favourable to the arts. Hill Strategies, a Canadian company that researches the arts, reports that in 2005 "21% of the population 15 and older attended a theatrical performance such as drama, musical theatre, dinner theatre or comedy (740,000 B.C. residents)" ("Provincial Profiles" 11), which is similar to the overall Canadian attendance figure. Since this province has several very prominent and active performance companies for young people, such as Vancouver's Green Thumb Theatre, which annually mounts extensive school tours that entertain "more than 125,000 children" (Green Thumb website) I can assume the figure of 21% is considerably enlarged. And people spend generously on culture. According to Hill, British Columbians spend the second highest amount on cultural goods and services in the country, $886, against the Canadian per capita average of $821 ("Consumer Spending," 14). Hill Strategies also reports that "BC residents spent 39% more on live performing arts ($160 million) than on live sports events ($110 million) in 2005... [and]... BC residents spending on cultural goods and services grew by 45% between 1997 and 2005" (14). More specifically, the per capita figure for consumer spending on art works and events, including live performing events, was $95 in 2005, the second highest in Canada, the national average being $88 (11). Because of these things, I might expect these three professional theatre companies to be flourishing arts organizations as well as highly engaged, contributory presences in their communities, deeply aware of their important role in the development and re-creation of their small cities.

Yet the companies operate somewhat in secret: their work is barely noticed. The activities of the companies on and off stage attract little exceptional notice beyond the usual promotional and occasional review articles in local newspapers. Nationally, they are rarely discussed in the critical literature; provincially, they are ignored: the annual BC theatre awards, the Jessies, for example, are given only to Vancouver professional companies. Even when a special effort to connect to a wider public is made, there is only perfunctory notice. Both plays named previously, *Ernestine Shuswap Gets Her Trout* and *Being Frank*, which should have garnered extraordinary attention because of their historical, regional relevance, and, in the case of *Ernestine*, the presence of a nationally-renowned playwright, Tomson Highway, failed to become the significant events of their promise, despite their being robust productions and being strongly promoted. No Vancouver or Toronto critics came to Kamloops to review *Ernestine Shuswap Gets Her Trout*; in Nanaimo, there was not even a local review of *Being Frank*, written by G. Kim Blank.

So while it is clear that all three companies have done impressive and valuable work, at the same time there is a troubling detachment from their communities. While it seems natural that these professional theatre companies are positioned to play a central role in the life of their communities, they remain, whether by choice or circumstance, somewhat peripheral to the central activities and concerns of the small cities they inhabit. For example, while the small cities are becoming increasingly interested in the diversity of their populations, the companies appear monocultural, adhering to a model that caters more to an exclusive demographic. While there is increasing energy in these cities to promote local heritage and culture, the companies continue to present images and narratives mainly of the outside, not dissimilar to that of their professional colleagues in the big cities.

Despite the small city location, their audience demographic seems typical to that of larger centres. Citing a Baumol and Bowern study of theatre audiences in Britain and the United States, Susan Bennett notes "that the audience came from a very narrow segment of the national population: 'In the main, it consists of persons who are extraordinarily well educated, whose incomes are very high, who are predominantly in the professions, and who are in their late youth or early middle age'" (94). This seems borne out locally, David Ross reporting that his typical audience member is "a woman, probably a school teacher, between thirty-nine and forty-three years of age, and she lives in Sahali…" (Interview, May 21, 2003). In his recent study of audiences, Richard Butsch reminds us that "dominant representations of audiences in the nineteenth and twentieth centuries were bourgeois…[tending] to equate good audiences with the middle and upper classes, Euro-Americans and males; bad audiences typically were identified with the working and lower classes, women and subordinate races" (4).

Perhaps most tellingly, there exists an uncertain mandate in the companies. The rhetoric of claims by artistic directors and statements in promotional materials often hint of a high level of community engagement, that their work goes beyond mere entertainment to include other functions of performance. TheatreOne's website talks about "enhancing the quality of life in Nanaimo by encouraging social interaction and developing Nanaimo's culture and its economy" (Website). Western Canada Theatre's mission statement promises to go considerably beyond entertainment, saying the company will "entertain, educate, enrich, and interact with the cultural mosaic of its Community" (website). Yet evidence of these suggestions of deep community engagement seems lacking. There seems little correlation between the current ethos of their communities and the focus of the theatre companies. Why is this? Could it be something in their historic structure, something in their generic condition, that acts as a hindrance to community engagement?

I am suggesting that we need to rethink the professional theatre in a small city, to ask a few questions about its identity and essential activity. The present generic classification, if I can offer one, seems to impose a set of standards and perceptions somewhat out of step with the community. For example, these organizations are understood primarily as "Professional Theatre Companies," which means initially that many of the key personnel will be members of professional unions or associations that represent their collective interests, such as Canadian Actors Equity Association (CAEA) and the Professional Association of Canadian Theatres (PACT). Although acknowledging, through the contractual Canadian Theatre Agreement (CTA), that "theatre makes an essential contribution to Canadian life on every level, cultural, social and economic" (2), groups such as the CAEA exist primarily to support the working conditions of its members. Canadian Actors' Equity has been criticized, by director and playwright Sky Gilbert, for stifling the work of smaller, artist-run companies, which often consist of equity and non-actors, the kind of people who tend to write and direct their own works, perhaps in a highly innovative manner, often with local community intonations. Adopting the market-driven model of American theatre can present difficulties in supporting a Canadian system that includes wider use of arms-length subvention. The Association has continued, despite opposition from several directors of small Canadian theatre companies, to lend its considerable support wholly to its own members, that is, to what it deems "professional" actors, directors, and stage managers, while at the same time denigrating non-members as "unprofessional" (Gilbert 17). Another critic finds that the CTA, while admirably attempting to be sufficiently inclusive "to capture diverse practices" in staging theatre in Canada, nonetheless adopts a "common-practice model that is not consistent with the current state of the Canadian theatre landscape," adding that "most producers view [the Canadian Theatre Agreement] as an encumbrance rather than an aid to their organizations" (Habel 13). I assume, then, that these organizations can act as somewhat of a restraint on the professional theatre companies in our study: what policy and bureaucratic curbs might they present, for example, should a company wish to radically alter its operation strategies?

Being professional means that these small city theatre companies participate in a certain funding arrangement common across Canada, by which, through various programs of direct and indirect government subsidy they are somewhat protected from the realities of the marketplace. The reasons for this financial intervention can be surmised as the companies' preservation of high art forms, with the consequent status this brings to the small city, their supposed potential to assert national and regional character, their assumed educational importance, as well as the financial benefits they bring to the community. It is estimated that about forty per cent of a company's funding comes from these grants. On the negative side, these companies spend an inordinate amount of time making grant applications. In doing so, they are susceptible to the fluctuating goals of national and provincial granting agencies and therefore must represent themselves favourably to the granting agencies, but not necessarily to their immediate community. I question to what degree this exercise assists or, as I suspect, compromises community-minded goals, especially when the various agencies might have conflicting criteria.

As professional, these companies are automatically tied to the theatre lineage of the big city, where operational and critical standards are set. Most practitioners, actors, designers and directors are for the most part big-city trained and experienced; most critics who write about the theatre also gain their insights and values from what they see in the big city. The prevailing attitude is that significant theatrical events occur in the big city: the small city simply benefits from what happens in the metropolitan centre. In a typical season, most plays are drawn from a canon of hits from big cities. Indeed, the much-favoured season of plays adopted by all three companies is derived from a big city, Chicago. Critic Mark Czarnicki suggests that this has been detrimental to the development of local drama (39). The subscription series, in which an entire season of plays is pre-sold to the public, usually with early signing discounts, is essentially an economic hedge in which losses are reduced for less successful plays while hits enjoy full houses. This model, taken initially from opera, has been criticized as encouraging a conservative season. Czarnecki has noted that locking each play into a fixed and limited time slot, "[denies] the opportunity to support and applaud a successful cultural endeavour…[it] curtails a community's potential to take pride in and enjoy its own work" (39).

With critic Alan Filewod, I have noted (2003) that Canada's professional theatre is inextricably linked in its origins to a colonizing mentality. The history of theatre in British Columbia reflects that its professional theatre was founded on principles barely acknowledging local community; in fact, according to theatre historians, its major focus was on importing the theatrical other. This was carried out in such a wholesale manner that even many of the province's theatre historians failed to assess the situation critically—where even a word such as "indigenous" is given an oddly non-home-grown denotation. In discussing the founding of what Chad Evans calls "indigenous" professional theatre in British Columbia, his seminal book *Frontier Theatre* describes his purpose as being "to evoke all forms of European and American theatre" (9). Similarly, while finding a "wealth of amateur and professional activity and the building of many theatres" (101), historian Andrew Parkin nonetheless concludes "Indigenous British Columbia theatre, as it exists now, is an offshoot of British and

American theatre, so far as they are distinguishable; it owes little or nothing to Chinese or Indian theatre" (102).

Clearly, both writers display a colonial attitude in their uncritical privileging of Euro-American culture and their erasure of truly indigenous performances. Other commentators, in categorizing and periodizing the province's performance activities, have paid "obsessive attention to firsts, to biggests, and to bests" (Hoffman 7); in doing so they have risked "reinstalling the very Euro-colonial tropes of exploration (hardship stories of early touring companies), discovery (naming first theatre groups, first shows), and conquest (building theatres, staging successful shows) that have thus far dominated theatre history and criticism in the province" (8). One might well ask: how much has this mindset changed in the theatrical practices of the early twenty-first century? And more pointedly, do the particular activities in several small cities show evidence of a postcolonial theatre?

As with much theatre in British Columbia, these local companies were formed in the ambivalent milieu of a postcolonial culture in which the theatre struggled to shed its colonial past. Significantly, each company, in its fairly short history, ranging from only fourteen years (Theatre North West) in Prince George, to twenty-four (TheatreOne) in Nanaimo, and thirty-three (Western Canada Theatre) in Kamloops, in a moment of neo-colonizing, whether by outright statement or simply by its production choices, identified its early mission as bringing the cultural other into the community by importing specific personnel and vision. The Nanaimo company, for example, was originally called Shakespeare Plus. Founded in 1984, it opened with a staging of *Romeo and Juliet*, under the artistic direction of Leon Pownall, an actor and director who had worked for eight seasons at the Shakespeare Festival in Stratford, Ontario. The company's purpose was "to bring professional theatre to the people of Nanaimo and the surrounding area with a focus on the works of William Shakespeare" (company website). For four summers, as a Shakespeare play was performed alongside a contemporary hit and a Canadian play, it became obvious that the Bard was not working for Nanaimo—but Canadian, and especially British Columbia plays were, especially Rod Langley's Dunsmuir plays, which narrated local history. Clearly a counter-discursive canon seemed more in keeping with community needs.

It should be remembered too that modern professional theatre in Canada participates in a form of cultural colonialism inherited from its formation in the mid-twentieth century. Founded in the late 1940s, the federal Massey Commission certainly reflected a colonial mindset: that Canada's theatre was of little significance and that a true the-

atre, indeed a much desired national theatre, must come from outside
the community; that the great tradition of world theatre, expressed in
the great dramas of all time, from Aeschylus to Shakespeare, was by-
passing Canada, a situation that could only be remedied by a system
of benevolent patronage. According to the Commission report: "this
great heritage is largely unknown to the people of Canada for whom
the theatre, where it maintains a precarious existence, is restricted to
sporadic visits in four or five cities by companies from beyond our
borders ("Massey" 176). Not only was the international canon unknown to Canada's citizens, but the report slighted what local theatre
did exist: "the professional theatre is moribund in Canada, and amateur companies are grievously handicapped" (177).

Thus was installed a federal system of support by which certain
professional theatre companies would operate as extensions of a national theatre – and indeed of the nation itself. This resulted in the
regional theatre system in which a number of landmark companies
in key population centres would become theatre centres: each would
carry out a variety of tasks, such as staging a central, canonical season of plays, touring some shows throughout the region, operating a
theatre training school, and running a "second" company of actors
who would present more recent and often edgier dramatic material
for younger, hipper audiences. In doing so, as when Vancouver's Playhouse Theatre Company (its present name) was grandly calling itself
in the 1970s "the Playhouse Theatre Centre of British Columbia,"
and Christopher Newton, one of its major directors, was declaring it
"a kind of 'national theatre' of B.C." (Page 48), the companies appropriated many of the extant theatrical activities in their communities
and beyond, one result being the diminution of the status of existing
theatre groups. Sonja Kuftinec reports that "Community theatre has
an image problem," in which "the difference between good (regional,
professional) and bad (community, amateur)…exemplifies a prevailing critical distinction" (23).

Similar to the other two companies, TheatreOne appropriated the
theatrical culture of its communities. It should be remembered that
there was no performance vacuum before the three companies were
established: each city had a flourishing pre-professional performance
culture largely consisting of amateur theatre groups (often there were
several), with a reach well into and beyond their communities, the latter typically demonstrated by participation in the regional, provincial,
and national drama festivals organized under the Dominion Drama
Festival. The existing companies, while tied to a conservative theatrical tradition, especially in their choice of the dramatic canon based

on established North American hits, nonetheless had strong connection to community in their ongoing use of local personnel and their appeal as a home-grown performing art.

Thus even as they were being founded, the regional companies were already constructed along certain lines and would make considerable demands. They would require a hefty chunk of available local funding and other material resources, they would need to occupy major performance and rehearsal venues, they would bring in their own acting and production personnel from outside the community, they would insist upon "professional" operational standards and skills, their manner of operation would be hierarchical and authoritarian, and their production methods would be text-based and focussed on the individual artist creator as sole authority. They would also have a common production strategy seemingly designed for a limited audience, and few would yield many defining narratives of their community. In short, they arrived in the city to impose (from without) rather than generate a cultural program (from within).

With these features, perhaps because of them, their purpose seemed primarily to offer entertainment. But there were other goals: performance scholar Richard Schechner lists six other functions. While he notes that "many performances emphasize more than one" (46), especially ritual events, he also notes that commercial theatre performances have the fewest: "A Broadway musical will entertain, but little else" (46). In their promotions, the small cities companies sometimes hint at functions such as "to make or foster community," or "to teach, persuade, or convince," (46) but come short of actual commitment to local issues or goals. Thus, while there is gesture to community, there is also a tentative nature to their work, especially since much of their emphasis resides in presenting narratives and issues from elsewhere.

A form of cultural neo-colonization therefore exists, even as each company functions more and more in rapidly changing communities that see culture as having an expanded role in their development. There is, for example, sudden interest from civic authorities: new opportunities seem to exist, as, for example, in the *Kamloops Cultural Strategic Plan*, which calls for "[supporting] the growth and development of our arts and heritage sector as a vital part of our community's economic, educational and social fabric" (Janzen 9). But how well are the companies equipped to respond? What is the future direction for these companies? Of course I am raising a number of difficult questions, such as the problem of making theatrical work significant culturally, perhaps even politically, in effecting genuine cultural/social change. It must be remembered that colonial powers maintained their hegemony by inscribing their own narratives, and that an essential task for cultural groups in a postcolonial territory like British Columbia is that of "examining and challenging those narratives, developing other ways of telling histories, and re-evaluating other ways of remembering" (Featherstone 167).

So where does this leave the professional theatre company in a small city? While attempting not to be overly prescriptive, I can posit several thoughts for consideration. The obvious direction for them is towards a more active participation in the cultural life of the community, where culture is understood not so much solely as art-based but as inclusive of the wider character and heritage of the community. The theatre companies then would need to re-think themselves as community performers and their audiences as more than mere consumers: their task would be to work in community development and to utilize their arsenal of theatrical skills and resources to be more responsive than they have been to historical and current cultural/social conditions. They would see their artistic personnel as public performers and collaborators, so that, for example, rather than preparing in isolation before presenting to their community, under the present model, they would find ways to perform within and for the community, the process becoming as important as the product. Critics Adams and Goldbard, specifically interested in community cultural development, note that the UN Declaration of Human Rights asserts that "Everyone has the right freely to participate in the cultural life of the community" (19). In this way, Adams and Goldbard point out, "Cultural action frequently serves as a form of preparation for social change" (21). Looking at theatre history, both past and present, provides many examples.

In *Bowling Alone*, his seminal study of the collapse of community life in America, Robert Putnam suggests a way to rebuild social capital, and therefore a healthy community life: "I challenge America's artists, the leaders and funders of our cultural institutions, as well as ordinary Americans: Let us find ways to ensure that by 2010 significantly more Americans will participate in...cultural activities from group dancing to songfests to community theatre to rap festivals. Let us discover new ways to use the arts as a vehicle for convening diverse groups of fellow citizens" (411). As an example of this in practice, he cites the work of Roadside Theater Company, which, founded in 1975, has derived its style and its content from the Appalachian culture in which it is based. The company uses storytelling, oral history, music, even mountain church forms to create and narrate plays based on the small towns and the farming and mining communities in which most members live. As Putnam notes, they "celebrate their traditions and restore community confidence through dramatization of local stories and music" (412).

The movement towards a true community theatre has been called many things—community-based theatre, theatre for development, popular theatre, social theatre, applied theatre, grassroots theatre, engaged theatre (see Kuppers 3; Leonard 3-9)—and its practitioners have been labelled "community artists" (in Anglophone countries), community animateurs (in francophone countries), but their goal has been the same: to locate their work more centrally within the actual life of their communities; in other words, to facilitate a genuinely community-based theatre. Examples of this are not hard to find; indeed, the initiative can be traced in North America to the early years of the twentieth century, when grassroots and folk theatre groups focused on geographic localities. The so-called Pageant Movement "was hospitable to such contemporary issues as urban expansion, the immigrant experience, regional culture, mass education," and "such pageants influenced the daily life of the community to work toward agricultural progress [and] appreciation of local history" (BF 279). At the same time, the Little Theatre Movement, in its idealistic beginnings in the US, believed that theatre could "explore social issues" and "improve American society" (Chansky 4). It is important to remember that while mainstream professional theatres such as those of Broadway or the West End are better known, there have also long existed alternate modes of theatrical production working at grass-roots activities in many communities across their countries. The existence of such groups, plus the increasing literature on their activities and rationales, is more and more mounting a challenge to the conventional practices of professional companies.

In his recent book, *Community Theatre, Global Perspectives*, Eugene van Erven calls this a "worldwide phenomenon...united...by its emphasis on local and /or personal stories (rather than pre-written scripts) that are first processed through improvisation and then collectively shaped into theatre" (2). This can be accomplished with the collaboration of professionals especially skilled in this manner of creation. The most notable example of this in British Columbia is the production of "Not the Way I Heard It...," a collaborative community play staged in Enderby in 1999. The program notes begin by locating the origins of the show: "The stories we share with you tonight are part of our combined communities' oral traditions" (2). Using the Colway style, which began in Britain in the 1980s, six specially trained professionals worked with diverse community (and neighbouring) groups to co-author and stage a script addressing local historical moments and myths. Following the Colway method, community members participated at every stage of the production, from providing input on the development of the script to finally performing the play. The result was a large, outdoor performance in a field next to the Shuswap River, using many actors (over 150), a host of technicians and crew (over 300), puppets, masks, dance, music, songs (nine original), a marching band, hundreds of specially built props, horses, wagons, stilt walkers, a pickup truck, all vividly and colourfully illuminating the area's oral history. The final work, reports Edward Little, "served to affirm common ground: the historical and contemporary challenges of isolation in small communities, concern for the environment, the deeply held appreciation of the area's natural beauty, respect for the spiritual connection of the Shuswap people to the salmon..." (57).

A range of other examples can be found across and beyond this country—one scholar estimates there to be "more than 50, but less than 100 professional grassroots theatres across the U.S." (Leonard 10). In Canada, Rising Tide Theatre of Newfoundland for over a decade now has animated the history and the economy of the small town of Trinity by presenting *The New Founde Lande Trinity Pageant*. On the other coast, in a more socially focussed manner, Vancouver's Headlines Theatre and its self-described group of "politically active artists" continues its mandate to stage "issue-oriented theatre" (Headlines website) focussed on specific communities, with plays such as *Out of the Silence* (about abuse in an Aboriginal family), *Meth* (meth addiction), and *NO XYA* (First Nations land settlement in northeast British Columbia). In their outreach to community, especially the last, groups such as these demonstrate "a commitment to audiences of every class and race [that] is contrary to mainstream theatre audience composition of the wealthiest 15% of the population" (Leonard 14).

Over the last few decades, a number of other Canadian theatre companies have been formed with a strong regional focus. In Nova Scotia, Guysborough County's Mulgrave Road Theatre, since its founding in 1977, has an impressive record of creating plays that recount the narratives of Atlantic Canadians, while Eastern Front Theatre, based in Dartmouth, similarly emphasizes the staging of new Atlantic Canadian plays. The Eastern Front also sponsors the annual SuperNova Theatre Festival, an eleven-day, cross-disciplinary series of performances, many about life in Nova Scotia, including at least one major premiere and several works specifically designed to encourage active community participation: an all-ages "Last One Standing" break dance competition and a ten-minute play writing contest for high school students. In Ontario, the Blyth Festival continues its long, impressive record of creating plays that "give voice to both the region and the country" (company website).

In Australia the so-called Verbatim performance, an intense form of documentary theatre, employs the use of interviews gathered from participants in a real life situation, as occurred after a Workers' Club in Newcastle was destroyed by an earthquake (see Makeham). In Britain, Reminiscence Theatre is a similar community-based movement wherein theatre practitioners record the memories of local persons who were involved in a narrative event, then use their actual words from recorded transcripts in the presentation of their public plays (see Schweitzer). This memory work represents a particular validation of community: "the very act of remembering, and the attention given to the specific person, can be empowering ... and it is in the connection between the banal or everyday and the 'elevated' realm of art as transformation that the power of community practice can reside" (Kuppers 146). Similar work has been performed by the Vancouver company Theatre Replacement in their recent performances of Bioboxes.

These are but a few of the possibilities open to a rethinking of the relationship between professional theatre in small cities in British Columbia and their "communitas." Certainly there are serious questions regarding theatre's role in the community: who should create theatre and why, how it should and shouldn't be made, the effects it should have beyond artistic ones, and the community's role in its creation. Of course there are many, many approaches in the literature and, admittedly, change may be difficult and slow in coming, but I believe that these professional theatre companies, located as they are in small cities in British Columbia, are well positioned to become more connected and vital players in the life of their communities. To do so, they must rethink their identity. One thing is certain: each must find its own way, keeping in mind the words of community artist and professor, Petra Kuppers, who has written, "Every community performance practitioner has to define for her- or himself what 'changing the world' means, what 'connection' means, and what 'community' means for them" (8).

James Hoffman

Works Cited

Adams, Don, and Arlene Goldbard. *Creative Community, The Art of Cultural Development.* New York: Rockefeller Foundation, 2001.

Bennett, Susan. *Theatre Audiences: A Theory of Production and Reception.* London: Routledge, 1990.

BF, rev. of *American Pageantry: A Movement for Art and Democracy.* UMI Research P, 1990. *The Journal of Aesthetics and Art Criticism* 49:3 (Summer 1991): 279.

Butsch, Richard. *The Citizen Audience: Crowds, Publics, and Individuals.* New York: Routledge, 2008.

Canadian Actors' Equity Association and the Professional Association of Canadian Theatres. *Canadian Theatre Agreement.* <http://www.fia-actors.com/uploads/CTA2003-2006.pdf>

Chansky, Dorothy. *Composing Ourselves: The Little Theatre Movement and the American Audience.* Carbondale: Southern Illinois UP, 2004.

Cohen-Cruz, Jan. *Local Acts: Community-Based Performance in the United States.* New Brunswick, NJ: Rutgers UP, 2005.

Czarnecki, Mark. "The Regional Theatre System." *Contemporary Canadian Theatre: New World Visions.* Ed. Anton Wagner. Toronto: Simon & Pierre, 1985.

Dubinsky, Lon. "The Culture of Participation." *The Small Cities Book: On the Cultural Future of Small Cities.* Ed. W.F. Garrett-Petts. Vancouver: New Star, 2005. 65-84.

Erven, Eugene van. *Community Theatre, Global Perspectives.* London: Routledge, 2001.

Evans, Chad. *Frontier Theatre, A History of Nineteenth-Century Theatrical Entertainment in the Canadian Far West and Alaska.* Victoria: Sono Nis P, 1983.

Featherstone, Simon. *Postcolonial Cultures.* Edinburgh: Edinburgh UP, 2005.

Filewod, Alan. *Performing Canada: The Nation Enacted in the Imagined Theatre.* Monograph in *Textual Studies in Canada* 15. Kamloops: U College of the Cariboo, 2002.

Gilbert, Sky. "Canadian Actors' Equity: Recognize What is 'Canadian' about Theatre Practice in This Country." *Canadian Theatre*

Review 123 (Summer 2005): 15-18.

Habel, Ivan. "Implementing Agreements." *Canadian Theatre Review* 123 (Summer 2005): 11-14.

Hill Strategies. "Consumer Spending on Culture in Canada, the Provinces and 15 Metropolitan Areas in 2005." *Statistical Insights on the Arts* 5.3 (Feb. 2007).

__. "Provincial Profiles of Cultural and Heritage Activities in 2005." *Statistical Insights on the Arts* 6.1-2 (Oct. 2007).

Hoffman, James. "Shedding the Colonial Past: Rethinking British Columbia Theatre." *BC Studies* 137 (Spring 2003): 5-45.

Janzen & Associates. *Kamloops Cultural Strategic Plan*. Kamloops: 2003.

Kuftinec, Sonja. *Staging America: Cornerstone and Community-Based Theater*. Carbondale: Southern Illinois UP, 2003.

Kuppers, Petra. *Community Performance: An Introduction*. London: Routledge, 2007.

Leonard, Robert H. and Ann Kilkelly. *Performing Communities: Grassroots Ensemble Theaters Deeply Rooted in Eight U.S. Communities*. Oakland, CA: New Village P, 2006.

Lippard, Lucy R. *The Lure of the Local: Senses of Place in a Multicentered Society*. New York: New Press, 1997.

Little, Edward. "Cultural Democracy in the Enderby and District Community Play." *Canadian Theatre Review* 101 (Winter 2000): 56-58.

Makeham, Paul. "Community Stories: 'Aftershocks' and verbatim theatre." Kelly, Veronica, ed. *Our Australian Theatre in the 1990s*. Monograph #7, Australian Playwrights. Amsterdam: Rodopi, 1998. 168-181.

"Massey Commision, The." *Canadian Theatre History, Selected Readings*. Ed. Don Rubin. Toronto: Copp Clark, 1996.

"Not the Way I Heard It..." By Cathy Stubington, James Fagan Tait, and Rosalind Williams. Programme. Enderby, British Columbia. 18 May 1999.

Page, Malcolm. "Change in Vancouver Theatre, 1963-80." *Theatre History in Canada* 2:1 (Spring 1981): 40-58.

Parkin, Andrew. "The New Frontier: Towards an Indigenous The-atre in British Columbia." *Theatrical Touring and Founding in North America*. Ed. L.W. Conolly. Westport, CT: Greenwood P, 1982.

Putnam, Robert D. *Bowling Alone: The Collapse and Revival of American Community*. New York: Simon & Schuster, 2000.

Ross, David. Personal interview. 21 May 2003.

Schechner, Richard. *Performance Studies, An Introduction*. 2nd ed. New York: Routledge, 2006.

Schweitzer, Pam. *Reminiscence Theatre: Making Theatre from Memories*. London: Jessica Kingsley Publishers, 2007.

Van Erven, Eugene. *Community Theatre: Global Perspectives*. London: Routledge, 2001.

Mervyn Nicholson

Babes in the Woods: Exotic Americans in British Columbia Films

"**L**otusland." That's what they call British Columbia – or the Coast part of it anyway – "the place where the bums don't freeze in the winter," as Al Purdy put it. Purdy was referring to Vancouver, not the British Columbia interior, which certainly does freeze bums in the winter. And, to be honest, Vancouver can be plenty freezing: it is not Hawaii, whatever Vancouverites may say. Vancouver is a more like Anchorage than it is like Honolulu. Nonetheless, the West Coast is a kind of *Canadian* Hawaii, the sort of Hawaii that would correspond to Canada, a Canadian version of paradise – in other words, there would, of course, be winter – there would have to be – but it would be a nice winter: with rain rather than snow, with temperatures above freezing rather than below it (and further below), and there would be lots of great trees and flowers and sublime scenery. Gardening would be good there. A modest sort of paradise, without any extravagant display of tropic excess, but still, a paradise. The very term "Lotusland" is interesting here. It refers to a paradisal island in Homer's *Odyssey*, where the sailors nearly sink into a life of irresponsible sensuality, encouraged by eating a plant ("lotos") that makes people forget ambition and just take it easy. Leisure, sensuality, and happiness are the order of the day. A definite moral disapproval can be detected, however, about the feeling that in Lotusland laziness is OK, the grasshopper thrives as much as the ant, and the productive and responsible Little Red Hen had better just move back to Toronto.[1] British Columbia is not really like this, but people still hope.

For Canada, there is something exotic, something magnetic, about British Columbia, especially the Coast, but also the Interior. The Okanagan Valley, for instance, has long had paradisal overtones. The saga of the Saskatchewan farmer who sells his land and retires to the Okanagan, with its fruit trees and heavenly clear lake, is well established in folk culture. Thus, in the Canadian context, British Columbia acquires what is termed a "pastoral myth." A "pastoral myth" is a vision of simplified life in the country: the main activities are making music and making love, alternately. The lovemaking gets great musical accompaniment, and music, adapting Shakespeare's phrase, feeds love. Every culture seems to have pastoral mythology. In western culture, the most influential example is the paradisal Garden of Eden, supplemented by Greek and Roman visions of an Age of Gold before there was history. British Columbia even has the appropriate association with gold: it is after all the fabled "gold mountain" as the Chinese once called it. In fact gold has huge political-historical significance. In particular, the great gold rush of the 1850s, drawing thousands from California (it had its gold rush a few years earlier), was instrumental in formalizing British control of what is to this day called *British* Columbia.

Pastoral myth [2] is by definition the fulfillment of desire, and love and music are only part of it. Desire finds satisfaction rather than frustration. In the pastoral myth, the scenery is fantastic, the food, typically fruit, is abundant and delicious, humans and animals live in harmony with each other, and people are good, basically: innocent, in short. There are problems, but they are nice problems, like the quarrels and embarrassments of young love. Spontaneity and impulse are essential to the pastoral myth, which prizes freedom. In the spirit of pastoral, the Bill Miner of Philip Borsos' movie *The Grey Fox* proclaims to his sister, "I'm just no good at work that was planned by other heads." Pastoral myth is about freedom; it eschews coercion and conformity; it prizes individuality. Everyone seems to have a pastoral myth, even if it only achieves reality in a summer camping trip or a cottage by the lake. Precisely such a vision meets us in the opening shot of Sandy Wilson's movie *My American Cousin*, a spellbinding vista of lake and trees and mountain. A "pastoral myth" is just that, a myth, something that isn't true, isn't real. But the word "myth" means something else besides untruth; it means literally story or narrative, not "untruth." In this sense, "British Columbia" becomes a *story*, something to visualize and think about, and not an actual place. As such it is a part of the Canadian imaginary, as it might be called: the psychological and imaginative Canada – not the geographical location but the one that maps emotion and expectation and personal experience. British Columbia becomes an event to enact, rather than simply a location. In this context, it is, like utopia itself, a place in the mind, whatever it is in reality. It is this mythic British Columbia, not just an actual socio-historical place, that is found in the British Columbia of Philip Borsos and Sandy Wilson.

Thus British Columbia has an "image," and this image is of a natural paradise, an image that has had a powerful influence on the way the province is viewed elsewhere in Canada. British Columbia does not, however, seem to have the same pastoral associations for Americans. The province, from an American point of view, is a northern extension of the cold, wet Pacific North West, ultimately the panhandle of Alaska. The Pacific North West has never had the appeal in the United States that its Canadian equivalent, British Columbia, has in Canada. A film that had, I would argue, significant influence, in terms of style and pacing, on Borsos' *The Grey Fox* is Robert Altman's 1968 *McCabe and Mrs. Miller*. This film was shot in British Columbia (mainly in West Vancouver), though the story is actually set in the United States, but closer to its northern border than is usual in American movies. The producer of *McCabe and Mrs. Miller*, David Foster, commented on the misery of having to endure "a brutal Vancouver winter" when making the film: hardly a way that Canadians would describe winter in Vancouver—wet and depressing, perhaps, but "brutal?" I don't think so.[3] Americans are typically unaware of Canada, often associating it simply with cold weather, as a kind of vast blank at the top of the weather map. British Columbia does not have the pastoral associations for Americans that it has for Canadians. But no wonder: Americans have a much more grandiose pastoral mythology. Pastoral myth is deeply embedded in American culture, from the earliest times, as if a new Eden could be found in America. The hunger for pastoral myth and the attempt to realize it are in fact obsessive, from Walt Whitman's *Leaves of Grass* to Jack Kerouac's *The Dharma Bums* and on to the 1960s, with its rebellious social and sexual energies, its "back to the land" and communal social experimentation. Such social energies have always been present in American culture, sometimes in conservative and fundamentalist forms.

To put it in the terminology Freud developed in his later writing, pastoral myth is the triumph of the pleasure principle over the reality principle. What we want trumps what is forced upon us. The pastoral myth is not only a nice place, it is also, more importantly, a *refuge*, a place to run away to. It is thus the place where you stop running, because you have found what you are seeking: freedom from the world's hostility. Pastoral is the place where difference is accepted, not hated; where there is room for everyone who is willing to get along. And British Columbia is curiously famous as a refuge. It is a refuge in the simple sense that it is the end of the line—there isn't anywhere else to go if you are heading west; and there isn't much left if you're heading north, from the United States, anyway. There is Alaska, but Alaska is still America, so if you are escaping the U.S., British Columbia is basically it. And Americans took this refuge seriously and literally and came to Canada during the Vietnam War, when thousands of draft resisters found a home in Canada. British Columbia was a favored destination. The era of the Vietnam War was also the era of the hippies and the social rebels, and they all wanted to go to British Columbia, and some of them did, and many stayed. This influx into British Columbia–this *finding* of British Columbia, so to speak–is the conditioning historical context of both B.C. film-makers Sandy Wilson and Philip Borsos. British Columbia becomes a place to pay attention to in their films.

As a place you go away *to*, it is not surprising that so much of the population of British Columbia are literally "from away," as Maritimers say; they are not natives of British Columbia, but have come here from somewhere else. It is a place you go to, and it's often not a place you go to in order to make money. That would be Alberta, which has very different symbolic overtones from B.C. Alberta is America North and only ambiguously Canada; again, it is not a place to escape to–Alberta is one of the places to escape *from*, Ian and Sylvia's *Four Strong Winds* song, with its "think I'll go out to Alberta" refrain, notwithstanding. You go to British Columbia for other reasons than making money. You go there to *live*, not to make a living. Often it is also a place *found*, so to speak, rather than sought out–some people drift here, simply by starting out at Steeles and Keele and pressing on the accelerator and seeing what happens. British Columbia is serendipitous, and what could be more consistent with the pastoral than serendipity? It is unnecessary to plan, because providence looks after you. That, at least, is the myth, the nature of pastoral.

Two important Canadian films draw upon this pastoral myth: Philip Borsos' *The Grey Fox* (1982) and Sandy Wilson's *My American Cousin* (1985), together with the sequel that Wilson made to *My American Cousin* released four years later in 1989 called *American Boyfriends* and set in the rebellious and wild 1960s[4]. The pastoral myth of *My American Cousin* is plain enough to see. It's the late 1950s, a decade that evokes a great deal of conservative.pastoral mythology, as the "Father Knows Best" decade of settled values and middle-class prosperity. The film opens as sublime scenery fills the screen–a panorama of lake and forest and peace and protection. It is also evening, the sign of things ending. Played by Margaret Langrick, the Sandy of the film is not quite thirteen years old, with an enclosing family of younger sisters and brother, an older brother, and strong parents with a prominent role in the action. The film closes with a voiceover by Sandy: the ranch was boring and frustrating to her as a girl, but in retrospect, it was a paradise – a paradise soon lost. The scenery is so magnificent that even Butch, the eponymous American cousin, notices it, and Butch has little room in his head for anything besides girls and fast cars. The name of Sandy's home is – surprise surprise – "Paradise Ranch." Even the making of the film had paradisal overtones, as Sandy Wilson remarked in recalling the production : "you couldn't have been in a more beautiful place. It was an exquisite summer, just one of our dry, high beautiful blue sky summers. We're sitting out overlooking Lake Okanagan and shooting a movie. I mean, It was just heaven" (qtd. in Gasher 81). Indeed, Wilson "shot much of the movie in the place where she grew up, Paradise Ranch" (Gasher 81).

The pastoral myth typically emphasizes animals as well as children, and this motif is conspicuous in *The Grey Fox*, as the title implies. The motif of animals is especially important in the form of horses. Horses are themselves nostalgic; they belong to a vanishing culture supplanted by the industrial age of mechanization. In a key scene, a train is pitted against horses, so as to recall Alex Colville's famous painting *Horse and Train* (1954), in which a horse gallops on the train track as a dark locomotive approaches.[5] There are no animals in *My American Cousin*, apart from Sandy's songbird and the prominent song "There's a bluebird on my shoulder." But the film does show the standard pastoral motifs of children, fruit trees, play. In particular it emphasizes picking, canning, and even *wearing*, cherries. The cherry is the emblem of innocent love. In this film, we are conscious of delicious food, play, and children more than hard work and routine, though we are aware of those too. The choice of projecting the action from the point of view of a loved, protected, and basically happy adolescent girl gives the movie its particular tonality of pastoral myth.

Childhood is itself often visualized in terms of pastoral myth, as a time of safety, freedom, innocence, and preoccupation with play and spontaneity. It is unusual to see in a movie such an emphasis on children engaged in play as in *My American Cousin*. But *Cousin* is also about childhood's end. Hence even more conspicuous than children having innocent fun is the rock and roll music alternating with love-making. By love-making, I do not mean actual intercourse, but constant sexual stimulation, sexual curiosity, experimental kisses, flirtation – innocent sex. Thus as soon as she crosses his line of sight, Butch falls in love with Shirley. Shirley is, she candidly explains, a virgin who is "saving it" for when she gets married – and she is indeed already engaged. Her boyfriend soon plunges into jealous rages about the interfering Butch, the California blond beach boy with the big muscles and the big red

Cadillac, who is no good at picking cherries. "Go back where you came from," he shouts at Butch. But nothing too unpleasant comes from this jealousy. Some shoving and name-calling—that's about it. Sandy's father makes a timely intervention and stops the hostilities, enacting his father-knows-best role very convincingly. The interloper American withdraws, and, as we learn later, the sensible Shirley does indeed eventually marry the hard-working young man she is engaged to. If there is a problem with pastoral myth, it is that, as young Sandy complains, " nothing ever happens." Paradise, it appears, is boring. It is a paradise only when it is gone. We don't recognize it until it is too late. Or is it really that paradise feels too good to be really true?

The sense of being in a protected space is characteristic both of childhood and of pastoral myth. In *My American Cousin* this protected space is emphasized by the presence of the parents and by all the British references in the film, notably the flags −conspicuous also in *The Grey Fox*−reminding us what a British country Canada was, even in the 1950s. But the "mother" country is as transitory as the protective if annoying mother figure in *My American Cousin*, the mother with whom Sandy is seen leaving in the final shot of the film. The British connection, needless to say, is the reason why there is a British Columbia at all, why there is a border between the province and the state of Washington. The names of the two jurisdictions tell us as much as geographical names can, indeed a whole history. The figure of the English grandmother, irritatedly correcting Sandy's pronunciation, is funny, but also emphasizes that Canada was still under the tutelage of a parental power. Of course, this tutelary view of British influence is itself a pastoral myth, given the struggle of Canadian culture to get free of colonial domination and find a national expression. The British never cared much about Canada, anyway. Ironically, as critics have remarked, the film projects the transition from colonial domination by England to colonial domination by the United States.[6]

The Grey Fox, starring Richard Farnsworth and directed by Philip Borsos, would seem to be totally different from Wilson's *My American Cousin*. *The Grey Fox* begins in 1903 and is a fictionalized account of Bill Miner−Canada's train robber, and, therefore, an American. Canadians don't do that sort of thing, after all. Miner has profound connections with Kamloops, and the setting of the film is mainly Kamloops and area, though the movie was not shot there (some scenes were shot on Douglas Lake Ranch , which is near to Kamloops). Miner had been jailed in San Quentin in the 1860s for robbing stagecoaches. After release from jail, he took up train-robbing. He eluded pursuit by escaping to British Columbia, Canada being the place where Americans never voluntarily go, and therefore an excellent hiding place. Canada, the invisible country, proves congenial to the foxy Miner; he robs a CPR train, and then finds refuge in Kamloops.[7]

He is almost in his 60s–old age for a man in 1903. But, improbably, he finds love here. In the movie, that is. He meets a brilliant female photographer and feminist, Kate Flynn, played with consummate charm and beauty by Jackie Burroughs. The film emphasizes their lovemaking, this time the real thing. Again, we get what a pastoral myth requires, delicious food (including a happy picnic), music and dancing. Music is emphasized–music that ranges from grand opera to Bill Miner singing in the bathtub. And then there is sublime, sublime scenery. As Allan Blaine puts it, in a fine essay on *The Grey Fox*, the "visual treatment of the B.C. interior may further support a general sensation of the region as heaven on earth"(129).[8] The pacing of *The Grey Fox* allows the full power of the incomparable scenery of British Columbia to be on display and to have its full effect.[9] Pastoral myth has always had an honoured place for the figure of the noble criminal–think Robin Hood, think Zorro. An "innocent criminal" is an oxymoron, but this paradoxical figure of the innocent criminal is essential to the mythology of pastoral. Butch in *My American Cousin* is also an innocent criminal. He has, after all, run away with his mother's Cadillac, not to mention having committed fornication. But that is the point: his crimes are innocent crimes.

The fact that a criminal can be innocent suggests a deeper aspect to pastoral mythology, namely a satiric impulse. Pastoral, unreal as it is, has always furnished a critique of the power relations in society, from Virgil's Eclogues through Swift's rational horses to Aldous Huxley's *Island*. Billy Miner in Borsos' film, portrayed by the handsome and sweet-voiced Richard Farnsworth, is clearly an innocent criminal. In one scene, Miner, acting on a spontaneous impulse, gives an orange to a young boy. An orange in 1903 was a spectacular gift to give a child; a child would definitely remember that stranger's generosity. Almost the last thing that happens in the film is that the same little boy reappears–and presents an orange to the now handcuffed Billy Miner as he is hustled on to the train heading for prison, having been caught after a final botched train robbery. The prominence of the child (and the exotic fruit) is indicator of the deep-level innocence of "the grey fox" himself, and marks the film's affinity with pastoral myth. In returning the fruit to the man who gave it to him earlier, the child affirms the essential goodness and innocence of the man, and proclaims the harmony between people, whatever their age or circumstances, that is characteristic of pastoral myth.

This exit scene is remarkable, too, for another reason. The whole town of Kamloops turns out—with a band playing, no less—to see Billy Miner off. The film accurately expresses the animus of the time toward the CPR—people joked that Bill Miner only robbed the CPR once every two years—the CPR robbed them every day.[10] Surprisingly, the local North West Mounted policeman, Lieutenant Ferney, turns up in the crowd of well-wishers. He is not in uniform when he does this, it should be noted. His real feelings are different from those that his official position demands of him: his presence in the crowd is significant. Miner is no criminal—not in the sense of being a danger to society. This Mountie not only likes Miner—he discreetly tips Miner off when the Pinkerton man comes sniffing around on the trail of a fox he regards as evil and dangerous, much as draft resisters were regarded by many Americans during the Vietnam war as the scum of the earth. The Pinkerton man, Seavey, has a totally different perception of Miner from that of Lieutenant Ferney. To Seavey, he is a terrorist capable of unlimited crime. He has actually attacked the railway, in its time the most monolithic of all concentrations of economic power. By contrast, Ferney sees him as a basically good man, a man who can be trusted when it counts.

The Grey Fox is typically discussed in the context of the Western and the vanishing frontier. Thus Miner represents the old wild west and is an anachronism in the "civilization" now descending upon him. But *The Grey Fox* is not really a Western or even a post-Western. Its conflict is not between the old and the new, between the frontier and "civilization," but between idealized values, represented by the pastoral myth, and the market system of impersonal forces, of control and coercion symbolized by the machine. That is why the most visually impressive scene in the film is that of the horses stampeded by the terrifying apparition of the oncoming train. The scene enacts the symbolic axis of the movie. This is the conflict between nature and an order that uses nature but does not love it, "nature" meaning human nature—human desires and needs—as well as nature in the sense of mountains and trees and rivers. Miner signifies aspiration for freedom and personal self-expression and security, in conflict with a social order that cares nothing about these things, because it only values property ownership, whether the railroad or the sawmill or the mine—all associated with drudgery and routine—and exploitation.

The theme of property ownership is represented in the film above all by the Pinkerton agent Seavey, but it also is represented by Miner's "friend" Jack Budd, the respectable hotel-owner who coerces Miner to steal for him. If you are powerful, others steal, manipulate, coerce for you, as the Pinkerton agent coerces for his masters (Pinkerton agents were typically employed as strike breakers and union busters). The film poses the question, who is the criminal? The true criminal is the system of coercion, with its Pinkerton agents, its hated CPR, its respectable hotel owners who steal by proxy.^{fl} That is why the film does not end with Miner being hauled off to jail. There is a coda: the story is not over. This story is never over. Miner must be shown escaping. Miner is not just a man; he is a myth: he is something that cannot be imprisoned, coerced, or controlled. Borsos ignored many facts in Miner's life, nowhere more blatantly than by allowing him to exit into a pastoral myth in Europe, no doubt with his true love. Pastoral myth, by its very nature, is a kind of denial of history. Miner did, of course, escape the B.C. Pen (causing a big scandal for the federal government, interestingly), but he was caught and again imprisoned back in the U.S., where he died. In Borsos, Miner, becoming a myth, enters a mythic world of freedom in the end. He can never be captured. He is the rebellious spirit of desire. No matter how many times he is imprisoned, he will always get free. That is why he deserves a movie about him. He is not really a man, at all. He is like Robin Hood or Zorro. Being an American merely heightens the mysterious quality of this figure in a Canadian context. He is exotic. He is timeless. Near 60, he is yet beautiful.

More important, in some ways, Borsos' Bill Miner allows us to understand our own country, and specifically British Columbia. Curiously, a similar insight appears in Wilson's *My American Cousin*. By introducing Americans into the center space of the film, we are enabled to see our own country differently, and, in a sense, to see it for the first time, what it is really like. We are so used to it, we do not see it at all. The presence of the magnetic American figure opens to us ourselves and the place where we live. *They* see us differently, and in a sense for the first time, since they are new here. For Canadians, Americans often connote power and beauty — power and beauty, that is, unavailable to the remote and peripheral and cold world of Canada, where as the bored Sandy of *Cousin* complains, nothing ever happens. Hence the two American leading men in these movies are both exotic, appealing, even charismatic, especially compared to every single Canadian male in either film. Both have an emotional aura that makes them visually magnetic on the screen itself. Butch ecstatically boasts, "Anything you want, you get it in the U.S.A.!" — and that means "in the States we got rock 'n'roll all day long!" This idealizing glow surrounds both Butch and Bill Miner.

But to notice the pastoral myth in both films is to notice also that the pastoral myth is undercut and ironic. Butch escapes to Canada because he is running away from home—he believes, as we learn at the end of the film, that he got a girl pregnant, and at 17 nearly 18 he can't face it. He has personal problems—the kind of problems that are the universal gauntlet that every young person runs in the passage through adolescence to adulthood. He is a refugee in a bright red Cadillac, and clearly no refugee at all. At the end of the film, his parents—both his mother and his father—arrive to take him home, as if he were regressing to childhood, to the control and tutelage of Mom and Dad (soon to divorce, we learn). Thus Butch with his mother parallels the departure at the end of the movie of Sandy with her mother. Neither is ready for adulthood; they must be rescued and controlled. (*The Grey Fox* also ends with the American being taken into custody and removed from the scene.)

But in *American Boyfriends*, the sequel to *My American Cousin*, Butch, now much older, gets married. He has transcended his adolescent runaway phase and is ready to assume the privilege and power of the fully adult American male, as signified by marriage. The movie emphasizes this transition to adult status with an elaborate ritual with lots of celebrators and celebration. Shrinking violet Butch is not. Ironically, however, growing up turns out to be deadly for him. Within days of his wedding and accession to full manhood, he is killed. So Butch never really does grow up. If only he had stayed in British Columbia!

Killing off Butch is unforgivable, but also revealing. It signals Wilson's intent to make a serious film in *American Boyfriends*, something totally unlike the nostalgia of *My American Cousin*, with its autobiographical reference.[12] Both *My American Cousin* and *The Grey Fox* have the pastoral orientation of an emphatically rural setting:1950s Kelowna in *Cousin* and 1900s Kamloops in *Fox* hardly count as cities. *American Boyfriends*, by contrast, is urban from the beginning, from Vancouver and Simon Fraser University through its pilgrimage to Los Angeles later: it inhabits a more serious world altogether. *American Boyfriends* puts paid to the saga of Butch, the muscular blond All-American golden boy, with the idealizing, erotic halo. He attains the adulthood he had lusted after in *My American Cousin* and, almost immediately, dies. But the chief irony is that young men Butch's age are being killed—killed in their tens of thousands—in Vietnam (not to mention several million Vietnamese). War is not just the backdrop of *American Boyfriends* but its determining context. At first the reality of the war is not noticed. As the action proceeds, however, the Vietnam War enters more and more into the centre of awareness of the film and even begins to usurp the interest in character, which is ostensibly the main focus in this film. Butch is killed, but he is not killed in the way that thousands of his fellows are being killed, in a pointless war fought on the other side of the planet, polarizing American society into patriot-fanatics and enraged rebels. But *My American Cousin* is also ironic. Thus, apart from how bored Sandy is, the first thing we hear about in the movie is the fact that the ranch is going broke. Even in the 1950s you can't make a living as an orchardist. The closing voiceover reveals that it was sold, so the paradise of Paradise Ranch is lost. It is a paradise that is just a function of the capitalist market, which may at any minute turn the occupants out of their happiness and security. The intrusion of the figure of the American into this pastoral scene suggests the commercial development that cares nothing for the people who live and work there. Thus critics draw attention to Butch's father, who immediately senses commercial possibilities in Paradise Ranch and wants to know how much it is worth. This has, he recognizes, the potential for prime real estate development.

The ironies of *The Grey Fox* are more obtrusive than in *My American Cousin*, because the action is so much more serious. Miner is, after all, a robber capable of shocking violence. But somehow we forgive him. The point is that British Columbia, beautiful as it is, where love, no matter how improbable, is found and realized, is also ruled by American Pinkerton agents, by giant corporations like the CPR, and by local crooks, like the so-called "friend" of Miner who owns the local hotel and blackmails Miner into rustling horses for him. He gets off scot-free, needless to say, while Miner is put on the CPR to jail. Kamloops is also a scene of devastating domestic horror: a Chinese man murders his desperate family, then cuts his own throat in a central passage of the film. Miner does not find refuge in British Columbia; he is used, even betrayed by a "friend"; the police—a special police squad sent from Alberta, where else—finally catch Miner. He is tried and condemned. He does escape from jail, however, and that is our final glimpse of "the grey fox," exiting to another pastoral myth, this time in Europe with the faithful love of Kate Flynn. At least that is what the film *tells* us. We are not shown this final exit and arrival, only informed by way of a written closing statement curiously parallel to the voiceover in *My American Cousin*. The free spirits do *not* find refuge in British Columbia, after all.

In both films, innocence turns out to be an illusion. There is no "escape to British Columbia" *in* British Columbia, no exit from American problems. The characters are compelled back to the past they have been trying to escape. But really, what self-respecting filmmaker is going to have a serious movie with a "they lived happily ever after" ending? *Of course* the pastoral myth is going to turn out to be an illusion. That is in a way *part* of the pastoral myth itself. It isn't real – it isn't really there, or *any* where, for that matter. It has to be an ideal, a place in the mind, not a place in geography. Hence pastoral myth is always close to satire. That is, it expresses a simple, powerful realization: there is something wrong with the attitudes and practices that control society. There is a reason why people are desperate to escape: there is something wrong with the U.S. Both of these movies have a satiric dimension. When the CPR wins, everyone else loses. Someone gains when Sandy's parents lose their orchard – but it isn't them. In this way, curiously, strangely, the pastoral myth does come true after all.

In this context *American Boyfriends*, the sequel to *My American Cousin*, comes into focus. The universal verdict on *American Boyfriends* is that it is a flop. *Boyfriends* is no match for *Cousin*. The plot construction is loose, the acting is all right but hardly inspired (at times amateurish), the scenario is contrived and, because there are too many characters, confused and confusing. Bursts of emotional excess are startling and actually embarrassing, especially a tear-jerking scene at the gravesite of Butch near the end of the movie. Veteran actors Richard Donat and Jane Mortifee, who add so much to *My American Cousin*, are absent in the sequel and badly missed. There are no actors of their stature or capacity in *American Boyfriends*. The star, Margaret Langrick, is good – but not as impressive as her much younger self in the earlier film.

Nevertheless, something about the later film makes it stay with the viewer: something about the sequel demands attention, something not easy to identify but something that gives it a value the original simply does not have. The expectation we have of the sequel is part of the problem. We expect, if not comedy, then at least a film of subtle humour and memorable characters – something like *My American Cousin*, in short. But *American Boyfriends* is not a comedy, despite expectations, despite funny moments, despite an upbeat ending. It is a film that begins with comic overtones but soon becomes serious, and then more serious. In this respect, it is totally different from the earlier *Cousin*.

Boyfriends is close in genre to the American road movie – the form that ranges from *Detour*, the notorious *film noir*, to the equally notorious *Thelma and Louise*. Christopher Gittings argues that *My American Cousin* is "an anti-road movie about the road not taken to the United States" (153) – perhaps; but if so, then the sequel really *is* the road taken to the United States. The road movie is a form characterized by the bonding of comrades, by nightmarish accidents, disillusionment, unexpected dangers, vicious personal conflicts, as well as camaraderie, humour, funny dialogue, moments of happiness and even joy, and interesting, varied scenery. Instead of freedom, what the protagonists find on the road, however, is trouble and crime. A Canadian example is Don Shebib's brilliant 1970 movie *Goin' Down the Road*. An influential American example is *Easy Rider* (1969), which made Jack Nicholson a star. *Five Easy Pieces*, also starring Jack Nicholson and partly shot in British Columbia, has similar overtones: an alienated protagonist wanders in search of something he knows not what, gets into trouble, and exits the scene of the story without having found purpose or direction – he merely exits.

The underlying point of the road movie is really the search for a pastoral myth: the search for a refuge, a place of happiness and safety and opportunity and freedom. In this sense, the road movie is typically a kind of *parody* of pastoral. It has the great scenery and the camaraderie of pastoral, but what happens on the road is typically disastrous. The sought-for pastoral myth turns out to be "nowhere." It turns out to be an illusion, and losing it is hard – a kind of final, often fatal blow. The road movie thus strikes at the heart of American "adjustment mythology," as Northrop Frye used to call it, the vision of the United States as the place of unlimited opportunity and freedom, the new Eden, the light to the world, the exceptional nation with the exceptional privilege, *summum bonum* of human social and individual desire: the place no one would want to leave, not in his right mind, anyway. Moving to Canada is a very serious thing for an American to do.

American Boyfriends begins with Sandy at Simon Fraser University, the utopian university planned ahead and created all at once (unlike staid U.B.C.), in the radical '60s, a period utterly different from the routine '50s of *My American Cousin*. In keeping with the times, she listens to impulse. With three girlfriends, she heads south for Butch's wedding and California. The film thus reverses the movement of *The Grey Fox* and *My American Cousin*, because it is about Canadians running away to California – not for refuge but in search of fun and, as the title suggests, boys, exotic erotic American boys. After all, for Canadians, California definitely eclipses British Columbia as a pastoral myth, or at least it used to. But the only boys the girls meet on the beach turn out to be Canadians from – where else? – Alberta, looking for California girls. (One should compare the same reversal in Margaret Atwood's *Surfacing*: the vulgar "Americans" on the lake turn out to be vulgar Canadians.) California, so often the pastoral myth of Canadians, turns out to be more myth than pastoral. The girls do finally meet some American boys, but these boys have other things on their mind than girls. They are the Vietnam generation, facing the draft and wondering whether to go to Vietnam – or escape to Canada. They are in conflict with themselves and with each other over the war, over America, over everything.

Thus, once we reach California, the film reverses mood as well as direction. The girls befriend a draft resister named Marty, from New York. Marty makes the decision to leave with them, in fact to escape. Where does he escape to? British Columbia – of course. There is, however, a near disaster at the border. Only because one of the Canadian border guards had been a picker on Sandy's father's ranch – Paradise Ranch, back in the Okanagan – do they all manage to get back across the Canadian border to safety and freedom. This unexpected friend intervenes to let the fugitive Marty slip into this country. In other words, this is another "innocent crime" of the type that pastoral demands. Significantly, it is the long-gone link with the pastoral-mythical world of *My American Cousin* – the fact that the border guard is an old friend from the ranch days and the ranch world – that saves them in the "realistic" world of *Boyfriends*. The film ends where it begins, with one difference: the American who has escaped to Canada stays, unlike the ending of both *My American Cousin* and *The Grey Fox*.

The close of *American Boyfriends* has deep political resonance. The very existence of English Canada is the direct result of American refugees escaping the United States, originally those who came in the wake of the American Revolution, and who were often robbed, attacked, and driven out in an act of ethnic cleansing that Americans don't like to acknowledge. Canada is *constituted* as a rejection of the United States. *American Boyfriends* is thus a profound *repudiation* of the "American cousin," in the sense of the United States that the American cousin represents. There is an ironic reference to note here: the title of the play Abraham Lincoln was watching when he was assassinated was *Our American Cousin*. In Wilson's film, then, as in Borsos' film earlier, British Columbia turns out to have an *openness to difference* that is such a precious feature of the pastoral myth. It turns out to be a genuine refuge after all, as it is for the paradoxical criminal-innocent, Marty, escaping at the end of *American Boyfriends*. Even in *The Grey Fox*, it is British Columbia that reveals to the American fugitive what real love and what real happiness actually look like, even if he cannot stay to enjoy it.

Perhaps that is the real point of the pastoral myth, the lesson of

British Columbia: it is better to know what we want, than to actually have it.

Notes

1. The association of British Columbia with drugs, and not just "B.C. Bud," is notable in this context. The renowned physician and author Gabor Maté describes some of the addicts he works with: "They are the hardcore injection users, and many will drift westward across Canada to the warmer climate and drug mecca of Vancouver's Downtown Eastside" (268).

2. The term "pastoral" does not have an exact meaning, even though it is one of the oldest strands of literature. In Western culture, it goes back to the Greeks, and to the Psalms in the Hebrew Scriptures, and even earlier to Egyptian and Mesopotamian precedents. The key point is that it is a simplified life close to nature, a nature which is in harmony with human beings. The term "utopia" is different in emphasis. "Utopia," Greek for "no place," is a term coined by Thomas More in the sixteenth century for his famous book of the same title. A "Utopia" is usually a political vision of a better system of social organization. Theory is an important aspect of utopian writing. Pastoral, by contrast, is anti-theoretical. It has anarchistic overtones: political systems lapse because social organization is no longer needed: individuals live in harmony with one another, spontaneously naturally. The numbers of people are usually small and cities few. By contrast, utopia implies conscious social construction, usually an urban orientation: systems of work and arrangements of power relations are the focus. The two terms are quite different, though they both refer to visions of a superior way of life, where people live happy, fulfilled, meaningful lives, and there is enough for everyone. My concern here is not with theorizing pastoral but with noting how its common images and motifs inform the work of directors Sandy Wilson and Philip Borsos.

3. Foster makes this comment in the audio commentary to the 2002 DVD of *McCabe and Mrs. Miller*. My concern in this article is *not* with the general question of how Hollywood has presented Canada, a question much discussed, beginning with Pierre Berton's pathbreaking *Hollywood's Canada* in 1975.

4. It is interesting that Wilson and Borsos grew up in the same area and knew each other as children (see Spaner 80), though there doesn't seem to be any influence by one on the other.

5. Compare also Colville's picture *Dog and Bridge* (1976). *Horse and*

Train may have inspired a memorable scene in Timothy Findley's novel *The Wars* involving a tragic confrontation between a horse and a train. The influential and nationalist Australian film *Breaker Morant* (1979) has a psychologically similar scene at the end.

6. Christopher Gittings notes, "If Sandra's parents and grand-mother are the allegorical figurations of an anglo-centric colonial Canada, then, Sandra herself allegorizes an adolescent Canada coming of age at mid-century, shifting her gaze from the UK to the US" (152).

7. Curiously, there was another exotic American visitor to British Columbia in 1903, one who also had a life-changing experience in B.C.: the Modernist poet Wallace Stevens. Camping in the wilderness in the province was a formative event for him (see my "Wallace Stevens and Canada, 1903").

8. Allen Blaine, "The Grey Fox Afoot in a Modern World" 129. Allen Blaine's earlier essay "Canada's Sweethearts, or Our American Cousins" notes the parallel between *The Grey Fox* and *My American Cousin* and some other films dealing with a central American character.

9. I suspect that the leisurely pacing of *The Grey Fox* owes a lot to Altman's *McCabe and Mrs. Miller*. The winter Borsos shows us in the Lower Mainland, when Miner gets a job in a sawmill, is hellish: incessant cold drenching rain under overcast sky. The scene could have been taken from Altman's movie *McCabe and Mrs. Miller*. Altman's earlier movie *That Cold Day in the Park*, shot in Vancouver (not West Vancouver, like *McCabe and Mrs. Miller*), is as cold, wet, and depressing as one could wish. For an interesting examination of Altman's movie-making in British Columbia, see David Spaner's *Dreaming in the Rain: How Vancouver Became Hollywood North by North West* (52-53). To Americans, the Pacific North West means rain rain rain—and what goes with rain: grey sky. The British Columbia scenes in *Five Easy Pieces* convey the same cold, damp, and alienating vision (though the story is set in Washington state). The scene is depressing enough for anyone to want to run away, as the Jack Nicholson character does. The depressing weather of *That Cold Day in the Park* would be enough to push any depressed person to, and over, the edge.

10. Mark Dugan and John Boessenecker emphasize the "sympathetic crowd" when Miner is taken to the train in Kamloops (130). They discuss the CPR joke (130). The scene of Miner being brought into Kamloops in the movie copies a famous photograph of the actual

event: Miner, under a blanket, in a wagon, with heavy rain pouring down. (Dugan and Boessenecker also pour cold water on the idea of Miner having a romantic love affair with an emancipated woman, which is such a memorable part of Borsos' film – Miner was, apparently, gay.)

11. Borsos' radical affinities are evident in his major film project on Norman Bethune, Canada's most famous leftist.

12. Wilson had made an earlier film, a short called *Paradise Ranch* (1977), based on home movies taken by her father.

Works Cited

Allen, Blaine. "Canada's Sweethearts, or Our American Cousins." *Canadian Journal of Film Studies* 2.2-3 (1994): 67-80.

___. "The Grey Fox Afoot in a Modern World." *Canada's Best Features: Critical Essays on 15 Canadian Films.* Ed. Eugene P. Walz. Amsterdam and New York: Rodopi, 2002. 117-46.

Berton, Pierre. *Hollywood's Canada: The Americanization of Our National Image.* Don Mills: McClelland, 1975.

Borsos, Philip, director. *The Grey Fox* [videorecording] . United Artists 1983.

Dugan, Mark, and John Boessenecker. *The Grey Fox: The True Story of Bill Miner – Last of the Old-Time Bandits.* Norman: U of OK P, 1992.

Foster, David. Audio Commentary to *McCabe and Mrs. Miller.* Warner Brothers 2002.

Gasher, Mike. *The Grey Fox Meets Jumanji: The Emergence of the Feature-Film Industry in British Columbia.* Ann Arbor: UMI, 1999.

Gittings, Christopher E. *Canadian National Cinema: Ideology, Difference and Representation.* London and New York: Routledge, 2002.

Maté, Gabor. *In the Realm of Hungry Ghosts: Close Encounters with Addiction.* Toronto: Knopf, 2008.

Nicholson, Mervyn. "Wallace Stevens and Canada, 1903." *The Wallace Stevens Journal* 25.2 (Fall 2001): 138-47.

Spaner, David. *Dreaming in the Rain: How Vancouver Became Hollywood North by North West.* Vancouver: Arsenal Pulp P, 2003.

Wilson, Sandy, director. *American Boyfriends* Backseat Production Ltd. 1989

___. director. *My American Cousin*. Borderlands Production. 1985.0

Contributor Notes

Pamela Cairns attended Langara Community College and UBC before moving to Kamloops in 1994 to start a business and family. In 2008 she graduated from TRU with a Bachelor of Education degree. Her research combines her love of history, education, and the interior of BC.

Nancy Duxbury is the Executive Director of the Centre of Expertise on Culture and Communities (CECC), at Simon Fraser University. She is also a member of the Small Cities reasearch alliance. For ten years she has been involved in launching and developing the Creative City Network of Canada, which links municipal staff with responsibilities for arts, culture and heritage development in about 140 municipalities across the country. She has done extensive research in the field of cultural indicators.

Gloria Filax is coordinator and professor of Equality Studies, Master of Arts - Integrated Studies, Athabasca University. Her recent writings are: *Queer Youth in the Province of the 'Severely Normal'* (UBC Press, Sexuality Series, 2006) and "'It's as if Canadians were born without tongues': An exploration of Canadian popular culture as critical pedagogy," forthcoming in *How Canadians Communicate: Popular Culture as Context.*

Anne Gagnon teaches History and Canadian Studies at Thompson Rivers University and has been coordinator of the Centre for Canadian Studies since 2006. She was a visiting professor in Germany for some eighteen months between 2000 and 2005. She was a contributing editor of *Textual Studies in Canada 17: The Canadian Studies Issue*, Summer 2004.

W.F. Garrett-Petts is Professor and Chair of English and Modern Languages at Thompson Rivers University, where he directs The Centre for the Study of Multiple Literacies and Mapping Quality of Life and the Culture of Small Cities (a national community-university research alliance). His recent books include *Artists' Statements and the Nature of Artistic Inquiry* (Open Letter), *The Small Cities Book* (New Star), *PhotoGraphic Encounters: The Edges and Edginess of Reading Prose Pictures, Visual Fictions* (U of Alberta P), and *Writing about Literature* (Broadview).

James Hoffman is Professor of Theatre at Thompson Rivers University and a member of the Small Cities reasearch alliance. He is the author of *The Ecstasy of Resistance: A Biography of George Ryga* (ECW Press) and has edited three books: *Playing the Pacific Province: An Anthology of British Columbia Plays, 1967-2000* (Playwrights Canada Press); *George Ryga, The Other Plays* (Talonbooks); and *George Ryga: The Prairie Novels* (Talonbooks). Hoffman was also one of editors of *Textual Studies in Canada*, 1997-2005.

Henry Hubert is Professor Emeritus at Thompson Rivers University, where he specialized in Rhetoric and Composition in the Department of English and Modern Languages, which he chaired prior to becoming Dean of Arts. He is the author of *Harmonious Perfection: The Development of English Studies in Nineteenth-Century Anglo-Canadian Colleges* (MSU Press), and co-founder of the publishing collaborative *Textual Studies in Canada*.

Terry Kading teaches Political Science and is a member of the Canadian Studies program at TRU. He is also a member of the Community-University Research Alliance (CURA) Mapping Quality of Life and the Culture of Small Cities research group investigating small city responses to social issues.

Tanis MacDonald is Assistant Professor in the Department of English and Film Studies at Wilfrid Laurier University in Waterloo, Ontario. She is the editor of *Speaking of Power: The Poetry of Di Brandt* (WLUP), and is the author of several scholarly articles on mourning and inheritance in Canadian women's writing. She is also a widely-published poet and reviewer.

Kelly-Anne Maddox is Assistant Professor in the Department of English and Modern Languages at Thompson Rivers University. Her research interests include Quebec migrant writing since 1990, as well as contemporary Quebec cinema. She has published articles on Anne Hébert, Ying Chen, Abla Farhoud, Lise Tremblay, Yan Muckle, and Sergio Kokis, and is currently focusing on representations of popular culture and consumer society in 21st-century Quebec literature.

Kimberly Mair is a doctoral candidate in Sociology at the University of Alberta. Her research is concerned with the aesthetics of representation and communication. She has recent articles in the following publications: *Senses and Society, Third Text. Critical Perspectives on Contemporary Art & Culture*, and *Interfaces, Word and Image: Intimacy.*

Ron McColl has recently retired as Manager of Corporate Programs and Projects for the City of Kamloops.

Alex Michalos is Chancellor, Emeritus Professor in Political Science, and Director of the Institute for Social Research and Evaluation at the University of Northern British Columbia. In 1974 he founded the journal *Social Indicators Research,* which is now in Volume 84. He has been working on quality of life measurement for many years.

Rachel Nash was born and raised in the west. She is currently Assistant Professor of English at Thompson Rivers University. Her recent research has focused on the artist statement and the nature of artistic inquiry. She is co-editor of an issue of *Open Letter* on that topic.

Mervyn Nicholson is Professor of English at Thompson Rivers University in British Columbia and author of *13 Ways of Looking at Images: Studies in the Logic of Visualization* and of *Male Envy: The Logic of Malice in Literature and Culture*. He completed his Ph.D. with Northrop Frye at the University of Toronto and has served on the executive of the Association of Canadian College and University Teachers of English. He has published widely in a range of journals, including *The Journal of the History of Ideas, Recherches Sémiotiques, Bright Lights,* and *LIT: Literature, Interpretation, Theory, Literature/Film Quarterly.*

Dan O'Reilly is Assistant Professor of Philosophy at Thompson Rivers University. He has been central in developing the Small Cities Online Research Community, which is an integral aspect of The Small Cities CURA Mapping Quality of Life and Culture Research Program investigating quality of life indicators relevant to online space. As part of this research project, he has leased land, developed resources and conducted workshops in Second Life.

Kalli Paakspuu is a Genie-winning filmmaker, cultural theorist and part-time faculty at York University. She soon expects to defend her doctoral dissertation "Rhetorics of Colonialism in Visual Documentation" at the University of Toronto. Her research examines early colonial cross-cultural photographic practices and North American Indigenous subjects, Indigenous peace activism, and the dialogical storytelling modes on both sides of the camera.

Ginny Ratsoy is Assistant Professor of English at Thompson Rivers University, where she has taught since 1980. A member of the Small Cities reasarch alliance, she has published articles on British Columbia literature and theatre. *Theatre in British Columbia*, a collection of eighteen scholarly essays which she edited, was published by Playwrights Canada Press in 2006.

Paul Stacey is from B.C. Campus in Vancouver and a partner with the Small Cities CURA initiative.

Andrew Tucker is the Director of Planning with the City of Nanaimo, Development Services Department.

Gilles Viaud is Assistant Professor of Geography at Thompson Rivers University and a member of the Small Cities reasarch alliance. His research interests include the social geography and quality of life in small cities, and social structure and change in urban residential areas. His research is published in both English and French journals.

Douglas Worts for 25 years was an educator/exhibit-developer/ audience-researcher/etc. at the Art Gallery of Ontario. He has recently embarked on a new and exciting path as a consultant in the area of "culture and sustainability" – much of which remains to be defined. His interests have been very much rooted in the cultural sector and for the past ten years he has been particularly interested in the relationship between culture and sustainability.

Yaying Zhang is Assistant Professor of English at Thompson Rivers University, where she teaches courses in rhetoric and composition. A member of the Small Cities reasarch alliance, her research interests focus on issues of language and culture at the intersection of rhetorical studies and postcolonial studies.